The Wa of Myanmar and China's Quest for Global Dominance

The Wa of Myanmar and China's Quest for Global Dominance

BERTIL LINTNER

Silkworm Books

ISBN 978-616-215-170-5
© 2021 Bertil Lintner
All rights reserved

First published in 2021 by
Silkworm Books
430/58 M. 7, T. Mae Hia, Chiang Mai 50100, Thailand
info@silkwormbooks.com
www.silkwormbooks.com

Cover: United Wa State Army (UWSA) soldiers stand guard during a welcome dinner, organised to commemorate the 30th anniversary of peace-building efforts in Wa State, in Panghsang on April 16, 2019. Photo by Ye Aung Thu / AFP

Typeset in Minion Pro 11 pt. by Silk Type

Contents

CONTENTS

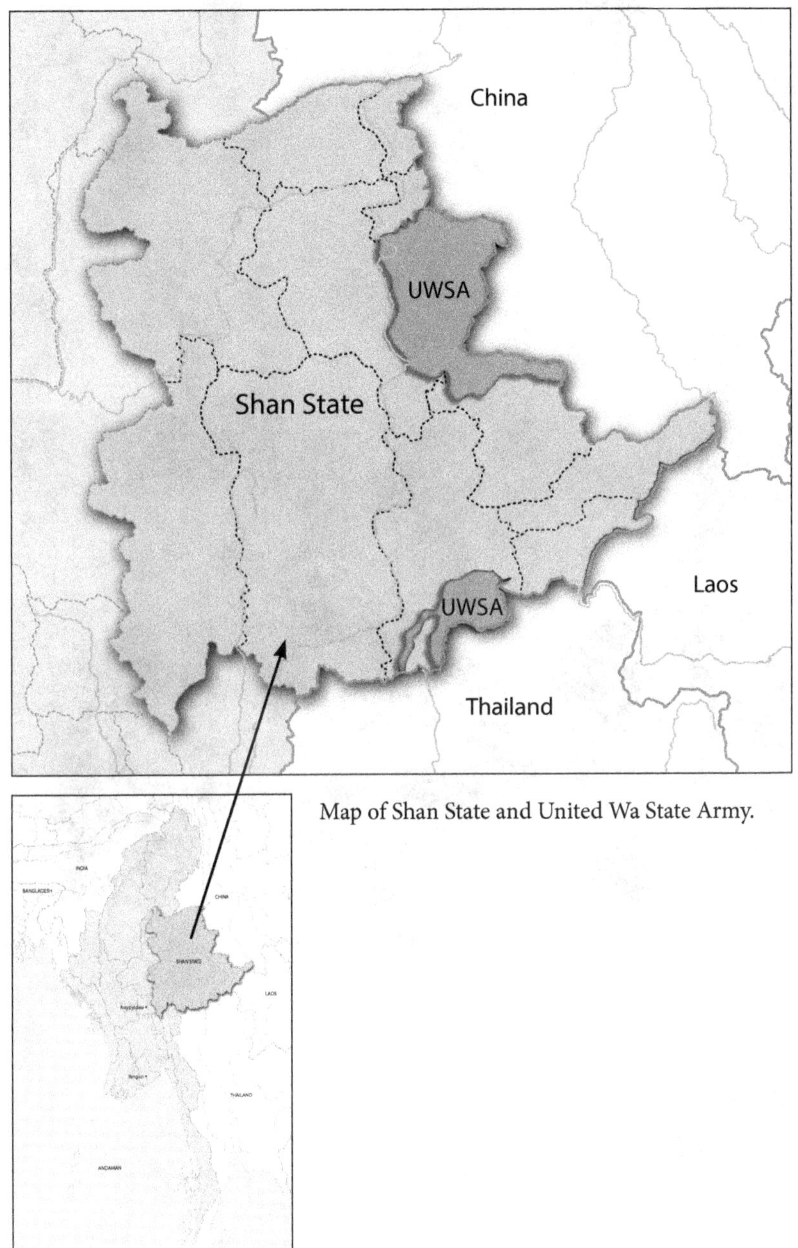

Map of Shan State and United Wa State Army.

Flag of United Wa State Army.

Introduction

Thousands of soldiers in impeccable uniforms goose-stepped in perfect formation past the grandstand where their leaders stood to attention. Then came an impressive and wide-ranging display of surface-to-air missiles, howitzers, mortars, rocket launchers, machine-guns, assault rifles, armored personnel carriers, and even a weaponized drone. Columns of civilians, mostly Wa tribesmen but also people from other ethnic groups in the area, made their way to the main parade grounds. Fireworks lit up the sky after dark and people cheered and danced through the night.

This event, on April 17, 2019, was not organized by the regular army of any recognized country. Rather, huge crowds of people had come together to celebrate the thirtieth anniversary of events that had led to the founding of the United Wa State Army (UWSA), an ethnic force made up of tribesmen from Burma's northeastern border mountains. In April 1989, the hilltribe rank-and-file of the insurgent Communist Party of Burma (CPB) had risen in mutiny against their mostly Burman, orthodox Marxist-Leninist leadership and had driven them into exile in China. The UWSA was born shortly thereafter, and grew to become what it is today: the largest and best-equipped military non-state actor in the Asia-Pacific region. The UWSA is believed to have at least 20,000 soldiers, with more in reserve. Their sophisticated weaponry has been supplied by China's security services. Just as the now defunct CPB was armed and equipped by the Chinese, so is the UWSA.

During the Maoist era, China wanted to export revolutionary communism. Today, their aim is economic expansion, and with it, political influence. It was to strengthen China's new role as a superpower that China's president, Xi Jinping, in 2013 launched an ambitious multitrillion dollar plan called the Belt and Road Initiative (BRI). Its short-term aim is to bring Asia, Africa, and Europe into a single mega-economic and trading area. This may seem innocent enough, but the ultimate goal of that new China-dominated partnership is to rival and eventually overshadow all those across the Pacific, Atlantic, and Indian oceans currently dominated by the United States, other Western powers, and Japan. China will become the world's dominant superpower, not just what it appears to be today, a trading nation, huge as it might be, expanding its political influence across the globe with the sole aim of protecting its economic interests.

Incongruous as it may seem, it is in this grand scheme that the Wa, a little-known people living in the northeastern borderlands of Burma, have come to play a pivotal role. With China's own ports being too distant and already overloaded with export item from the coastal provinces, the landlocked inland provinces need other outlets to the sea. Only two neighboring countries can provide that: Pakistan and Burma. But the route through Pakistan down to the coast goes from Xinjiang in China's westernmost region over the Karakoram Mountains, reaching an elevation of nearly five thousand meters above sea level, a dangerous climb for any commercial vehicle, before reaching the lowlands.

China's security services do not want to see a new war on its southwestern border. Peace was established when the Wa, tired and weary after years of fighting, entered into a ceasefire agreement with the government within weeks of setting up the UWSA. It would have been a mistake for China to give up the foothold they had enjoyed inside Burma since the CPB days. The UWSA could be a trusted and useful geostrategic ally in the quest for dominance in Burma and beyond. The UWSA began to acquire sophisticated weaponry from China, and soon became even stronger and better equipped than the CPB ever was.

Chinese support for the Wa gives Beijing leverage inside Burma, the neighbor that provides China with the easiest and most convenient access to the Indian Ocean. The so-called China-Myanmar [Burma] Economic Corridor from Yunnan down to the Bay of Bengal, has therefore become one of the most important features of the BRI.

Under the terms of the peace agreement with the Burmese government, the Wa were permitted to retain control over most of the CPB's former base area along the Chinese border. Consequently, they established their own self-administered buffer state between Burma and China. They were also allowed to engage in any kind of business to sustain themselves. In these remote mountains, the main source of income used to be the cultivation of opium poppies. For more than two decades, the UWSA and its allies were Asia's main producers of opium and its derivative heroin, though they later turned to manufacturing methamphetamines and other synthetic drugs. Today, it appears that the Wa earn more from tin and rare earth mining than from the trade in opium, heroin, and methamphetamines, commodities that may not be that important to them anymore.

So who are the Wa? They speak several Mon-Khmer dialects and are thus very distant relatives of the Khmer empire builders in Cambodia as well as the Mon, who once had their own kingdoms in what are today Burma and Thailand. But the Wa never had their own kingdoms and have never been ruled by any central Burmese authority. Burma became a British colony after being conquered in stages in the nineteenth century. However, governmental presence in the Wa Hills, as they were called, was limited to annual flag marches up to the Chinese border.

At that time, the Wa were still head hunters and feared by the people of the plains, and thus the British troops that carried the Union Jack up to the border were always heavily armed. The Wa Hills were only nominally included in the Shan States of Burma and had their own chieftains who did not heed any central or regional authority, which was the reason the Wa Hills were in colonial records sometimes referred to as 'the Wa states.' But most of the Wa Hills remained marked 'un-administered' on colonial maps.

In the 1950s, large tracts of the Wa Hills were occupied by renegade Nationalist Chinese Kuomintang forces who had retreated across the border into Burma following their defeat by Mao Zedong's communists in the Chinese civil war. They established bases in the Wa Hills and other mountainous areas of the Shan States from where they tried to invade Yunnan but were repeatedly driven back to the Burmese side of the border. The parts of the Wa Hills where the Kuomintang were not present were controlled by various local, mostly Wa, chieftains-cum-warlords. The Kuomintang, as well as the region's warlords, financed their respective struggles with income derived from the cultivation and sale of opium, the only cash crop viable in these remote mountains.

The Kuomintang's presence in northeastern Burma was a major reason China decided to lend all-out support to the CPB. Burmese communists had been living in exile in China since the early 1950s, but it was not until a decade later that military training camps were established for them in Yunnan. Following several years of preparation, they made their move on January 1, 1968. Communist forces streamed across the border and the old Kuomintang bases were some of their first targets.

While the political commissars were CPB cadres, the foot soldiers were almost exclusively 'volunteers' from China. It was only when the CPB had captured the Wa Hills in the early 1970s that its 'people's army' began to consist of local recruits. Before long, the bulk of the CPB's fighting force was predominantly Wa. China poured in more aid to the CPB than to any other communist force outside Indochina. By the mid-1970s, the CPB had established control over more than 20,000 square kilometers of territory in northeastern and eastern Shan State, including most of the Wa Hills.

Although the Kuomintang threat was eliminated, the CPB had no intention of remaining in these remote border mountains. Its goal was to push down to the Burma lowlands and seize power in the capital, Rangoon (now Yangon). The Wa, on the other hand, only wanted to defend their homes in the hills. Not surprisingly, the plan to conquer the lowlands failed, and as China's policy changed after Mao's death in 1976 and with the rise of 'the capitalist roader' Deng Xiaoping, the CPB had outlived its usefulness for the Chinese.

Things came to a head in March and April 1989, when the hilltribe rank-and-file of the CPB's army rose in mutiny and drove the aging, mostly Burman leadership of the party into exile in China. It may be assumed that the mutineers had been given the go-ahead by the

Chinese. No longer interested in promoting revolution, they wanted to open the border for trade and exploit the natural resources in the frontier areas.

Thus, the UWSA was born from the ashes of the old CPB. Other ethnic groups in the CPB also formed their own armies which made peace with the government. What those groups earned from their various commercial activities was used to build roads, hospitals, and schools in the area, the development of which had been grossly neglected by the CPB. The UWSA and its ex-CPB allies also built casinos and hotels inside their respective areas to lure tourists from China, who began arriving by the busload not long after the 1989 mutiny.

In the process, the UWSA has become exactly what the Chinese wanted: a useful bargaining chip when they want to put pressure on the Burma government not to stray too close to the West. The UWSA is also a useful tool when the Chinese want to protect their investment in Burma. This became especially important after Burma's then president, Thein Sein, decided in September 2011 to suspend a US$3.6 billion Chinese hydroelectric power project in the far north of the country. The Chinese also have to deal with ongoing protests against a Chinese mine project in Letpadaung, northwest of the central city of Mandalay. Most importantly, China is engaged in, and wants to control, the construction of a deep-sea port at Kyaukphyu in Burma's Rakhine State, and to build high-speed railways that will connect the port with Kunming, the provincial capital of Yunnan.

For these reasons, China has also become involved in Burma's so-called peace process, or talks between the central government, the military, and the country's many ethnic armed groups. Initiated by Thein Sein after he assumed the presidency in 2011, the task of ending decades of civil war in Burma has now fallen on Aung San Suu Kyi, who after an election in 2015 became 'state counselor,' or the country's nominal leader (Burma's constitution prevents her from becoming president because her two sons are not Burmese citizens). Her party, the National League for Democracy, scored another landslide victory in the November 8, 2020 election, ensuring that there will be no change in official policies: the country's ethnic armed organizations are supposed to sign a ceasefire agreement with the government before any substantial negotiations can take place. That, many observers argue, is placing the cart before the horse and will not work. Beijing, on its part, has outmaneuvered a host of Western peacemakers who became involved in the process after Thein Sein's announcement and the formation of a government headed by Suu Kyi, and because of the close relationship that exists between China's security services and the UWSA as well as its allies, the Chinese have emerged as the sole arbiter of the talks. However, China is not necessarily interested in a final, peaceful solution to Burma's civil wars. It wants stability which it can use to protect and enhance its geostrategic goals, now under the aegis of the massive, all-encompassing BRI.

I was the only foreign journalist to visit these border areas when they were controlled by the CPB. In 1986–87, I trekked through the entire CPB territory, from Panghsai in the north where the fabled Burma Road crosses the Chinese border, to the Mekong River and the border with Laos. I also spent three months at the CPB's (now the UWSA's) headquarters at Panghsang where I interviewed all the leaders of the party. These were the only interviews ever granted to a foreign journalist. I spent months in the field with the Wa troops of the CPB, and thus the 1989 mutiny came as no surprise. I know how much the Wa hated their Burman leadership. I wrote about that, and predicted the mutiny, in a cover story for the *Far Eastern Economic Review* in May 1987, two years before the collapse of the CPB. I also broke the news about the mutiny in March 1989. That story, also for the *Far Eastern Economic Review*, was the first to appear in the international media as I was the only foreign journalist informed by the mutineers about the uprising. The message came to me via radio and telephone as I was then living in Bangkok.

Since then, I have maintained contacts with Wa and their allies. The UWSA leadership has kept a hostile distance, though, because of what I have written about their involvement in the drug trade. However, in August 2019 the UWSA leadership allowed me to visit their area. Although I did not get to see Bao Youxiang, the top leader, I met almost everybody else. The UWSA leaders wanted to present their side of the story, which I appreciated, and my visit to their area was even shown on their own television station: 'A friend of the Wa people returns after 32 years.'

The Wa are a proud people and, as Bao said in his speech at the April 2019 celebrations, "The Wa people are the masters of their own destiny." That may not be entirely correct given their dependence on China for almost everything, apart from trade and the supply of weaponry. The Chinese *yuan*, not the Burmese *kyat*, is the only currency that is used inside their area. Mobile phones and Internet connections are provided by Chinese servers. The Chinese language is more widely spoken than Burmese. Having had many meetings with Wa from all walks of life from the 1980s to today, it is also my impression that they may be puppets of the Chinese. But they are not Chinese stooges. The Wa are aware that the Chinese feel superior to them and in many instances refer to them as 'uncivilized savages,' and they despise that. It is my hope that this book will present a better understanding of the Wa, who they are, and how China's leaders are using them to promote their own economic and strategic interests. The Wa deserve a brighter future than that.

The Wa: Wild Men of the Mountains

As Burma, as it was then called, was heading for independence in the years after World War II, representatives of its many ethnic minorities were summoned by the British colonial power for talks at Maymyo, a picturesque hill station in the highlands east of Mandalay, now called Pyin Oo Lwin.[1] The hearings were called the Frontier Areas Committee of Enquiry, and leaders of the non-Burmese peoples who lived in territories far away from the country's heartland on the plains of the Irrawaddy River were invited to present what they expected from the proposed Union of Burma. Did they want autonomy for their respective areas? A federation of equal states? Or even their own independent nations, separate from Burma? Under British rule, central Burma had been ruled as a colony while the more than forty Shan principalities, or the Federated Shan States, were protectorates. Other areas were called 'designated' or 'un-administered.' It was a patchwork of different jurisdictions, which now had to be brought under some kind of unified, central administration.

Talks with major non-Burmese ethnic groups—the Shan, Kachin, Chin, and Karenni (or Kayah)—went relatively smoothly. They came prepared and asked for autonomy within a proposed federal structure. The Karen, who had been fiercely loyal to the British colonial power and even fought with them against the Japanese-allied Burmese during World War II, did not participate in the talks. Instead, they sent a letter stating that they wished "to be in a distinct territory under the direct control of the Governor," or a dominion that would be self-governing but remain under British sovereignty.[2]

The Wa sent four delegates. Two of them represented Mong Lun and Hsawnglong, relatively developed Wa principalities in the southern hills, while the other two came from the wilder and more remote northern states of Mong Kong and Mong Mon. The hearings were headed by U Nu, who later became independent Burma's first prime minister. The southern Wa did not have any specific request. Naw Hkam U from Mong Lun stated only that "we are not well educated in politics but we are willing to abide by the decision of the Federated Shan States Council,"[3] while Sao Naw Hseng from Hsawnglong stated that "Was are Was and Shans are Shans. We would not like to go into the Federated Shan States."[4]

If that were not puzzling enough, the talks with the northern Wa revealed a wide gap between the Wa way of looking at life and the committee's perception of it:

Do you want any association with other people?
Hkun Sai (for the Wa): We do not want to join anybody because in the past we have been very independent.

What do you want the future to be in the Wa states?
Sao Maha (for the Wa): We have not thought about that because we are very wild people. We never thought of the administrative future. We think only about ourselves.

Don't you want education, clothing, good food, good houses, hospitals?
Sao Maha: We are very wild people and don't appreciate all these things.

Have you got any ideas as to how you would like the Wa states to be administered in future?
Sao Maha: No.[5]

This exchange of views may appear farcical, but in retrospect it shows that the Was did not think of themselves as citizens of Burma, and that was not going change after independence in 1948 or when the name of the country was changed to Myanmar in 1989. The Wa did not have any concept of nations or states, nor were they ever ruled by any outside power. The Frontier Areas Committee of Enquiry's report even stated that "there are no post offices but mails are accepted and distributed if addressed care of the Administrative Officers"[6] which, in any case, would not have been relevant to them. Wa literacy in any language was extremely limited so they would hardly have been any avid letter-writers among them. The report went on to mention that "the only medical facilities are those provided by the Frontier Constabulary outpost Medical Officers and by itinerant Chinese practitioners (non-certificated) … there is no organized education service in the Wa states."[7]

The early history of this idiosyncratic and isolated people is shrouded in mystery. There is no doubt that they are related to the Palaung, tea growers in northern Shan State, and the Lawa in the hills of northern Thailand. The Mon and the Khmer may speak related languages, but that is the only similarity between them and the Wa.

The Mons in Burma and Thailand and the Khmer of Cambodia not only established their own kingdoms but also have their own literature and are Buddhists. Even the Palaung have converted to Buddhism. But most Wa have remained faithful to their animistic beliefs throughout history, and it is only in recent years that some of them have become Buddhists or Christians. What we know for certain is that the Wa and their Lawa relatives have inhabited northeastern Shan State, southern Yunnan, and northern Thailand for centuries. They may even be the original inhabitants of those areas as the old Lanna kings of northern Thailand and the Shan *saohpa*, or princes, in the eastern state of Kengtung paid a token yearly tribute to the Lawa and the Wa respectively as the "original owners of the land."[8]

When a Kengtung prince was crowned, two Wa always took part in the ceremony and the Shan chief would consider his coronation incomplete without them.[9] The Wa may have been despised as 'savages,' but the Shan had to recognize their special status as a truly indigenous people. In Lanna, Thai historian Sarassawadee Ongsakul noted "that the Lua [Lawa] were accepted as the original owners of the land can be seen in the coronation procession, in which a Lua walks with a dog ahead of the king into the city,"[10] which was present-day Chiang Mai. The Wa and the Lawa may not have lived in the fertile valleys where the Shan and Thai settled, but they were certainly the first to form communities in that part of Southeast Asia.

Chronicles compiled by the Shan rulers, and research done by British colonial administrators and Chinese officials, provide some clues, but it is far from certain that those accounts are accurate. Based on interviews and oral history, they also contain widely differing accounts of the origin of the Wa. The intrepid British colonial officer James George Scott, who traveled extensively in upper Burma at the end of the nineteenth century, claims that the Wa believe they originated from tadpoles and "spent their earlier years on the lake at Nawnghkeo, an uninviting-looking oval lake at the top of a mountain seven thousand feet high … the lake is about half a mile long and two hundred yards wide. It is said to be enormously deep, and so cold that no fish can live in it."[11] When they "became frogs they moved to a place called Nam Tao where, in the progress of time, they grew to be ogres,"[12] and eventually morphed into human beings. According to Scott, they were head hunters, but definitely not cannibals, as rumored among the Shan who lived nearby and feared these ferocious tribesmen.

A second version, put forth by V. C. Pitchford in a 1937 essay, mentioned that lake as well. The name Nawnghkeo is Shan for 'green lake' while the Wa call it Kaing Kret. But Pitchford's essay has no reference to tadpoles, instead recounting that "from its primaeval waters sprang the forebears of the Wa race and when they became men, they lived in the cavern of Pakkatei and there they learned the mystery of head hunting, whereby they waxed fruitful and multiplied exceedingly."[13] On the other hand, Willy-André Prestre, a French researcher, was told a story while smoking opium with some tribesmen that they were descendants of frogs. He also recorded references to some kind of evolution that eventually resulted in human beings. According to a fourth, Chinese version, "mankind came from a cave called Yang-ho."[14] That version of the origin of the Wa makes no mention of tadpoles, frogs or head-hunting.

Needless to say, all those versions are part of local mythology and, as Scott once remarked, Wa belief systems are "a jumble of Buddhism, totemism, and simple fantasy."[15] Buddhism entered their belief systems through contacts with the Shan, called Dai in China, lowlanders living mostly on the western side of the Wa Hills but also in the east where they lived together with Han Chinese. The Shan, the British, and the Chinese divided the Wa into 'tame' or 'big' Wa, those who had lived close to Shan or Chinese civilization and adopted some of their respective customs, including Buddhism, and 'the wild Wa,' tribesmen who were still animists with some elements of Buddhism, and also head hunters. It is head-hunting and the presumed wildness of the Wa that has caught the imagination of people in the outside world and instilled fear among the neighbors of these fiercely independent tribesmen.

Scott noted in his book *Burma and Beyond* that "the fact is there has always been a fascination about the Wa. They were first heard of by Europeans in the days of Vasco da Gama. At least, there seems no reason to doubt the assertion about his experiences made in Camoëns' *Lusiads* that among the 'thousand unknown natives' he came across the Wa. He calls them Gueos, and said they were cannibals, and that certainly was the belief even amongst their nearest neighbours, the Shans and the Burmese, until 1893, when a British party went across the centre of their country,"[16] and, presumably, discovered that they did not eat human flesh but were not averse to the habit of chopping off people's heads.

The origin of the Wa head-hunting tradition is obscure and will probably never be fully fathomed. One theory was produced by Alan Winnington, the Beijing correspondent for the British communist paper *The Daily Worker* in the 1950s. Armed with his communist credentials, he was the only Westerner at that time who was allowed to travel extensively in remote parts of Yunnan. He later wrote a book called *The Slaves of the Cool Mountains*, and although the title actually refers to the Norsu tribe in northwestern Yunnan, it also includes a unique account of the Wa. Winnington retells a Wa legend according to which decapitation began with a trick played on them by Zhuge Liang, the famous Chinese warrior at the time of the Three Kingdoms, or AD 220–280. In order to make them fight each other instead of their Chinese neighbors, Zhuge is said to have given the Wa boiled rice to plant, which, naturally, did not grow. He then told the Wa that their rice would grow only if they sacrificed human beings and cut off their heads. After the tribesmen heeded this advice, Zhuge gave them proper rice seeds, which grew.[17] Chinese chronicles provide a similar account of the origin of head-hunting, but there the evil trickster is a Shan, not a Chinese.[18]

On the Burmese side—and before independence in 1948—colonial presence in the area was limited to occasional visits by adventurers like Scott and annual flag marches up to what the British perceived as the border with China. The Shan writer Sao Saimong Mangrai, a member of the Kengtung princely family, relates in his book, *The Shan States and the British Annexation*, that "during the Wa Hills tour of a British officer in 1939, a Sikh doctor had to be rushed out of the head-hunting area under an escort of a platoon of troops when it was learned that the Wa had come and offered 300 silver rupees to some of the camp followers for his head, which, with its magnificent beard and moustache, they said would bring enduring prosperity to their village."[19]

Saimong Mangrai's tale, as well as Western and Chinese accounts of head-hunting among the Wa, tend to describe it in the context of fertility rites and wishes for good harvests. Magnus Fiskesjö, a Swedish anthropologist, disputes this theory and argues that it had more to do with the collection of trophies in war with rival villages. There was no fertility god or deity that figured in the head-hunting rituals because, as Fiskesjö writes, "the pantheon of spirits … had no direct part in the arrangements of enemy heads and skulls. Wa warfare practices of the past must be understood within the social and regional context of conflict over land and resources, not 'customs.'"[20]

Whatever the case, warfare between different Wa villages was prevalent, and given the tribal nature of Wa society it would not have been necessary for someone like Zhuge or anybody else to play tricks on them with boiled rice to pit one community against another. As Winnington describes, "the Wa people live on the jungle hilltops in fortified villages of bamboo, thatched houses built on stilts."[21] A Wa village called Urnu he saw in China in the mid-1950s was no different from those across the border in Burma at the same time and earlier:

> Like all villages, Urnu is surrounded by a high growth of dense thornwood between 15 and 20 yards thick, with dead and living thorn intertwined to form an impenetrable natural barbed-wire barrier. At opposite ends of the village two tunnels are cut through the barrier, closed on the inside by massive doors hacked out of large trees—hinges, door and bolt slots all cut from a single piece of hardwood—giving the village the advantage over attackers in the tunnel.[22]

Skulls of decapitated enemies were put on display outside the village to warn off intruders. Each village would have a drum house, and the sound of drums would he heard when there was a festival, or if people from a hostile village were spotted in the vicinity. The Wa also displayed heads of buffaloes, complete with impressive horns, as trophies suggesting wealth and successful hunting trips. The horned buffalo has, in modern times, become the symbol of the Wa nation.

According to Scott, "Most villages count their heads by tens or twenties but in some cases they run into many more, according to the age of the village, and whether, as sometimes seems to be the case, the trophies or, as one might say, the guarantees, of one village run into and combine with another."[23] The Chinese, Scott noted, knew the Wa best "since they have dealings with them in opium and salt."[24] Opium was a major cash crop in the hills and as such sold to Chinese merchants and their contacts spread far and wide in the region. G. F. Hudson, another British colonial officer who wrote about the Wa during the early colonial era, identifies the Panthay— Chinese Muslims from Yunnan who had fled into Burma after rising up against the emperor, which lasted from 1855 to 1873—as the main buyers of Wa opium. Historically, they have been excellent muleteers and controlled much of the caravan trade in the region, not only the opium business. Other goods they transported as far south as Chiang Mai in northern Thailand included salt, tea, minerals, precious stones, and consumer goods. But opium was a major commodity, and according to Hudson, the Panthay, the opium traders, were "financed by Singaporean Chinese and they had 130 Mauser rifles with 1,500 mules, exporting opium by the hundredweight into French, Siamese and British territory, each muleload escorted by two riflemen."[25] For the little money the Wa opium farmers got from selling their crop, they were able to buy salt, rice, and a few other necessities from the same Chinese merchants.

Silver mining was another source of income, and again the buyers were mostly the Panthay and other Chinese from Yunnan. Large-scale silver mining was carried out between 1650 and 1800, and even gave name to what now is a town in the Wa Hills: Vingngun, Shan for 'silver town.' It is not unusual that towns and areas in the Wa

Hills have Shan names, and the partial conversion to Buddhism among some of them led to the adoption of Shan political systems. While some Wa chieftains did pay tribute to more powerful Shan *saohpa*, Fiskesjö also notes that "these Wa deflected Shan dominance by seizing on their geographical position to set themselves up as Shan-style princes, on the model of those same threatening Shan States, so as to be able to compete with them."[26] The outcome was the emergence of what became known as the Wa states, sometimes even spelled with a capital 's'.

The best organized of those Wa states was Mong Lun in the southern hills. Tawang, or Ta Awng as he is sometimes called, proclaimed himself *saohpa* in the early nineteenth century. He died in 1822, and having no sons was succeeded by his nephew Hkun Hseng who had a Shan name, and who became a Buddhist and made the village of Pangyang the capital of his state. After the British annexation of the Shan States in the 1880s and 1890s, Mong Lun maintained cordial relations with the various Shan *saohpas* as well as the colonial power. Several of the children in the ruling family were sent to schools in the Shan States, and it was not unusual that they, apart from their native Wa, could speak Shan, Chinese, Burmese, and even English.[27]

Thus, it would not be fair to the Wa to say that they were a backward tribe who, apart from some interaction with their Shan and Chinese neighbors, lived in total isolation in their mountains with little or no understanding of the outside world. The Wa were smarter than that and, in fact, even the 'wild' ones had a notion of being a people at the center of the universe. In his Ph.D thesis, Fiskesjö noted:

> The most salient feature of the general situation of the Wa during
> the last few centuries is the persistence of an autonomous Wa

centre, which was politically and economically independent. This centre was surrounded by a Wa periphery, in which people lived under the tenuous rule of state societies yet farther beyond. The Wa people living in the central Wa lands take it for granted that they live at the origin of the world, at which they themselves have remained.[28]

Other sections of the human race, the Wa believe, have emerged later out of holes in the Wa mountains "from which all humanity come forth [and they] have proceeded farther away—because the land was already occupied. This applies to such non-Wa others as the Shan and the Lahu, the Chinese and the Burmese, as well as any others still."[29] According to Fiskesjö, "the Wa also see themselves as living at the top of the world, since it is where the highest and most imposing mountains are."[30] The Lahu, who speak a Tibeto-Burman language, are not ethnically or linguistically related to the Wa, but the two hill peoples have always been close and are in some mythology regarded as brothers.

The special status the Wa enjoyed among the Shan and the northern Thai is well documented and may have enhanced that worldview. Their relations with the Chinese are also well-established, but modern Chinese sources exaggerate that relationship in order to fit it into the notion of a unified nation-state that encompassed all the peoples living within China's present boundaries. If official Chinese sources are to be believed, the Wa "came under the rule of the Han Dynasty"[31] in the second century AD: "Thereafter, through the Tang, Song, Yuan, Ming and Qing dynasties, the Va (Wa) people have had inseparable ties with other peoples in the hinterland."[32] That, of course, is pure fantasy as not even Yunnan came under direct

Chinese rule until the fourteenth century, and the very existence of a Wa people was virtually unknown to the emperors in Beijing until the late eighteenth century.[33]

Colonial Britain, rather than China, was the first outside power to claim the Wa Hills. After deposing Thibaw, the last king of Burma in 1885 and sending him into exile in India, the British went on to conquer the Shan States. They wanted mainly to avoid the emergence of an uncontrollable buffer area between them and the French, who at about the same time were establishing their colonial rule in Indochina, which included present-day Laos. Sir Charles Crosthwaite, British Chief Commissioner of Burma in 1887–90, described the situation in this way:

> Looking at the character of the country lying between the Salween and the Mekong, it was certain to be the refuge of all the discontent and outlawry of Burma. Unless it was ruled by a government not only loyal and friendly to us, but thoroughly strong and efficient, this region would become a base for the operations of every brigand leader ... or pretender ... where they might muster their followers and hatch their plots to raid British territory when opportunity offered. To those responsible for the peace of Burma, such a prospect was not pleasant.[34]

Consequently, the Shan States were 'pacified' over the years 1885 to 1890, and those areas achieved a status different from that of Burma proper. While Thibaw was deposed, the Shan princes were permitted to retain their titles and rule their respective states in a manner similar to that of the Indian maharajas. As protectorates and not colonies, the Shan States had their own administration, police forces, civil servants, magistrates, and judges.[35]

Hudson wrote that "the annexation of Upper Burma in 1885, gave us a frontier with China, much of it so undefined that we had to arrange for its delimitation by joint commissions of British and Chinese officers. Neither side wanted the Wa States, a singularly unattractive area, a liability, not an asset, and the Chinese, when discussing the map, agreed to leave them on our side of the frontier."[36] The British, Hudson said, were "left with the burden of policing them and preventing their annual raids into civilised territory."[37] Scott had already concluded that "the Wa never stood against us, even in their permanently fortified villages. Their shooting was puerile, and our casualties were a mere handful, but their constant sniping and ambushes were distracting … [but] since they will never stand, it is impossible to punish them save by burning their villages."[38]

But Hudson also concluded—and that was as late as the 1930s—that "throughout history, the only administered area on either side of the Burma-China frontier were the valleys and a few main routes. The hills were No Man's Land, even for the Chinese, and the Wa massif was especially *terra incognita*. Nobody ever went there and even the approaches were dreaded, the Salween and Mekong valleys being malaria-ridden—Chinese officers regarded the whole area as a penal station."[39]

The presence of the Wa, and prevailing myths about them, was another reason why Chinese administrators did not venture into these remote mountains. Dorothy J. Solinger wrote in her study of ethnic minorities in Yunnan:

The wild Kawa [i.e. Wa], living between the Salween and the Mekong Rivers, were head-hunters. Their fondness for warfare, and their superstitious belief that Chinese heads were the most efficacious for their sacrifices, had historically kept the Han out of their hills quite effectively … these Kawa hated the Han and never came under their influence. Only a few scattered Shan settlements dotted the otherwise homogenous, isolated and mountainous wild Kawa homeland on the Burma border.[40]

There is, in fact, no historical evidence to suggest that the Wa saw Chinese heads as especially preferable, or that heads were used in religious rites, but just the notion that it could be true was enough to keep all Chinese except some brave and locally connected silver and opium traders out of the Wa Hills. Interaction with the Shan was mostly in the valleys, and then when Wa came down from their hills to buy or barter certain necessities.

Britain, however, had a fundamental strategic interest in controlling the Chinese frontier. That meant establishing a semblance of stability along the border, and leaving the Wa to run their own affairs as long as they did not raid the lowlands. There was also nothing there of any commercial interest. By the end of the nineteenth century, the silver deposits had been depleted, and the opium that was grown in the Wa Hills was of poor quality and most of it was consumed locally.

The British policy towards the Wa was to contain them rather than try to administer their hills. Peace in the frontier areas was important because Britain's interest in Burma as a whole was as a backdoor to China for trade and commerce. The strategic importance of Burma was recognized by other colonial powers as well, and some of them had been in the region even before the British arrived on the scene. One of the first was the Vereenigde Oost-Indische Compagnie (VOC), or the Dutch East India Company. Having lost Formosa, or Taiwan, to rebellious Chinese forces from the mainland in 1662, and then been excluded from Chinese ports as well, the Dutch went looking for alternative trade routes to China. Burma seemed an obvious route from the Bay of Bengal to the vast Chinese market, and that was why the Dutch maintained a significant presence in Burma for nearly half a century. Their eye was on the northern Irrawaddy River port of Bhamo at the beginning of an old trade route called the 'ambassadors' road,' which ended in Yunnanfu, today's Kunming. Bhamo, in today's Kachin State, was as far north as the influence of the Burmese kings stretched in those days.

However, the VOC did not succeed. "Time and again," Dutch historian Wil O. Dijk wrote, "the Company's factors in Burma pleaded with the King to allow the VOC a trading post on the Sino-Burmese border, but to no avail. Eventually this ban became a major factor contributing to the Dutch decision to abandon Burma."[41] That was a major setback for the Dutch because, as Dijk writes, "there is perhaps no route by which overland traffic between southwestern China and any point on the Bay of Bengal can so readily be carried than the Bhamo route."[42]

Nevertheless, Dutch merchants stayed on in Burma even after the British conquest in the nineteenth century, and the colony attracted a wide range of other merchants from all over the world. Rangoon, the capital of British Burma since 1853, became one of the most cosmopolitan cities in Asia, with significant foreign communities of Indians, Chinese, Armenians, Jews, Persians, Europeans, and Eurasians. It was, of course, not because of trade with China, but all kinds of commercial activities benefited from Burma's strategic location at the crossroads of South and Southeast Asia.

Some modern Chinese writers are eager to find historical justifications for President Xi Jinping's Belt and Road Initiative (BRI). Pan Qi, a former vice minister of communications, wrote for the September 2, 1985 issue of the official Chinese weekly *Beijing Review*, that "there was a road connecting western Yunnan with southeast and west Asia quite early in history: Zhang Qian, a Han Dynasty (202 B.C.–220 A.D.) diplomat, helped open a southern 'Silk Road' from Sichuan, and the artery was travelled for centuries."[43] There is no doubt that Zhang Qian wrote extensively about trade routes to and from China, Central Asia, and beyond.[44] But his attempts to forge a route from Sichuan to India proved unsuccessful.

There may never have been a 'southern Silk Road' but the 'ambassador's road,' sometimes called the 'tribute road,' was real, although it could hardly be described as a highway even by eighteenth- or nineteenth-century standards. It got is name because some Burmese kings and Shan princes paid tribute to the Chinese emperor, which, in modern China has been interpreted as a kind of recognition of Chinese sovereignty over those regions. But this tribute payment should be seen as a bribe rather than a sign of acceptance of the authority of a higher power: take this and leave us alone. It was meant to keep the Chinese at bay, nothing else. Several Shan princes paid tribute to the Burmese kings for precisely the same reason.

British rule in Burma—and the Shan States—was meant to change all that. On March 1, 1894, China and the United Kingdom signed a convention that was meant to regulate, and perhaps even stimulate, cross-border trade. There was even talk about building a railway from Burma to China. From 1894 to 1900, Major Davis, a British official, made a remarkable series of surveys of the northern Shan States and Yunnan for possible railway routes. He found that the most convenient route would be from Mandalay over the hills to Lashio and then on to Kunlong on the Salween River. From there, along the Nam Ting River, a Salween tributary, the terrain was relatively flat all the way into Yunnan, where mountains once again dominated the landscape.[45] Davis argued that the railway should be built on both commercial—to facilitate cross-border trade—and political grounds: to control the backdoor to China in order to secure British influence over Yunnan and other restive provinces.

Unfortunately for Davis, his final surveys of the projected railway across Yunnan were lost when his colleague, Captain W. A. Watt-Jones, was killed during the Boxer Rebellion in Beijing in 1900. If the plan had materialized, the railway would have skirted the northernmost fringes of the Wa Hills. The cost of such a railway would also have been prohibitive. Davis estimated that a meter-gauge line would cost 20 million pounds and that the construction would take at least ten years.[46] A railway was built from Mandalay to Lashio, and that included the spectacular Gokteik viaduct, which was built in 1899 and opened in 1900. Components for the 689-meter-long bridge were made by the Pennsylvania Steel Company and shipped to Burma. The height of the bridge is 102 meters, the highest in Burma and, at the time, the largest railway trestle in the world.

But after that, nothing more happened on the railway front. Overall, trans-Burma trade with China proved disappointing and Burma Railways abandoned all plans of construction beyond Lashio to the Chinese frontier. John LeRoy Christian, a US army major, wrote in 1940 that even jade from the mines around Hpakan in Kachin

State was no longer sent along the ancient routes through Guangxi in southern China, but went by sea from Rangoon to Guangzhou and "Britain and France forgot Yunnan and their rivalry for its trade."[47]

It was not until 1937 that China and Britain awakened to the importance of the Yunnan gateway. China was at war with Japan, Shanghai was attacked, and China's maritime ports were blockaded by the Japanese navy. Work then began on building an all-weather highway from Burma to Yunnan to supply the Chinese forces that were resisting the Japanese advance in the east. It was not only a matter of cutting a road over the mountains of Yunnan. The Salween and the Mekong, two great rivers, also had to be spanned by modern steel-cable suspension bridges. Anywhere from 150,000 to 300,000 men using the most primitive of engineering equipment went to work, and as soon as it was opened in 1939 hundreds of trucks sped off on the 1,145-kilometer run from Lashio to Kunming. Even after its completion, no fewer than 30,000 men were kept constantly at work on maintenance and improvement of the surface to make sure it could carry heavy traffic.[48] That was, of course, the famous and fabled Burma Road that wound its way in numerous switchback curves over the mountains.

Then, the Japanese invaded Burma in January 1942. The Burma Road was cut and the allied forces—the United Kingdom and the United States—had to look for an alternative route to send supplies to the Kuomintang forces in China's interior. The American commander, General Joseph W. Stilwell, who earned the nickname 'Vinegar Joe' for his short temper and abrasive manner, came up with a bold solution: to cut an entirely new road from the small town of Ledo in Assam in northeastern India across northernmost Burma into China, where it would link up with the older Burma Road. He argued that it would be possible because the Naga and Kachin hills in the north were never fully conquered by the Japanese. There, local Kachin guerrillas, supported by the United Kingdom and the United States, were constantly harassing the Japanese, and with some more Allied support they should be able to maintain reasonable safety for the road construction crews. Stilwell, who had served as a military adviser to the nationalist Chinese leader Chiang Kai-shek, did not want to abandon him and his forces in their fight against the Japanese. He had also brought with him Chinese soldiers to India, where they were being trained and equipped to assist the Allied forces. For the British, it was also the beginning of the campaign to reestablish their rule over Burma.

First went Stilwell's American-trained Chinese divisions, driving the Japanese before them. On either side, in flanking movements, Chinese and American patrols provided security for the road construction teams. On the heels of the Chinese divisions came the trailblazers, marking out the line with axes for the armored bulldozers that followed. Last came the main labor force, who blasted the road, paved it, and constructed steel bridges across the innumerable streams and rivers along the way.

While the Burma Road was built by Chinese labor, Stilwell's road construction effort was one of the most mixed anywhere in the world. Lieut.-Col. Frank Owen, a British officer in one of the teams, described the laborers: "Chinese, Chins, Kachins, Indians, Nagas, Garos slashed, hauled and piled, Negroes drove machines. Black, brown, yellow and white men toiled shoulder-deep in the streams, belt-deep in red mud. On one camp, 2,000 labourers spoke 200 different dialects."[49]

It was the British Empire, with considerable American support, that struck back against the Japanese. Soon weapons carriers, guns, tanks, and infantry columns flowed down the ten-meter-wide double-tracked, metaled, trenched, banked, and bridged road which Stilwell had initiated. Town after town was conquered, and even the administrative center of the Kachin Hills, Myitkyina, fell on August 3, 1944 after a seventy-eight-day siege by the Allies. The road, which was known as 'the Stilwell Road' or 'the Ledo Road,' became a new highway stretching from Ledo to Kunming, a total of 1,726 kilometers.

Other dry-weather roads were built by Allied engineers and local labor from India into the Chin Hills, from Manipur to the Chindwin River, and to the Arakan region across the border from East Bengal. The Japanese were forced out of Rangoon in May 1945, and on August 15 their last units surrendered to the Allied forces at the southeastern city of Moulmein. As LeRoy Christian remarked in 1945, "Altogether, the isolation of Burma had been destroyed by the current war."[50]

The same held true also in the Wa Hills. But their contacts with the outside world had actually already entered a new stage when the first Western missionaries arrived there in the 1930s. The trailblazer was Marcus Vincent Young, an American Baptist, whose father William Young had come to Burma in 1892 and began spreading the gospel in Kengtung in 1901. After failing to convert any Buddhist Shan, he turned to missionary work among the Lahu in the hills surrounding Kengtung city. The Lahu, like some other Southeast Asian peoples such as the Karen further to the south in Burma, held a legend predicting that a white man holding a big book would one day arrive to bring salvation among people who could not read and write.

Adoniram and Ann Judson, American Baptist missionaries, became aware of that tale when they arrived in southeastern Burma in 1813, and to their initial astonishment Karen came down in the thousands from their hills to welcome the white foreigners.[51]

Similarly, thousands of Lahu flocked to Kengtung to see and listen to Young, a white American who wore a white tropical suit and, like the Judsons, carried his Bible wherever he went. He capitalized on the fact that the Lahu had a similar belief, and his conversion rate was so high that a delegation was sent to Kengtung to investigate. According to US researcher Alfred McCoy:

> Although the investigators concluded that Reverend Young was pandering to pagan myths, Baptist congregations in the United States were impressed by his statistical success and had already started sending large contributions to 'gather in the harvest.' Bowing to financial imperatives, the Burma Baptist Mission left the White God free to wander the hills.[52]

Young put the Lahu language into roman script and his son Vincent, who went to work mainly among the 'tame Wa' in 1920s, did the same wherever he went. In 1933, Vincent Young and his Wa colleagues romanized the Wa language and published the first book in this new script, a collection of hymns, identified on its title page as being written in the 'Kaishin dialect.'[53] A complete translation of the Bible into romanized Wa was published in 1939. Vincent Young also founded a church and a missionary school in Menglian in the Wa area of southern Yunnan. The school educated hundreds of Wa and Lahu students, many of whom became pastors of Christian congregations in Menglian itself and in Gengma, Cangyuan, Shuangjiang, and Lancang, all counties now on the Chinese side of the Sino-Burmese border.[54]

A constant problem for the British nominal overlords was to determine the exact location of that border which led to confrontations with the Chinese when they, in the nineteenth century, began to claim the mountains on the southern fringes of Yunnan. The British had made some attempts to penetrate the area already before World War II. A body called the Inselin Commission was appointed to more firmly demarcate the border between Burma and China, and in 1935–36 attempts were made for the first time to survey the Wa Hills. The British also stationed two officers in the Wa Hills to "introduce light administration."[55]

The road that was built into the northern Wa Hills in 1941 was part of those efforts. However, large tracts of the Wa Hills remained inaccessible. It was simply too dangerous for any outsider to venture into the areas where head-hunting was still rife. Finally, in 1941, the British and the Chinese agreed on where the border should be. But then the war broke out and the British were forced to leave Burma. Rangoon fell to the Japanese on March 8, 1942 and the rest of the colony was soon overrun as well. It was only in the far north that the Japanese did not establish control, and in some parts of the Shan States.

The Burma Independence Army (BIA), led by Burmese nationalist hero Aung San, had assisted the Japanese when they marched across the border from Thailand and occupied Burma. But wary of local, ethnic sentiments—many of the non-Burmese nationalities tended to be anti-Burmese as well—the Japanese kept the BIA out of the Shan States when they tried to enter the area in 1942.[56] It was not until September 22, 1943 that Japan decided to transfer "the Karenni states, Wa states, and the whole of the Shan states with the exception of Kengtung and Mong Pan states"[57] to a Burmese puppet regime which the Japanese had established in Rangoon on May 8 of that year. That regime continued to 'govern' Burma until the end of the war and was dissolved only when the British returned. It was the Imperial Japanese Army that remained the most powerful institution in Burma throughout the occupation.

Kengtung and Mong Pan were given to Thailand, a Japanese ally, whose support was necessary to secure the borders of the occupied territories. As the British had evacuated Burma and the Shan States in 1942, they sought help from Chiang Kai-shek who sent the 93rd Division into Kengtung while the 249th and 55th Divisions moved into the Karenni States and the southern Shan States. According to Shan historian Sai Aung Tun, "the Chinese soldiers were generally not well trained or well-equipped like the Japanese. The Chinese were badly defeated by superior numbers and mechanised equipment, including airplanes, against which they had no defence."[58]

On May 3, 1942, twenty-seven Thai airplanes flew over Kengtung where the Chinese troops were stationed and bombed the town's market. The bombardment inflicted heavy casualties on the Chinese, who withdraw to the north, close to the Chinese border. A few weeks later, Thai troops led by Field Marshal Pin Choonhavan and his son, Chatichai Choonhavan, marched into Kengtung and the Thai flag flew over the town.[59] Kengtung, with 31,000 square kilometers, the biggest of the Shan States, and the much smaller Mong Pan State across Thailand's northwestern border, were both placed under Thai administration, which the Japanese recognized the following year. Thailand was also given areas in northern Malaya and western Laos as part of the Japanese scheme to establish what they called 'The Greater East Asia Co-prosperity Sphere.'[60]

Fierce fighting raged for months in the north. As the British and their mostly Indian troops retreated either towards India or China, they were bombed by the Japanese. According to Sai Aung

Tun, "corpse after corpse lay scattered in towns, especially Lashio, Hsenwi,"[61] and along the Burma Road, "which came to be known as the Road of Death."[62] The Wa Hills, however, were never the scene of any serious warfare. The Japanese were probably as afraid as anybody else to enter the area. The only recorded exception occurred in the northern Wa Hills shortly after the Japanese invasion. A small contingent of Japanese troops, escorted by a Shan from west of the Salween River, attacked a Wa settlement near Mong Mau and killed twenty-one villagers who, presumably, were armed as well.[63]

The situation was different in Kokang immediately to the north of the Wa Hills. There, the local Chinese population resisted the Japanese when they tried to enter the area at Kunlong on the Salween River. The local ruler of Kokang, Yang Wen-pin, allied himself with the nationalist Chinese, and in 1943 he and his then twenty-three-year-old son Yang Kyein-sein, or Jimmy Yang, were invited to visit Chiang Kai-shek at his wartime capital of Chungqing.[64] Jimmy Yang later became a prominent businessman and politician in Burma, and in the 1960s and 1970s joined a rebel army opposed to military rule.

Kengtung and Mong Pan were returned to the Shan States when the British returned in 1945, not to reestablish colonial rule but to prepare for Burma's independence of which the Frontier Areas Committee of Enquiry was an important part. The Karen never joined the talks and did not, in 1947, go to the small market town of Panglong, north of the Shan States capital Taunggyi, to sign an agreement which paved the way for Burma to become a democratic federal republic with local autonomy for the frontier areas. The day representatives of the Shan, the Kachin, and the Chin signed the Panglong Agreement with Aung San. February 12 is still celebrated as Union Day, a national holiday.[65]

The Shan *saohpa* also asked for, and were granted, the right to secede from the proposed Union of Burma after a ten-year period of independence, that is, in 1958, should they be dissatisfied with the new federation. This right was ensured under the first Burmese Constitution, Chapter X, but applied only to the Shan and Karenni states. The 1947 Constitution stipulated that other states could also be formed, the first would be for the Kachin and the Karen, but those states would not have the right to secede from the Union.[66]

Talks with the Wa did not produce any tangible results or recommendations. Based on the Panglong Agreement and the 1947 Constitution, Burma became an independent federal republic on January 4, 1948, but it had no real jurisdiction of the Wa Hills. During the last years of colonial rule, the British had attempted to establish some kind of indirect rule by appointing Harold Young, William Young's son and Vincent's brother, as assistant superintendent of Mong Lun and adjacent areas. Although he was American, he had been given the rank of captain in the British Army and was put in command of two battalions of mostly Shan soldiers who fought against the Japanese when they occupied most of Burma during World War II. Harold Young's knowledge of the area and of local languages were invaluable assets to the British. He also saw action together with the Americans and the British against the Japanese in the Kachin Hills in the far north of the country, and was there recruited by the US Office of Strategic Services, a forerunner to the Central Intelligence Agency (CIA).[67]

After the war, Harold Young tried and convicted several local warlords who were suspected of having collaborated with the Japanese. Among them was Khun Ja, the uncle of Khun Sa, who became a prominent drug trafficker in the 1960s and ran his own private army in the Golden Triangle, the notorious drug-producing area where Thailand, Burma, and Laos meet, until he eventually surrendered to the Burmese government in January 1996. Khun Ja was executed by a gunshot to his head on the banks of the Irrawaddy River.[68]

Whatever control the British, and after 1948 the government of independent Burma may have had in some outlying areas, was abandoned when, in the early 1950s renegade nationalist Chinese Kuomintang force overran large tracts of the eastern Shan States. Beaten and defeated by Mao Zedong's communists in the Chinese civil war, they had been unable to join the main force that retreated, along with Chiang Kai-shek, to Taiwan, and the only alternative to surrender was to regroup in the mountains across China's southwestern border.

Kuomintang solders first entered the northern Wa Hills and then marched through Mong Lun, where the local ruler, however, managed to protect his people and their area. The nationalist Chinese pushed on to the mountains north of Kengtung, the home of Akha, Palaung, and other hill peoples. That area was easier to control than the wild Wa Hills. The Kuomintang also established a presence in Kokang, a district north of the Wa Hills populated by ethnic Chinese of Yunnanese stock. Even if the Kuomintang presence in the Wa Hills was relatively limited, the Wa, who had been largely spared the devastation of World War II, found themselves caught up in the intricacies of world politics.

The Kuomintang built an air base at Mong Hsat near the Thai border and soon supply flights began to arrive from Bangkok and Taiwan, where the Republic of China, defeated by the communists on the mainland, lived on under the leadership of Chiang Kai-shek and his main Kuomintang force. The effort was supported by the United States and its Central Intelligence Agency (CIA), and the plan was to reconquer the mainland from those bases in the northeastern mountains of the Shan States. It was, in a sense, the CIA's first secret war, and General Li Mi, the Kuomintang officer in charge of the operation, was proclaimed commander of the 'Yunnan Province Anti-Communist National Salvation Army'[69]

This was at a time when the United States and its allies were fighting under the United Nations banner against North Korean and Chinese forces on the Korean peninsula. Claire Chennault, a hard-line former US general and World War II hero who had served as an adviser to Chiang Kai-shek, later admitted publicly that a plan existed to wage a broader war against China, using Burma as a springboard:

> It is reported—and I have reason to believe it is true—that the Nationalist [KMT] Government offered three full divisions ... of troops to fight in Korea, but the great opportunity was not putting the Nationalists in Korea. It was a double envelopment operation. With the United Nations forces in Korea and the Nationalist Chinese in southern areas ... the Communists would be caught in a giant pincer ... this was a great opportunity—not to put the Nationalist Chinese in Korea, but to let them fight in the south.[70]

Between 1950 and 1952, the Kuomintang army in Burma's Shan States tried no fewer than seven times to invade Yunnan but was repeatedly driven back across the border. The Burmese Army then entered the Shan States to rid the country of its uninvited guests, and that in turn led to an unprecedented militarization of the Shan States. But the areas east of the Salween River were too remote to be affected by the buildup. There, the Kuomintang reigned supreme through alliances it had established with local warlords, most of them from Kokang and the eastern Shan States, but some of whom were also Wa.

The Burmese government raised the issue in the United Nations, and on April 23, 1953 the General Assembly adopted a resolution stating that "these foreign forces [i.e. the Kuomintang] must be disarmed and either agree to internment or leave the Union of Burma forthwith."[71] At first the UN resolution seemed to have had some impact on the situation. On October 29, a joint US-Thai-Taiwan communique was issued in Bangkok stating that 2,000 nationalist soldiers, including their families, would be withdrawn. Taiwan also pledged it would no longer supply the troops in Burma with weapons, and those who remained there would be disowned.[72]

The evacuation began in February 1954 and lasted for a month. Kuomintang soldiers were brought by truck from the border to Chiang Mai in northern Thailand where, for the benefit of the media, they were paraded through the streets dressed in smart uniforms and newly issued tennis shoes before they boarded US aircraft destined for Taiwan. Other units left via Chiang Rai north of Chiang Mai and Lampang to the south.

The evacuation no doubt weakened the Kuomintang, but several thousand of its troops still remained in the hills of the eastern and southern Shan States. It was also becoming increasingly clear that not all the troops that were sent to Taiwan were genuine Kuomintang soldiers. The US researcher Alfred McCoy noted:

"Many of the troops carried rusting museum pieces as their arms. The Burmese observers, now allowed into the staging area, frequently protested that many of the supposed Chinese looked more like Lahus or Shans. Although other observers ridiculed those accusations, the Burmese were correct. Among them there were large number of boys, Shans and Lahus. Even by 1971 there were an estimated 300 Lahu tribesmen still living in Taiwan who had been evacuated during this period.[73]

The Yunnan Province Anti-Communist National Salvation Army was officially disbanded, but thousands of nationalist Chinese soldiers remained in the Shan States and in settlements on the border with Thailand. The hill peoples living in the areas where they operated were the most tragic victims of the war, which continued for years after the so-called repatriation in 1954. Elaine Lewis, an American Baptist missionary working first in Kengtung and then in northern Thailand, wrote in 1957 that "at the time the Chinese Communists occupied Yunnan Province to the border of Kengtung State in 1950, a great flood of hill peoples came down to Kengtung State."[74] According to Lewis, the Kuomintang invasion forced many of them to flee again:

> For many years there have been large numbers of Chinese Nationalist troops in the area demanding food and money from the people. The areas in which these troops operate are getting poorer and poorer and some villagers are finding it necessary to flee … many hill people from the area have found their way into the hills of northern Thailand, so that now one may find substantial numbers of Lahus, Akhas, Meau [Hmong], Was, and other hill tribes originally from Kengtung in the hills of northern Thailand.[75]

Even if some villagers fled across the border when soldiers from the Chinese People's Liberation Army (PLA) entered southern Yunnan in the early 1950s, they were at first quite lenient in its treatment of the hill peoples. Hardly any Chinese had been there before, which was the reason some fled. The PLA was seen as a foreign force, so people did not know what to expect and were afraid of them. But the main reason the PLA had entered the area was to prevent the Kuomintang from crossing the border with Burma, and for that they needed the support of the local people. In his account of his travels in the Chinese Wa Hills, Winnington met a Wa leader called Jabuei, who told him that the PLA first came into the area in 1950 and called him and other village headmen to a meeting:

> They said they were against the Kuomintang and so we listened to them, although they were Hans [Chinese]. They told us that once the Kuomintang was driven out, there would be no more oppression of the minority peoples by the Hans. We should be masters of our own lives and they would co-operate with the headmen and bring a better life to all the Wa people. Instead of stealing from our people they would bring gifts and new doctrines that would help the Wa to grow rich like the Hans.[76]

In order to spread literacy among the Wa in China, the new communist authorities introduced a new writing system for their language in 1957. Like the Wa script invented by Vincent Young and his Wa workers, it was also based on the roman alphabet but was designed to be closer to the then new *pinyin* romanization of Chinese characters.[77]

China's own way of romanizing the Wa language was, as Fiskesjö points out, part of a broader scheme "to support the political and military consolidation of Chinese rule over the area, and the introduction of social and economic reforms."[78] Primarily, it included the establishment of Chinese rule where there had been none before, including crushing what the Chinese communists labeled *canfei*, 'bandit remnants,' or the remnants of the Kuomintang.[79]

After a few years of leniency, and as soon as the Kuomintang threat had been eliminated, the Chinese authorities introduced an entirely new oppressive system. Weapons in the possession of Wa tribesmen, who were used to being armed because they depended on hunting, were confiscated, and according to Fiskesjö all paraphernalia associated with head-hunting was thoroughly destroyed, along with the social institutions that sustained independent Wa society:

Drum-houses were torn down, along with any *njouh* head-poles [a head-hunter's head-container] planted near them; the log drums were thrown out, or burned (only surviving in a few faraway museums, such as the display at the museum of the Yunnan Nationalities University in Kunming, the provincial capital). The roadside *a nog* [head-container posts planted along the approach to a village] were destroyed or abandoned; the fortifications protecting villages were broken up and demolished. The major rituals of the past were abandoned. Chief ritualists and other leaders of were demoted, marginalized, or even persecuted.[80]

Wa elders Fiskesjö spoke to regarded 1958 as the key watershed "since in that year the Chinese shifted policy from reconciliation to enforcement."[81] Even the Wa had to become Chinese communists and were herded into people's communes.

In the Shan States of Burma, discontent was simmering. As the Shan's constitutional right to secede from the Union was coming into force in 1958, meetings were held in many towns and demands were raised for independence. The Burmese Army's war against the Kuomintang meant that the Shan had become squeezed between two forces, both of which were perceived as foreign and oppressive. The government tried to suppress the growing nationalist movement by using the army and its dreaded intelligence service which, in effect, functioned as a secret police force. But the outcome was counterproductive. Groups of young people moved into the jungle, where they organized armed guerrilla units. One such group was called Noom Suk Harn, or 'The Young and Brave Warriors,' and was led by a man called Saw Yan Da. His other name was Sao Noi, and he was a Shan from Yunnan. He was joined by some university students who had fled the towns when the Burmese Army began its campaign to suppress the Shan nationalist movement.

In 1959, a well-known Union Military Police officer named Bo Mong joined the rebellion. He was an ethnic Wa, and with a band of Wa warriors and Shan students he launched a surprise attack on the garrison town of Tang-yan. They managed to capture Tang-yan while another group tried, unsuccessfully, to attack Lashio in the north. It was not a well-planned and synchronized military campaign and the Burmese Army eventually managed to recapture Tang-yan. But the authorities in Rangoon were taken aback by the sudden outburst of violence in the Shan States. The battle of Tang-yan marked the beginning of a long war between the Union Government and various Shan rebel armies.

In 1959, the Shan *saohpa*-whose attitude to the rebellion had been ambivalent—some supported it while others wanted to remain within the Union—formally renounced all their powers at a grand ceremony held at the state capital of Taunggyi and attended by all the *saohpa* as well as the commander of the Burmese Army, General Ne Win, who was then heading a caretaker government. The duties of the *saohpa* were taken over by the elected Shan State government. The Shan States became Shan State, and it was hoped this would satisfy the aspirations of the nationalists. It did not. In April 1960, a new, better organized rebel force, the Shan State Independence Army, was formed by Shan students who, dissatisfied with the authoritarian rule of Sao Noi, had broken away from his Noom Suk Harn.[82]

In the early 1960s, the Kachin in the far north were also getting prepared to rebel. General Ne Win had allowed elections to take place in 1960, and U Nu was returned to power. But one of his election promises had been to make Buddhism the state religion of Burma, a move seen by the predominantly Christian Kachin as an open provocation.

In 1960, the Burmese and Chinese governments had at last managed to demarcate their common border. As part of the deal, three Kachin villages and the Panhung-Panglao area in the Wa Hills had been handed over to the Chinese in exchange for Burmese sovereignty over an area northwest of the town of Namkham known as the Namwan Assigned Tract, a 220-square-kilometer area, which the British had leased from China in 1897. The village tracts in Kachin State encompassed 152 square kilometers and the Wa territory that was ceded to China was 189 square kilometers in area.[83] The deal was not unfair by international standards, but rumors soon spread across Kachin State to the effect that vast tracts of Kachin territory had been handed over to China.

On February 5, 1961, in response to the question of making Buddhism the state religion and the border issue, a group of Kachin led by World War II veteran Zau Seng formed the Kachin

Independence Army (KIA). It soon took over large tracts of land in Kachin State as well as the Kachin-inhabited areas of northern Shan State.

On the Thai border, Karen, Karenni, and Mon rebel armies had been active for years. Burma was in turmoil, and on March 2, 1962 General Ne Win stepped in, overthrew the elected government of U Nu and introduced not a caretaker government, as in the late 1950s, but a straightforward military dictatorship. While it was meant to contain and eventually crush the ethnic insurgencies, the outcome was just the opposite. Those rebellions flared anew as opposition grew against the new military government, which had abolished the limited autonomy the ethnic areas had enjoyed under the 1947 Constitution and replaced it with strict centralized rule. The 1962 coup also led to the rebirth of the insurgent Communist Party of Burma, which from powerful beginnings in the early 1950s had dwindled into a rag-tag army holding out in isolated pockets in central Burma.

2

The Plan that Failed

Incongruous as it may seem, an event that would much later determine the Wa's place in history began on August 15, 1939 in a small flat in Rangoon's Barr Street. Thakin Kodaw Hmaing, a writer and a major figure in Burma's nationalist movement lived there, and on that day a small group of young nationalists gathered in his home for an important meeting. They wanted to form a Burmese communist party. But since Barr Street is just around the corner from where the British authorities had their spies, the nationalists moved to a more discreet location in Myay Nu Street. It was a small wooden house, long gone, where one of them, Thakin Ba Hein, lived with his family. There, the Communist Party of Burma (CPB) was formed, and this unpretentious meeting in Rangoon is called the CPB's first congress.[1] Aung San became the first general secretary of the party.

Apart from Thakin Ba Hein, a young, talented, and well-known leftist intellectual, three other members of what was called the 'Thakin Party' were also present—Thakin Aung San, Thakin Hla Pe (Bo Let Ya) and Thakin Bo—as well as two ethnic Indians, Naag, a medical doctor, and the theoretician Hamendranath Ghoshal. *Thakin*, or 'master,' the Burmese equivalent of *sahib* in Hindi, was a title reserved for the British in Burma, but the young nationalists used it show that they, and not the colonial administrators, were the real masters of their country. Ghoshal and Dr. Naag were never members of the Thakin Party or the Dohbama Asiayone ('Our Burma Association'), an organization consisting solely of ethnic Burmans.[2] The leftists were staunch nationalists as well and had little regard for members of other ethnic communities. When Thakin Kodaw Hmaing, the learned Grand Old Man of Burmese nationalism, was offered the position of chief minister of the Shan State of Yawnghwe in the 1920s, he refused to accept the post, saying he had no wish to serve under "a foreign ruler"[3] and, as a nationalist "to kneel down before a Shan *saohpa*."[4]

Quite independently from the radical student movement among the Burmese intellectuals, communist ideas also penetrated Rangoon's Chinese community in the late 1920s. 'Chinese communism' was first introduced into Burma by a man called Wu Wei Sai (alias Wu Ching Sin) and his wife, who arrived in Rangoon in May 1929 from Shanghai. Wu became the editor-in-chief of *Burma News*, a Chinese-language newspaper, and his wife, who is not named in British police documents, found work as teachers at the Chinese-medium Peng Min School in Rangoon. The couple distributed communist leaflets in Rangoon's Chinatown and built up a small circle of followers. This clandestine group of ethnic Chinese members was discovered when, in December 1929, the Special Branch of the British police intercepted a letter Wu Wei Sai had written in invisible ink to the regional communist headquarters in Singapore.[5]

Wu left Burma in 1930 and was never heard of again. Only half a dozen followers remained in the cell he had established. A Chinese cell was also established in the central town of Pyinmana, but neither this group nor the one in Rangoon had any contact with the radical

Burmese nationalist movement; instead, their links were with the Chinese-dominated communist movement in Malaya and Singapore.

Had the two groups established contact in the late 1930s, communism in Burma could have taken a very different course. Despite being inspired by the communist movement in India, of which Burma formed a part until 1937, the Burmese radicals also pinned their hopes for help in their struggle against the British on Mao Zedong and his communist army in China. However, they had no means of contacting Mao's communists, something which Wu and his group could have helped with. Nevertheless, the *thakin* met in Rangoon in 1940. At the advice of Thakin Kodaw Hmaing, they decided to send CPB general secretary Aung San and Thakin Hla Myaing (Bo Yan Aung) to Shanghai, where they knew the Chinese communists were strong.

Eager to elude the British police, the duo disguised themselves as Chinese deck passengers and took the first ship to China they could find in Rangoon's port. It was, however, destined for Amoy, or Xiamen, a coastal city in China's Fujian Province, which was then occupied by the Japanese. The two young Burmese—Aung San was twenty-five and Thakin Hla Myaing thirty-two—found jobs as English teachers on Gulangyu Island, part of Xiamen but historically with an international settlement similar to that in Shanghai.

A letter they sent back to their comrades in Burma was intercepted by Japanese agents in Rangoon, and they were tracked down to the room they had rented on Gulangyu. Japanese agents based in Xiamen visited them and listened carefully to what they had to say. Aung San and Hla Myaing were told to forget the Chinese communists. The Japanese would provide them and their comrades with arms and military training, and they were brought on a Japanese ship to Tokyo.[6]

The Japanese took them to Thailand, and while Thakin Hla Myaing remained behind in Thailand, Aung San, again in disguise, returned to Burma in February 1941. The following month, he left on a Japanese freighter with four of his comrades. In April, another batch consisting of seven young *thakin* were smuggled out of Burma. More followed in June and July, helped out of Burma by Japan's intelligence services. A Burmese drama student in Tokyo, Ko Saung, had joined the initial meeting but never took part in the military training that followed the arrival of the others.

In July, an unexpected batch of eleven arrived, and that group included several members of a right-wing minority faction of the Dohbama. It was clear that the Japanese did not fully trust Aung San and his left-leaning comrades. The July batch included Thakin Shu Maung, who would later be known as Ne Win. Not surprisingly, friction soon arose between the original group and the latecomers. Thakin Shwe, who later became Kyaw Zaw, remembers that Aung San and Shu Maung (Ne Win) quarreled quite often when they were at a training camp on the Chinese island of Hainan, which was occupied by the Japanese. Thakin Shwe, or Kyaw Zaw, remembers that Aung San objected to what he saw as Shu Maung's immoral character: "He was a gambler and a womaniser, which the strict moralist Aung San, and the rest of us as well, despised. But for the sake of unity, we kept together as much as we could."[7] They thought they would be fighting for independence from the United Kingdom, but the Japanese had other plans. They wanted to occupy and control Burma in order to cut American and British support for the Chinese nationalists who were battling the Japanese in China's interior. That support was coming from India to Burmese ports and then overland to Yunnan.

Although Ko Saung remained behind in Tokyo and one of them died from malaria while on Hainan before he could return to Burma, the group became known as 'The Thirty Comrades,' the total number of young Burmese who had been recruited by the Japanese. Throughout modern Burmese history, they have enjoyed a cult-like status, and despite their alliance with the Japanese are seen as the fathers of the country's independence.

In December 1941, the remaining twenty-eight of the Thirty Comrades were transferred to Bangkok where the Burma Independence Army (BIA) was formally set up on the 26th. They took a blood-oath, promising each other to fight until death for freedom for Burma. One more died of illness in Thailand, so only twenty-seven of them entered Burma together with the Japanese in early 1942. Many more Burmese joined on the border or as soon as they had crossed it. The number of BIA fighters had swelled to thirty thousand when Rangoon fell on March 7. The BIA itself did not actually do much fighting; they followed on the heels of the Imperial Japanese Army, which drove the British out.

On August 1, 1943, the Japanese granted 'independence' to Burma and a cabinet, made up of Burmese nationalists, was set to govern the country. In reality, Japanese occupation had replaced British colonial rule, and that soon became obvious to Aung San and his comrades. An emissary, the communist Thakin Thein Pe, was sent secretly to Calcutta to contact the British, and in 1944 a front organization called the Anti-Fascist People's Freedom League (AFPFL), was set up to coordinate the planned uprising against the Japanese. On March 27, 1945, the Burmese nationalists eventually turned their guns against the Japanese, and fierce battles were fought in many parts of central Burma. The Karen and the Kachin, though, had never accepted the Japanese as some kind of 'liberators.' All along they had, with Allied support, carried out guerrilla warfare against the Japanese.

On May 1, 1945, Rangoon was liberated. British rule was restored, but the fight for independence was not over. The CPB, now a legal political party, was a member of the AFPFL and the communist leader, Thakin Than Tun, was Aung San's brother-in-law, so there were, in the beginning, no serious problems within the front. The party had its headquarters in a building at 130 Bagayar Street in Rangoon's Sanchaung township from where it organized labor strikes in the capital and movements among landless peasants in the countryside. But that was not enough for communist hard-liner Thakin Soe, who accused the party leadership of being guilty of advocating 'Browderism,' or the kind of peaceful transition to socialism that Earl Browder, general secretary of the Communist Party of the United States, had come to believe in.[8] This led to a split in the CPB in 1946, and Thakin Soe set up his own outfit called the Communist Party (Red Flag).[9] He and his followers went underground in the Irrawaddy delta to wage a guerrilla war against the British colonial power.

However, the CPB was expelled from the AFPFL in October that year, and its shift from being a legal political party to an organization that was prepared to go underground began in April 1947 when it decided to boycott the elections to the new Constituent Assembly. 'Browderism' was gradually being given up as the CPB increased its contacts with communist parties in other countries. In 1947, politburo member Thakin Ba Thein Tin and *yebaw* (comrade) Aung Gyi, another senior party cadre, represented the CPB at the British Empire Communist Conference in London.[10] A few months later, on January 4, 1948, the British left Burma, which became an independent republic outside the Commonwealth. Communist pressure on the AFPFL not to accept any 'sham independence' was a major reason Burma did not, like other former colonies that had achieved independence, become a dominion where the British monarch remained Head of State.

A month after independence, CPB general secretary Thakin Than Tun and politburo member Thakin Ba Thein Tin went to Calcutta to attend the second congress of the Communist Party of India (CPI). Another group of four Burmese radicals were also in Calcutta at that time, but to take part in an Asian youth conference organized by the Soviet-controlled World Federation of Democratic Youth. Some historians claim that the CPI congress and the youth conference were used by the Soviet Union and Cominform, a new international communist organization set up by Moscow, to draw up a master plan for armed communist rebellions all over Southeast Asia.

There is, however, no historical evidence to back up this claim. The CPI congress did result in the dismissal of CPI's moderate secretary P. C. Joshi and the election of B. T. Ranadive, a much more radical leader, and calls for armed uprisings were heard at the youth conference. But that falls far short of a communist strategy for the entire region. The almost simultaneous outbreak of communist uprisings in Burma, Malaya, French Indochina, and the Philippines in the 1940s had other causes, specific to those countries. Communist forces had played important roles in the struggle against the Japanese occupation of their respective countries. They had weapons, and they did not think that the struggle for their goals, socialism, and communism should be forgotten just because they had been instrumental in driving out the Japanese.

The CPB had nevertheless become radicalized, and condemned what they called 'Burma's sham independence,' which led to a serious conflict with the AFPFL and, especially, the socialist stalwart Kyaw Nyein, who served as home minister in independent Burma's first cabinet. But the radicalization was caused more by domestic issues than by attending meetings in Calcutta. On July 19, 1947, half a year before independence, Aung San had been assassinated by a team led by the rightist politician U Saw. Thakin Than Tun, Aung San's brother-in-law, and other communist leaders were convinced there was a British plot behind the assassination, in which another seven national leaders and a young bodyguard were also gunned down.[11]

Independent Burma's first prime minister, U Nu, was a talented intellectual but hardly the strong leader the country needed during its troubled first years of independence. In an attempt to placate Burma's restless ethnic minorities, Sao Shwe Thaike, the Shan *saohpa* of Yawnghwe, had been appointed president of the new Union of Burma. But that was a ceremonial title with limited political significance. The Karen, the Karenni, and the Mon were ready to rebel against the government, which they did not long after Burma's independence.

In mainstream politics, the situation was becoming more tense as Kyaw Nyein's socialists rallied in the park outside the city hall and attacked the editorial offices of left-wing publications. At first, the CPB had no guns at its office in Bagayar Street, but as the situation deteriorated they began to stock rifles and pistols on the premises. The party also organized labor strikes and began to attack U Nu personally, branding him a 'fascist.' Then, on March 25, 1948, U Nu ordered the arrest of Thakin Than Tun. In a show of defiance, Thakin Than Tun addressed a crowd of three thousand people in downtown Rangoon. Three days later, the police raided the CPB headquarters. It was early in the morning, so the leaders had not yet arrived. At 11.30 am, the party's politburo issued instructions to all leading cadres to leave Rangoon as soon as possible and move to rural areas, where armed struggle was to be organized. This decision to go underground was much more serious than that taken by Thakin Soe two years earlier, which had led to only a few skirmishes with the police. The CPB was one of the most powerful political organizations in the country. Now it was civil war.

Some leaders left in different cars while Thakin Than Tun went in disguise by train. Ghoshal simply caught a bus to Toungoo. Hundreds of other party workers left by whatever means possible. They were all headed for the Pegu Yoma, a densely forested mountain range north of Rangoon. On April 2, in a village near the town of Pegu, the first shots were fired in a civil war between government forces and communist rebels that was to last for several decades.

By the end of April, only a few underground party activists remained in Rangoon to act as the party's 'eyes and ears,' while in the Pegu Yoma the CPB formed its own 'People's Liberation Army of Burma.' The uprising spread quickly across the country, and within a year the CPB had managed to raise a force of 15,000 armed partisans. Guns were snatched from police and army outposts or came from caches various anti-Japanese forces had hidden in forested areas when World War II was over and the British had returned to Burma. CPB units were now active not only in the Pegu Yoma but also in the Irrawaddy delta region, in Tenasserim in the southeast, in the Arakan Yoma in the west, in northern Sagaing Division, and even in parts of central Shan State.

Several Western writers on Burmese history, among them the German scholar Klaus Fleischmann and a British author, Martin

Smith, have argued that a thesis, purportedly written by Ghoshal in December 1947, played an important role in the CPB's decision to resort to armed struggle. Titled *On the Present Situation in Burma and Our Tasks* and referred to as 'the Ghoshal Thesis', it outlines the strategy for a prolonged Maoist-style armed uprising in the countryside. Fleischmann believes it reflects a "more extreme policy of the CPB," which led to the party's "taking up armed insurrection against the government."[12] Smith calls it "historic."[13]

It is, however, highly unlikely that Ghoshal, an ethnic Indian whose main constituency was among the Indian working class in Rangoon and other major cities, would have advocated peasant-led guerrilla warfare in the Burmese countryside where he had no following. Smith acknowledges that there is a "lack of references to the document" in the CPB's own publications before the collapse of the party in 1989.[14] He then goes on to state that "Bertil Lintner has speculated that the absence of copies of Ba Tin's [Ghoshal's] thesis on the CPB side has meant the document might not be authentic. Ba Thein Tin does not support this view,"[15] and then comes a reference to his alleged correspondence with the CPB chairman.

I find this statement astonishing because it was Thakin Ba Thein Tin who told me—and I am the only foreign journalist to have met and interviewed the now late CPB chairman—that he had never heard of such a thesis. Other party veterans were equally bewildered when I asked them about it. I therefore promised to send the CPB leaders a copy of it when I was back in Thailand, which I did. Khin Maung Gyi, the CPB's last general secretary, wrote in a letter to me dated April 15, 1992: "Many thanks for this document. As for us, this is the first time that we have got the opportunity to read the so-called 'Ghoshal Thesis', which was non-existent inside our party and is merely a fabrication with the aim of accusing the CPB as the instigator of the civil war in Burma."

Khin Maung Gyi, then a close acquaintance of Ghoshal, should have known if it were a party document and had been written by him. Both of them were in Rangoon when the party leadership decided to leave for the Pegu Yoma mountains. According to both Khin Maung Gyi and Thakin Ba Thein Tin, Ghoshal was unwilling to go with them and the other party leaders and cadres because he was busy organizing a strike among ethnic Indian dock workers in Rangoon. Instigating a civil war in the countryside would have been far from his mind.[16]

Thus, it is impossible that Thakin Ba Thein Tin himself wrote what Smith claims he did. In fact, Smith had no contacts with any CPB leaders until I introduced him to a cadre in Yunnan in 1988. Smith says he corresponded with Thakin Ba Thein Tin in the period 1988–1990,[17] which is also unlikely because the Chinese dispatched the old chairman to Hunan Province after the April 1989 mutiny, and he was kept there, incommunicado, until he died in 1995. It is more likely that a much younger party member, who was not in Rangoon in the late 1940s, wrote those letters, perhaps on behalf of Thakin Ba Thein Tin.

That, however, leaves an intriguing question: who wrote the so-called Ghoshal Thesis and why? A party veteran, now living in Rangoon, points at a strikingly similar document with an almost identical title written by Mao Zedong in December 1947: *The Present Situation and Our Tasks*.[18] Khin Maung Gyi might be right. It was fabricated by someone to discredit the CPB, and that 'someone' could only be in the psychological warfare section of the military intelligence service or perhaps in a department under Burma's then hard-line interior minister Kyaw Nyein, who led the campaign against the communists. Whatever the case, Ghoshal did not write it and it is not a genuine CPB document. But it shows how sophisticated Burma's security services already were at that time.

Despite its initial successes on the battlefield, the CPB made some serious political blunders. In late 1951, at the height of its strength, its central committee decided to launch an entirely new policy. The Chinese revolution had succeeded because the communists had joined hands with the Kuomintang against the Japanese, and then, when the foreign invader had been defeated, they turned against their erstwhile Kuomintang allies and drove them into exile on the island of Taiwan. At this time, there was a strong belief that a similar strategy could be put into practice in Burma. The CPB leaders suggested that their forces should forge a united front with the Burmese government's army against the Kuomintang invaders in the northeastern and eastern Shan States. If successful, the Burmese communists would attain a stronger position and be able to turn against the government.

In line with this new policy, called 'PCG' (Peace and Coalition Government), the CPB as a conciliatory gesture began to return to the landlords the land they once had confiscated from them and given to the cultivators. The inevitable outcome was that many CPB fighters, who were sons of peasants, became disillusioned and returned to their home villages. The government never accepted the CPB's offer of a united front and, consequently, the party lost nearly half of its fighting force in the process. The communist insurrection had failed.

Moreover, not everyone in the party agreed with the new policies. Shortly after the meeting in late 1951 at which the leadership had decided on their new line, groups of hard-liners began to leave secretly for China to seek support for the continuation of their armed struggle. The first batch of thirty Burmese communists led by *yebaw* Aung Gyi traveled north and managed to cross the border into Yunnan. Early the following year, Thakin Ba Thein Tin, then vice chairman of the party, set out on what was going to be an arduous year-long journey by elephant and on foot towards Yunnan. His party crossed into China near Laiza in Kachin State, then a small border village. They were escorted by Chinese border guards to the town of Baoshan, where they boarded a plane for Kunming and, later, Beijing. One more group followed shortly afterwards, bringing the total of CPB cadres in China to 143. The group also included Bo Zeya, one of the Thirty Comrades and the chief of staff of the CPB's army, politburo member Thakin Than Myaing, and Thakin Baw, a senior member of the central committee.[19]

The Burmese communists were well received by the Chinese and allowed to remain in Chengdu in Sichuan Province, where they were given political training. But no military aid was forthcoming at this time; the government in Beijing was not willing to sacrifice its friendly relations with the U Nu government for the sake of a relatively small group of Burmese communists who were dissidents even within their own party.

Much to their surprise, however, the newly arrived CPB cadres were introduced to an old comrade who had disappeared almost a decade earlier—Aye Ngwe, a Sino-Burman party member and former student at Rangoon University. When it became clear that Aung San had failed to reach communist-controlled areas in China in 1941, the CPB had sent Aye Ngwe overland to Yunnan, a safer bet than going by ship to some little-known Chinese port.

In September 1941, Aye Ngwe had walked across the border bridge at Kyuhkok-Wanting, where the Burma Road crosses the international frontier. It took him five years to contact the Chinese communists, by which time he had lost touch with the CPB. In 1947, he became a member of the Communist Party of China (CPC) and learned to speak standard Chinese. In Burma, he had spoken only one of the southern dialects. When the CPB cadres began arriving in China in the early 1950s, Aye Ngwe was called upon to act as interpreter.[20]

Unbeknown to the CPB cadres in Sichuan at that time, there was also another group of former fighters from Burma in China. Naw Seng, a Kachin World War II hero who had fought with the British against the Japanese during the war, had at first been a Burmese army officer leading several campaigns against the CPB in the Irrawaddy delta but then turned his guns against the government. He led a band of Kachin and Karen warriors who captured one town after another in northern Burma and the Shan States. His goal was an independent country for the Kachin, which he called Jinghpaw Pawngyawng. But after several initial successes, his group, the Pawngyawng National Defence Force, was eventually cornered at Mong Ko in the northeasternmost corner of the Shan States. In April 1950, Naw Seng and about three hundred of his followers retreated across the border into Yunnan. They were allowed to remain in China, but while the CPB exiles in Sichuan were allowed to study at various institutions in Chengdu and some were even sent to the central party school in Beijing, Naw Seng and his men ended up in a people's commune in rural Guizhou, one of China's poorest and most neglected provinces.

Back in Burma, the CPB was, at last, outlawed in 1953. At the same time, relations between China and Burma were excellent. The

Burmese Army had fought valiantly against the Kuomintang, which Beijing appreciated. On April 22, 1954, China and Burma for the first time signed a bilateral trade agreement. Then, on June 28–29, Chinese Premier Zhou Enlai visited Burma at the invitation of the Burmese government and held talks with U Nu. A joint Sino-Burmese declaration was signed by the two leaders on June 29, endorsing the 'Five Principles of Peaceful Co-existence': Mutual respect for each other's territorial integrity and sovereignty, non-aggression, non-interference in each other's internal affairs, equal and mutual benefits, and peaceful coexistence.[21]

The next issue was to settle the disputed border, which U Nu discussed in detail during a September 1956 visit to China. The border was settled in 1960, but that only led to more turmoil along it as the Sino-Burmese border agreement was one of the factors which led to a new rebellion among the Kachin. Whether Naw Seng was aware of this is unknown, but it is plausible to assume that they did not receive any news from home as he and his followers were toiling in their people's commune in Guizhou, cut off from the rest of the world.

The Burmese communists, though, were much more connected with the outside world. In 1957, three promising younger cadres were selected to further their studies in Moscow. There they were joined by two other Burmese communists who had made it to the Soviet Union from Burma in the early 1950s. The most outstanding of the five were the young intellectual Khin Maung Gyi and San Thu, a party worker from Pyawbwe in central Burma. Khin Maung Gyi attended the Academy of Social Sciences in Moscow and wrote a thesis on 'Agrarian Problems in Burma.'[22]

The Burmese communists were active in their exile, but whatever they were doing had no impact on the situation inside Burma until general Ne Win seized power on March 2, 1962. The Chinese had long been wary of the ambitious and sometimes unpredictable general, and some important events, which reflected the fact that a new chapter in China-Burma relations had begun, took place shortly after his coup. The first rather innocuous step was taken when, on August 1, 1962, the CPB exiles published a document in English titled *Some Facts about Ne Win's Military Government*, denouncing the new regime. Until then, they had not been allowed to print any propaganda material in China. Now they were, and it would soon become even clearer that China's policy towards Burma was undergoing some fundamental changes.

The most urgent task was to find a way to contact the CPB units that were still holding out in the Pegu Yoma and other places in central Burma. There had been no links between them and the exiles since the latter had trekked to China in the early 1950s. By a strange twist of fate, it was the new military regime in Rangoon that unwittingly provided an opportunity for the Burmese communists in China to reestablish contact with the forces at home. Probably hoping that the country's many communist as well as ethnic insurgents would give up when faced with the massive force of the new military government, Ne Win called for peace talks after about a year in power. In July 1963, the CPB, Thakin Soe's much smaller Red Flag communist party, the Karen, Mon, Shan, and Kachin rebel armies, and some smaller groups attended the negotiations in Rangoon, with guarantees of free and safe passage to and from the peace parley, regardless of the outcome.

The colorful Thakin Soe probably attracted the most attention when he arrived accompanied by a team of attractive young girls in khaki uniforms. He placed a portrait of Josef Stalin in front of him on the negotiating table and then began attacking the 'revisionism' of Soviet leader Nikita Khrushchev and the opportunism of Mao Zedong's China. Not surprisingly, Thakin Soe was soon excluded from the talks.

However, twenty-nine CPB members arrived by air from China, ostensibly to participate in the peace talks. Among the 'Beijing returnees,' as they came to be known, were *yebaw* Aung Gyi, Thakin Pu, 'Thirty Comrade' Bo Zeya, a woman cadre called Sein Win, and Thakin Ba Thein Tin, who did not actually participate in the talks but seized the opportunity to sneak out of Rangoon and visit the CPB's headquarters in the Pegu Yoma. He had brought with him radio transmitters from China, and the communist fighters in the Pegu Yoma were shown how to use them so they could communicate with the exiles in Sichuan. They were also told to be patient. Big plans were being hatched in China, and help would soon be forthcoming.[23]

According to CPB documents, the government demanded that the communists should concentrate all their troops and party members in an area stipulated by the authorities, inform the government if there were any remaining guerrillas or cadres elsewhere, stop all organizational activities of the party, and cease fund-raising.[24] The intransigence of the military regime was a blessing in disguise for the CPB. The talks broke down on November 14, and the various insurgents returned to their respective jungle camps. Thakin Ba Thein Tin and another CPB cadre flew back to China, while the remaining twenty-seven 'Beijing returnees' went to the Pegu Yoma where they assumed de facto leadership of the party at home.

Following the split in the international communist movement at about the same time, Khin Maung Gyi, San Thu, and a third party member called Thein Aung were forced to leave Moscow. The CPB had sided with China in the split and were no longer welcome in the Soviet Union. The other two Burmese communists in Moscow, Aung Win and Kyaw Zaw (not the same Aung Zaw as the one from the Thirty Comrades), who had married Russian women, were allowed to remain in the Soviet Union. They later became Burmese language teachers at a school in Moscow where the Soviets trained diplomats and intelligence agents.

A 'leading group of five' to direct the work in China was set up in Beijing shortly after Thakin Ba Thein Tin's return from the peace talks in Rangoon. This group, which became the nucleus of the new leadership of the CPB that emerged in the 1960s, consisted of Thakin Ba Thein Tin as 'leader,' Khin Maung Gyi as his personal secretary, and Thakin Than Myaing, Than Shwe, and Tin Yee as members. Than Shwe was a World War II veteran who had been educated at an officers' training school in Rangoon during the initial stages of the Japanese occupation. Tin Yee was a CPB cadre from Pegu, who had joined the party in 1943 when some of the communists had begun guerrilla warfare against the Japanese. Both had gone to China in the early 1950s.

In late 1963, San Thu, one of the Moscow returnees, was put in charge of a team that began surveying possible infiltration routes from Yunnan into northeastern Burma.[25] The Chinese also built a network of new asphalted highways leading from Kunming to various points along the borders with Burma. Warehouses were stocked with arms and ammunition in preparation for a China-supported thrust into Burma, which would usher in a new era in the history of the CPB insurgency.

The problem was that the CPB cadres in China, with the exception of Than Shwe and a few others, were well-read Marxist intellectuals with little or no military experience. On the other hand, Naw Seng's Kachin were excellent fighters. In early 1963, even before the peace talks began in Rangoon, Naw Seng was brought to Chengdu to meet what had become known as 'the Sichuan *laobing*,' or the Sichuan veterans. He was introduced to Thakin Ba Thein Tin and told that the time had come to go back to Burma and fight. Naw Seng, eager to leave his people's commune in Guizhou, readily agreed. He assembled his men, known now as 'the Guizhou *laobing*,' or the Guizhou veterans, and their military skills were enhanced at a training camp in Yunnan. Aye Ngwe gave them political lectures in Marxism-Leninism.

More alliances were forged in the early 1960s as the small cells of ethnic Chinese communists were for the first time put in touch with the CPB. They were few in number, but the Chinese embassy in Rangoon arranged for ethnic Chinese from the capital and some smaller towns in the Irrawaddy delta to go to the CPB's then base area along the Shweli River in northern Shan State and wait for further instructions.[26]

In preparation for the momentous events that were being planned in Beijing, the time was also ripe for a major shakeup of the party at home. The CPB exiles in China declared in 1964 that the party was "struggling against revisionism or right-wing opportunism as the main danger in the international communist movement and inside our party."[27] There were no more connections with the Communist Party of India, which had been close when the CPB in the years after World War II operated openly in Rangoon and elsewhere. Now, the

CPB was firmly on the Chinese side in the split in the international communist movement and condemned Khrushchev and the 'Soviet revisionists.'[28]

In 1965, a prominent central committee member, Thakin Pe Tint, was sent overland to Yunnan to cement ties between the units in the Pegu Yoma and elsewhere in Burma and the 'leading group of five' in China. Not long after, Aung Sein, a young Burmese communist who had been a soldier in the group that had escorted Thakin Ba Thein Tin to China in 1953, was sent back along the same overland route, using old networks of local contacts, to the Pegu Yoma. He carried with him a letter in which Thakin Ba Thein Tin and the other leaders in China outlined the 'invasion plans' in detail. In 1963, the Pegu Yoma-based headquarters had been informed only in general terms of what was going to happen.[29]

Internally, China was about to embark on a decade of chaos and destruction. In May 1966, Mao called on young people to rise up against what he termed 'counter-revolutionaries' within the Chinese leadership.[30] Then, on August 12, the official weekly *Beijing Review* published a sixteen-point declaration that the Central committee of the Communist Party of China (CPC) had passed on August 8, launching what was called the Great Proletarian Cultural Revolution.[31]

The Beijing returnees, inspired by Mao's Cultural Revolution and assigned the task of similarly 'cleansing' the CPB of 'rightist deviationists,' staged grisly trials in the Pegu Yoma. They enlisted the support of militant *tat ni lunge*, or Red Youth Guards, who often were orphans raised by the party and led to regard it as their 'parent.' Hence, they were immensely loyal to their new masters. *Yebaw* Htay, who had headed the CPB's delegation to the 1963 peace talks, was branded 'Burma's Deng Xiaoping' after Mao's main 'rightist' rival in the CPC, and executed. The veteran Ghoshal was denounced as 'Burma's Liu Shaoqi' after China's disgraced president, and also killed.[32] Bo Yan Aung (Thakin Hla Myaing), one of the Thirty Comrades who had gone with Aung San to Xiamen in 1940, was also among those executed, which meant bludgeoned to death by the *tat ni lunge.*

Many of the intellectuals who had joined the CPB in the wake of the 1962 coup were purged and killed as well. The policy was unofficially referred to as *pyouk-touk-hta,* or, in English, 'the Three Ds': dismissed from office, dispelled from the party, and disposed of (that is, executed.) In 1986, when I asked Thakin Ba Thein Tin about the purges, he was unrepentant and referred to them as a "revolution within the party," and claimed that no more than fifty-three people were executed.[33]

One of the most hard-line of the Beijing returnees was Taik Aung. Born into a peasant family in Waw near Pegu, he had joined the party as a young man and was considered a ruthless fanatic. He led the *pyouk-touk-hta* purges and seemed to take a delight in having veterans as well as younger cadres killed by the *tat ni lunge.*[34]

Of the other Beijing returnees, Bo Zeya was killed in action in 1967 near Tharrawaddy, *yebaw* Aung Gyi fell in battle in 1968, Thakin Pu succumbed to illness in 1969, and Sein Win, the only woman among them, died fighting in the Irrawaddy delta. Among the exiles in China, Thakin Than Myaing was dismissed from the party and languished in a Chinese labor camp until he was released and 'rehabilitated' in 1973.[35] He was fortunate to have survived his ordeal, but the CPB at home experienced five years of extremely bloody purges before the master plan that had been drawn up in Beijing was put into practice. Moreover, that plan went far beyond revitalizing the CPB insurgency.

Kang Sheng, at the time China's intelligence chief and the mastermind behind the formation of a 'new' CPB, had grander plans. During the Vietnam War in the 1960s and 1970s, the Americans talked about what they called 'the domino theory'; if communism was not stopped in Vietnam, it would spread to the rest of Southeast Asia and perhaps even beyond. That theory may have been correct, but for Mao's chief strategist Kang, the North Vietnamese leadership and the National Liberation Front in the south were too close to the Soviet Union to be trusted. Kang's plan was to spread revolution to the region through the CPB and then down to Thailand, Malaysia, and Indonesia, where Maoist-leaning communist parties were active. The plan, absurd as it may seem, also included the Communist Party of Australia (Marxist-Leninist), a tiny group of pro-Beijing Australian radicals. One of Thakin Ba Thein Tin's closest foreign associates was its chairman, a Melbourne lawyer called Edward Fowler Hill. Thakin Ba Thein Tin told me: "Ted Hill and I were together in Beijing. We wrote appeals against the Soviet Union and for world revolution. He was a fine, cultured kind of man."[36]

The plan was put into action early in the morning of January 1, 1968. Naw Seng and his Kachin fighters crossed the border into Burma at Mong Ko, the very same place he had retreated from in 1950. But this time, his men were heavily armed, and within hours overran the Burmese Army garrison there. Heavy fighting continued in surrounding areas, and for the first time in the history of the country's civil war, the Burmese Army found itself outgunned, and in some cases even outnumbered as thousands of Chinese 'volunteers' streamed across the border to fight alongside the CPB.

Most Western historians have assumed that China's decision to lend all-out support to the CPB was prompted by riots in Rangoon's

Chinatown in mid-1967.[37] Ne Win's disastrous economic policies, based on what he called "the Burmese Way to Socialism," which, in effect, meant that everything in sight was nationalized and handed over to the military, had resulted in acute shortages of rice and basic foodstuffs in Rangoon. At the same time, the Chinese community in the capital had also been influenced by the Cultural Revolution, and many young Sino-Burmese began wearing Mao badges. This violated an official Burmese regulation, and the young 'Red Guards' in Rangoon were ordered to remove their badges. When some of them refused, anti-Chinese riots swept the capital in June and July. Chinese-run stores were ransacked and looted, and many Sino-Burmese were killed in their homes. The authorities did not intervene until the mobs stormed the Chinese embassy in Rangoon. The riots were clearly orchestrated by Burma's military authorities to deflect attention from the food crisis, and the Sino-Burmans were easy targets because many of them were merchants and controlled a large chunk of the black market that had emerged after the 1962 coup. But by attacking the embassy, mob violence had got out of hand and had to be curtailed.

Ne Win's military government was denounced as "counter-revolutionary, fascist and reactionary"[38] over Radio Beijing, and anti-Burmese demonstrations were held in the Chinese capital. Secretly, more Sino-Burmese from Rangoon and elsewhere were helped by the Chinese embassy to reach the CPB's base area along the Shweli River, to join their comrades who had fled some years before.

A few months after the Chinatown riots in Rangoon, Radio Beijing began accusing the Burmese Army of "border violations," saying that Burmese forces had intruded into Yunnan and that Burmese aircraft had violated Chinese air space. Foreign observers were somewhat disconcerted, but no one seems to have understood that all this, and the Chinese reaction to the riots, amounted to little more than pretexts for Beijing's move to support the CPB, which came across the border on New Year's Day 1968. That decision was taken in 1962, not in 1967. Moreover, preparations on the ground, such as surveying infiltration routes, had been made well before the Chinatown riots.

For Kang's masterplan to succeed, however, the Chinese and the CPB understood that the 'new' communist insurgent movement in Burma could not rely solely on the Burmese intellectual *Sichuan laobing* or even Naw Seng's *Guizhou laobing*, who, apart from a handful of Karen, were exclusively Kachin. From the very beginning, the CPB contacted local ethnic warlords who operated in the border areas. They were not communist but would most certainly become allies if they were offered new automatic weapons from China, which the CPB had in abundance.

In July 1967, CPB cadres contacted Peng Jiasheng, an ethnic Chinese warlord in Kokang, and brought him to Beijing. He did not become a party member but accepted CPB leadership, and in return received a generous supply of Chinese weapons. Five days after the capture of Mong Ko, he and his troops entered Kokang from the Chinese side of the border. By August most of Kokang had been overrun.

West of Mong Ko and opposite the town of Namkham, there were two enclaves north of the Shweli River which belonged to Burma. Ohn Kyi, a party veteran, came across the border from China in February and linked up with Saya Mong and Bo Kang Yoi, two local Shan rebel leaders. Those two enclaves, Khun Hai and Man Hio, were also in CPB hands by August. Around Mong Ko itself, the CPB expanded the territory under its control to include the valleys of Mong Hom and

Mong Ya, which were overrun in 1969. The communist juggernaut rolled on, and there seemed to be nothing the Burmese Army could do to stop it. In early 1970, communist troops took over Mong Paw, a small town west of Mong Ko. Then, on March 27, CPB troops armed with mortars, recoilless rifles, and machine-guns launched an all-out attack on Panghsai, a garrison town next to Kyuhkok where the Burma Road crosses into China. It took the CPB only a day to capture it. The CPB now controlled territories stretching from the enclaves opposite Namkham to a contiguous area around Panghsai, Mong Ko, and Kokang in the East.[39]

The CPB also managed to establish a base area in Kachin State. In November 1967, two local commanders in the Kachin Independence Army (KIA), Sakhon Ting Ying and Zalum, had broken away and been contacted by the CPB. The dispute with the KIA leadership was over tribal issues. Most KIA leaders were Jinghpaw, which some Maru were unhappy with. Zalum, a Maru, and Ting Ying, who belonged to the closely related Ngoshan, set up a new base area for the CPB in the mountains around Kambaiti, Pangva, and Hpimaw on the Chinese border in eastern Kachin State.

Fierce battles were fought with the KIA, which, hardly surprisingly, resented communist incursions into what the Kachin considered their territory. That was also a problem for Naw Seng. He was unaware even of the existence of the KIA when he and his men entered Mong Ko on January 1, 1968. Although located in northeastern Shan State, the mountains around Mong Ko are populated by Kachin tribes. Naw Seng found himself fighting his own kinsmen and he resented it. But he had no choice. He had to follow orders from the CPB leadership and their masters in Beijing. In 1969, he was appointed chief of what was named the Northeastern Command of the CPB's army.

The CPB's tactics, which were to win over local warlords, appeared to be working. In 1967, some Akha tribesmen in the mountains near the Burma-Laos-China triborder junction northeast of Kengtung, had risen up against the Kuomintang in reaction to heavy tax collection and general abuse. Led by Lao Er Ji Pyao and armed with homemade flintlocks, spears, and knives, they ambushed and harassed the Kuomintang incessantly without any outside support. In 1970, the CPB invited Lao Er Ji Pyao and a few of his men to China. According to him, "We were told that we would get modern arms if we joined hands with the CPB."[40] They agreed, and in October 1971 Pe Thaung, the CPB's political commissar in the area, proclaimed the formation of 'War Zone 815.' The term probably had no meaning to the local Akha; it was named after the founding date of the CPB, August 15, 1939.

In October 1969, the CPB made its first foray into the Wa Hills. The party sent Mya Thaung to the Mong Mau area in the north as he was one of the few of the *Sichuan laobing* who had any military experience. He came from Bassein in the Irrawaddy delta and was trained by the British Army in Dehra Dun in India after World War II. After returning to Burma, he had served with the Burmese military and joined a unit that mutinied after independence in 1948. That unit merged with the CPB, and Mya Thaung went to China in the early 1950s.

He had never seen any Wa before he ventured into their hills to contact local warlords. His assignment was to offer support to any Wa chieftain who was waging guerrilla war against government-sponsored militia units.[41] Taking advantage of tribal rivalries, he managed to win over two prominent Wa warlords, Zhao Yilai and Bao Youxiang. Zhao was born in 1940 in a small, poor Wa village near the Chinese border. When he was sixteen, his family moved across the frontier to Cangyuan in Yunnan, a town and an area which also had a sizable Wa population. According to his official biography, Zhao worked for a while in a people's commune before being recruited into a local police force. During that time, he also fought for a while with the Chinese against a Kuomintang unit that had managed to cross the border into Yunnan.[42] Back in the Saohpa area of the northeastern Wa Hills in 1967, Zhao and some of his comrades organized a local guerrilla unit that fought against local government-sponsored militia units.

The much younger Bao, who was born in 1949, came from Hkwin Ma in the northern Wa Hills and had also spent some time in Cangyuan in his youth. According to the same official account, Bao attended a Chinese primary school from 1959 to 1961, and then returned with his family to Hkwin Ma. At only seventeen years of age, Bao and some other young Wa formed a band that fought against the government's militias.[43]

It is plausible to assume that China's intelligence services were aware of Zhao's and Bao's past and current activities and had briefed Mya Thaung before he crossed the border from China and marched into the Wa Hills with a small group of Burmese communists. Such a venture would have been suicidal without prior knowledge of local conditions and who to contact.

In December 1969, Zhao Yilai and CPB commissar Kyaw Htin, one of Mya Thaung's officers, launched their first attack. The target was Saohpa, which was defended by a small garrison of government troops supported by a militia led by Saw Lu, a twenty-seven-year-old Wa who had been educated by missionaries at the Karen Baptist School in Myaungmya in the Irrawaddy delta. The much better equipped CPB force overran Saohpa without much difficulty. The CPB had gained its first foothold in the Wa Hills.

However, the advance from Saohpa into other areas of the Wa Hills was slow. Saw Lu was not the only Wa who resisted the newcomers. Throughout history, these fierce and proud tribesmen had managed to resist any outsiders who had come to subdue them. Fighting between the CPB and local bands broke out across the Wa Hills. According to Mya Thaung, "In the Hkwin Ma area, an entire village, including women and children, put up a last stand, barricading themselves inside a longhouse. We fired a B-40 rocket through the door at the end of the longhouse. That finished them all off."[44]

Within a year or so, local resistance had subsided, and the Wa came to accept the CPB's dominance through its superior firepower. Many Wa were now recruited into the CPB's army, and they turned out to be excellent fighters. But most of them were privates while many of the officers were Kokang Chinese. Nearly all the political commissars, though, were Burmese.

A clandestine radio station, the People's Voice of Burma, was officially inaugurated on March 28, 1971, the 23rd anniversary of the CPB uprising, and began transmitting from Mangshi in Yunnan in April. Fighting bulletins were mixed with choirs singing revolutionary songs and announcers extolling the virtues of Marxism-Leninism. The broadcasts were in Burmese and a number of minority languages, including Wa, whose support was crucial for the survival of the CPB in the northeastern border mountains.

Everything seemed to be going to plan. But those remote areas in northern, northeastern, and eastern Shan State were seen as nothing more than springboards from which the communists would march down to Burma proper and seize major population centers.

With that in mind, in November 1971 the CPB launched a surprise attack on a Burmese army base a few kilometers east of the town of Kunlong on the Salween River. The aim was to capture a strategic bridge that connected Kokang with areas west of the river. At that time, the Kunlong bridge was one of only two on the Salween River in Shan State. The other was at Ta Kaw on the main highway from Taunggyi to Kengtung in the south. The one at Ta Kaw was old but, ironically, the impressive suspension bridge at Kunlong was built by the Chinese when U Nu was Burma's prime minister and relations between Rangoon and Beijing were good.

The Burmese army outpost was annihilated after a savage eight-hour battle. There were no survivors; all three commanders and their eighty soldiers died in the fighting. The CPB pushed on and took up positions on Shan Tele Mountain, overlooking the Salween River and the bridge. There are very few places where it is possible to cross the fast-flowing Salween and, if the CPB managed to capture the bridge and secure it, it would be an easy task to send thousands of troops to the west bank of the river. From Kunlong, it is only seventy-five kilometers to Hsenwi and another fifty to Lashio, the main town in northern Shan State. A victory at Kunlong would have left the entire northern Shan State open for the CPB, and they would have been able to march on to Mandalay and the Pegu Yoma, where their old comrades were still holding out.

The government was clearly aware of this and threw in all possible resources to defend the bridgehead at Kunlong. "The whole area became a war zone," remembers Aung Myint, a Burmese army officer who took part in the campaign. "Convoys of trucks rumbled down the road to Hsenwi to the river carrying reinforcements and ammunition to the front. Command posts were established everywhere, and daily weapons drills were conducted by the roadside."[45]

The Burmese commander, Tun Yi, was nicknamed 'Napoleon' because he was short and rotund. His first tactic was to charge Shan Tele peak with infantry forces. With fixed bayonets, the soldiers ran uphill, shooting as they advanced through the forested slopes of the mountain. But the well-entrenched CPB troops on the top of the mountain repelled more than forty such attacks, inflicting heavy casualties.

The firepower of the communists seemed inexhaustible, as was their logistical advantage. Shan Tele was close to the Chinese border, and fresh supplies of bullets and even rations for the CPB solders were sent in daily. Wounded CPB soldiers were treated in Chinese hospitals across the border. It also became obvious that most of the CPB's troops were actually regulars from the Chinese army, or so-called volunteers, mostly Red Guards, who had joined their Burmese comrades in their fight against Rangoon. "We found telltale bodies in the forest on the hillsides," recalls Aung Myint.[46]

When the communist forces resorted to Chinese-style human-wave tactics, the situation at Kunlong became desperate. Some defenders fled in disarray, while others deserted and were never seen again. 'Napoleon' Tun Yi ordered his men to mine the bridge with dynamite sticks and blow it up if the outer defenses fell to the CPB. Each battalion commander was ordered to keep one bullet for himself to commit suicide rather than be captured alive by the CPB or, alternatively, have to return in disgrace to Rangoon where court-martial was awaiting everyone who deserted his post. It was a do-or-die battle, the biggest and fiercest the Burmese army had ever fought.

A local militia force, led by a Kokang warlord called Luo Xinghan, also took part in the battle, but mostly as local guides to help direct infantry assaults and artillery barrages rather than as conventional soldiers. Their knowledge of the terrain was far superior to the Burmese commanders' who all came from central Burma and did not even speak the local languages. In return, Luo was permitted to use army vehicles to transport his opium out of the area. Government soldiers would sometimes even come along to assist in protecting his convoys of mules and lorries that carried opium from his base in Lashio down to the Thai border.[47]

It was the artillery that finally turned the tide at Kunlong. Howitzers were positioned around Shan Tele, and as the CPB soldiers came charging down the mountain in human waves, air-burst shells were fired. They proved effective even against CPB troops inside bunkers. The concussion when the shells exploded in the air caused bleeding from the nose and mouth. Hundreds of CPB soldiers died, though the human waves never seemed to end. But the artillery had had its impact and, on January 7, 1972, after forty-two days of continuous heavy fighting, the CPB eventually pulled back from Shan Tele. The Kunlong bridge was safe, and so was the road to Hsenwi and Lashio. It was the Burmese army's first major victory in the northeast and the morale of the troops was boosted tremendously.

Despite the success at Kunlong, the Burmese military realized that it could not defeat the CPB in the northeast and drive them out of the base areas they had established along the Chinese border. But the CPB could be flushed out of its much weaker areas in central Burma, which had not benefited from the supply of Chinese munitions, and in that way the grand plan to link up the 'new' forces with the 'old' would be thwarted. With the CPB isolated in the northeastern border mountains, central Burma would be secure.

The first target was the Pegu Yoma. The *pyouk-touk-hta* purges had depleted the ranks of the units there, and effectively alienated the CPB from the urban intelligentsia. On September 24, 1968, less than a year after the thrust into Mong Ko, the CPB's official chairman, Thakin Than Tun, had been assassinated in the Pegu Yoma by a government infiltrator. He was succeeded by Thakin Zin, who tried to get support from the new powerful forces in the northeast. In 1969, 'the Butcher' Taik Aung and about ten cadres were sent to Mong Ko. They did not come back, and by the early 1970s the government's offensive against the CPB's old strongholds was in full swing. Communist as well as Karen insurgents were forced out of the Irrawaddy delta and the Pinlebu area in the north. The old Red Flag faction, never very influential in any case, had almost vanished after its maverick leader, Thakin Soe, was captured in his last base in the Arakan Yoma in November 1970. He was taken to Rangoon and jailed.

In early 1975, a major offensive was launched in the Pegu Yoma. All remaining CPB camps there were overrun, and on March 15 the Burmese army even managed to kill Thakin Zin and his secretary Thakin Chit. The survivors either surrendered or fled to the Pokaung range in Magwe Division, where a handful of CPB soldiers managed to hold out until 1979. Very few CPB cadres, probably not more than ten or twenty from the old base areas, ever made it to the new base area in the northeast.[48] One of the few who did was Kyaw Mya, the leader of the CPB forces in Arakan. He left his area after the Burmese army had mounted a major offensive there in 1979. But he crossed the border into Bangladesh and went to Dhaka, where the Chinese embassy put him on a plane to Beijing. From there, he went down to the base area in northeastern Shan State. Kyaw Mya told me that was easy: "The Bangladesh authorities were very close to the Chinese. They let me through although I didn't even have a passport."[49]

The battle at Kunlong bridge and the ensuing eradication of their old base areas in central Burma turned out to be a turning point for the Burmese communists. The government's army had managed to contain them in remote mountains along the Chinese border, such as Kokang and the Wa Hills, where they did not belong and had never intended to stay. Kang Sheng's plan to spread revolution to Burma and beyond had also failed.

3

The Wa and the Communist Party of Burma

Having failed to cross the Salween River at Kunlong, the Communist Party of Burma (CPB) realized that it had to turn its attention to less well-defended government positions. In April 1971, a combined force of Zhao Yilai's Wa troops and Chinese volunteers had attacked Mong Mau in the northern Wa Hills. It was captured on May 1 (Labour Day), a day especially chosen by the CPB's Burmese political commissars. Presumably, though, that was of little significance to the Wa troops who marched into town on that day. For them, it was a battle against central authorities which most Wa despised, and the CPB had given them guns to fight with. Nevertheless, that victory meant that the only motor road into the Wa Hills, from the town of Panglong south of Hopang to Mong Mau, had been cut.[1]

After the battle at Kunlong, the CPB marched on, south from Mong Mau, encountering little or no resistance along the way. The aim was to link up with Pe Thaung's newly established War Zone 815, and thus wrest control over the entire border from Panghsai on the Burma Road in the north down to the Mekong River and the Laotian border. In rapid sequence in June and July 1972, the CPB took over three townships east of the Salween: Na Hpan, Man Hpang, and Pangyang. At the same time, the market towns of Loi Leun and

Vingngun were captured and then, finally, the town of Panghsang on the Nam Hka River, which marks the border between Burma and China.

Only one area now separated the Wa forces in the Wa Hills from War Zone 815: the hills surrounding the Burmese garrison town of Mong Yang. That area was controlled by a Shan army led by Khun Myint, a warrior who had been fighting against the Burmese government since the early 1960s. He had been contacted by emissaries sent by Pe Thaung in 1971, and by November 1973 most of the area was controlled by the CPB. But it was not until 1975 that Khun Myint agreed to merge his forces with those of the CPB. After all, he and his fighters were Shan nationalists, not communists. In April 1976, they became the 768 Brigade of the CPB's 'People's Army.' The commander of the brigade, Sao Noom Pan, was a Shan Christian, and his deputy, Michael Davies, the son of a Shan mother and a Welshman who had worked as a forestry officer in the Kengtung area in the 1950s.

The CPB could now concentrate on consolidating their new contiguous base area along the Chinese border. Altogether more than twenty thousand square kilometres of territory were now under their control, and more than half of it consisted of the Wa Hills. For the Wa, it meant that for the first time in history they came under what could be described as a central governmental authority.

One of the first edicts issued by the Wa's new masters was a ban on head-hunting. Officially, that was done by 'educating the masses,' but according to the Wa leader Zhao Yilai, his men simply shot those seen carrying severed heads.[2] Just as the Chinese communists had done in Wa areas on their side of the border, the CPB also destroyed head-poles, drum houses, and other paraphernalia associated with head-hunting. But heads continued to play an important role in Wa ceremonies, and instead of cutting new ones, some villagers took to unearthing buried corpses and decapitating them.[3] After the 1989 mutiny, it also became clear that the Wa had kept skulls hidden in their villages, out of sight of the CPB's political commissars.[4]

The CPB divided the Wa Hills into two districts, a northern district with its center at Mong Mau and a southern district headquartered at Panghsang. The districts were divided into townships, which in turn were made up of village tracts. On the district level, however, there were in the beginning few Wa in leading positions. The new rulers were the CPB's political commissars.

Panghsang, located in a horseshoe bend of the Nam Hka River with Chinese territory everywhere except to the west, was an ideal place for a major base. In April 1973, what was called the Northeastern Command moved from Mong Ko to Panghsang. A hydroelectric power station was built by the Chinese on the outskirts of the village, which soon came to resemble a small town. The top party leaders stayed in small individual concrete buildings behind a well-stocked armory at the far end of the horseshoe. A printing press was also built with equipment provided by China.

After the death of Thakin Zin in March 1975, a hastily convened party congress was held in Panghsang, and Thakin Ba Thein Tin became the new chairman of the CPB. He and other central committee members stayed in the secluded headquarters area in Panghsang. Central Burma was lost, and the CPB had to adjust to having base areas in these remote areas along the Chinese border.

Despite the setback at Kunlong, Chinese support continued unabated. Kang Sheng and the hard-liners had not given up their strategy for spreading revolution to Southeast Asia and beyond. During the decade 1968–1978, the Chinese poured more aid into the CPB effort than into any other communist movement outside Indochina. Unlike the old units in the Pegu Yoma, who were dressed in Burmese *longyi* (sarongs) and sandals and were armed with little more than old World War II-era rifles and shotguns, the new troops in the northeast had new Chinese uniforms with red stars on their caps, and were well-equipped with modern Chinese weapons: semiautomatic and automatic rifles, light machine-guns, 12.7mm anti-aircraft guns, 60, 82 and 120mm mortars, and 75mm recoilless rifles. Radio equipment, jeeps, trucks and petrol, as well as rice, other foodstuffs, cooking oil, and kitchen utensils, were sent across the border into Panghsang, which after the loss of the Pegu Yoma in 1975 was designated the official headquarters of the CPB. The Chinese even sent a truckload of detailed military maps, covering all the border areas and parts of central Burma.

On the other hand, the CPB did very little to develop the Wa Hills and other areas the party had captured. The Wa and other recruits from the non-Burmese ethnic peoples in the new base areas were thus viewed as little more than cannon fodder for its army. As Tom Kramer points out in his study of the Wa movement, when the Chinese volunteers began to return to China in the mid-1970s, Wa troops in particular formed the bulk of the fighting force: "The organisation made modest attempts to bring health and education to the area, but for the CPB the Wa region was never a priority and was always a stepping stone to reach the central plains."[5]

The printing press in Panghsang mainly churned out propaganda leaflets and ideological studies in Burmese, which very few Wa were able to read, if they could read at all. Textbooks used in the CPB's village schools were also in Burmese. Conspicuously absent were publications in Wa or any other minority languages. But like the 'old'

CPB in the Pegu Yoma, the 'new' party also collected orphans who received some basic education in Burmese and were told that the party was their parent. The ability to read and write non-Burmese languages was kept alive only in Christian churches, Buddhist monasteries, and small schools run by the villagers themselves.

Almost all political posts in the CPB's leadership and top positions in the civil administration were filled by Burmese communists. The top leadership in Panghsang seldom ventured out of the heavily guarded headquarters area at the end of the horseshoe bend in the Nam Hka River. Although Thakin Ba Thein Tin was the chairman of the party, he is not known to have ever visited a Wa village. The only times he left Panghsang were when he traveled through China to Mong Ko in the north, or went to visit Chinese communist leaders and high-ranking cadres in Kunming and Beijing.

Many of the military officers in the CPB's army were Kokang Chinese. A few who had come with Naw Seng in 1968 and from Ting Ying's and Zalum's CPB unit in Kachin State were Kachin. Then, on March 9, 1972, Naw Seng, the ethnic Kachin military commander in the northeast, died under mysterious circumstances near Mong Mau. The first internal announcement from the CPB claimed that he had died when falling off a horse "on the way to the frontline."[6] However, the official version of his death soon changed to a tale of how he had fallen off a cliff while hunting in the Wa Hills. Many Kachin, however, believe that he was murdered by the CPB because he refused to fight against his kin in the Kachin Independence Army (KIA). In the late 1960s and early 1970s, the two rebel forces were engaged in heavy battles in the hills south of Mong Ko and in Kachin State itself.[7] Nevertheless, on July 6, 1976, the Kachin rebels and the

CPB signed an alliance ending the war between the two groups. The agreement was written in pure Maoist language:

> Today, throughout the world the two superpowers—the Soviet social-imperialists and American imperialists—are trying to divide and rule the world between them … it is necessary to decisively stand on the side of the world's peoples headed by the socialist People's Republic of China … both parties totally agreed that the common enemy of the people of all nationalities—the Ne Win-San Yu military government—is the chief representative of the three main enemies: imperialism, feudalism-landlordism and bureaucrat capitalism.[8]

Had the ardent Christian Kachin become communists? Despite the Maoist rhetoric, and despite invitations to all Kachin rebel leaders to visit China, little had actually changed inside the KIA-controlled areas of Kachin State and northern Shan State. But Chinese-made assault rifles, machine-guns, mortars, and ammunition began flowing in. The CPB forged similar alliances with the Shan State Army (SSA) and smaller bands of Pa-O, Padaung (Kayan), and Karenni (Kayah) rebels. These groups also benefited from arms supplies from the CPB in return for allowing the communists to operate in their respective areas.

A new CPB Brigade, 683, was set up for a fresh attempt to push into western Shan State. Militarily, it was led by Bao Youxiang, one of the first Wa warlords to have merged his band of tribesmen with the CPB, and Li Ziru, who belonged to the group of Chinese volunteers who had come across the border in the late 1960s and later decided to stay in Burma. After more than a year of fighting alongside the

SSA, the 683 Brigade had been unable to push further than Loi Tsang ('Elephant Mountain') in western Shan State, overlooking an old CPB area near the towns of Mong Kung and Lai-Hka.

The Shan and other minority peoples in the area clearly favored the non-communist rebel groups and viewed the arrival of the CPB with suspicion. As a result, the SSA was forced to distance itself from the CPB in order not to lose the support it was still enjoying. This second attempt to push westwards with the aim of reaching central Burma failed, and thus the alliance with the SSA was in jeopardy. The SSA also had a camp on the Thai border and was dependent on supplies coming from that side as well, and the Thais were not pleased to see their Shan cousins linking up with a potent communist force.

The Chinese must have been frustrated with the CPB's lack of success. The CPB was recognized as a fraternal communist party, and unlike the KIA, the SSA and other allies dealt directly with Kang Sheng's security apparatus and his International Liaison Department (ILD) of the Communist Party of China (CPC). The ILD reported directly to the CPC's central committee, and as the researchers John Byron and Robert Pack put it, it "had an almost unlimited charter in external affairs during the 1950s and 1960s, wielding far greater influence than the government counterpart, the Foreign Ministry."[9]

In line with Kang Sheng's grand plans, Panghsang was not only the CPB's headquarters but also played host to about a dozen activists of the Communist Party of Thailand and more than twenty cadres from the Communist Party of Indonesia (Partai Komunis Indonesia, PKI), including the two daughters of its once powerful chairman, D. N. Aidit. The Communist Party of Malaya's *Suara Revolusi Malaya* ('Voice of the Malayan Revolution') broadcast from Hengyang south of Changsha in Hunan Province, but its leader, Chin Peng, often visited Kunming where he met CPB cadres.

Those connections were far more important to the CPB, and the Chinese, than the welfare of the Wa and other nationalities among the rank-and-file of the party's army. Whenever the CPB fought against the Burmese army, it used senseless human-wave tactics, which may well work in a country like China with a population of more than a billion people, but when employed in this very different contact, what happened to a small, poor people in the Wa Hills was nothing short of a demographic disaster. When I trekked through the northern and southern Wa Hills in 1986, there were hardly any able-bodied males between the ages of ten and fifty in the villages. The others were either in the CPB's army or dead.[10]

At that time, most Wa depended on opium as a cash crop because their mountains were too high, and the soil too poor, for the cultivation of rice and vegetables. They had to buy food from the lowlands using the meager income they got from cultivating opium poppies and harvesting the sap. That was also true in Kokang, the highlands around Mong Ko, and the mountains north of Kengtung. In the late 1970s, an estimated 80 percent of all poppy fields in Burma were under the CPB's control. But that led to a security problem, given that outside merchants had to enter the CPB areas to buy raw opium, which they then convoyed down to the Thai border where it was refined into pure white heroin. In order to do so unhindered, those merchants were well-connected with Burmese army commanders, and in an exchange of favors provided them with useful intelligence about the CPB. The CPB collected taxes on the opium farmers as well as the traders, but it was an income they could well do without.

Shortly after the Burmese communists had wrested control of the Wa Hills, Chinese experts helped them to introduce high-land wheat, which they had hoped would become the new cash crop. But not many Wa knew how to prepare the new crop, and the CPB and its Chinese advisers had not taken into account that bamboo flowers every fifty years or so, and that it attracts rats in hordes which multiply and destroy crops and food stocks. In 1976, that was precisely what happened in the Wa Hills. The wheat was wiped out and there was famine.

The CPB assisted the famine victims by distributing 60,000 Indian silver rupees, at that time still the most commonly used hard currency in the Wa Hills as they were made of real silver, not paper, and 1,600 kilograms of opium, which the party had stockpiled at Panghsang. As soon as the crisis was over, most families reverted to growing opium poppies, which are less vulnerable to pests than wheat or any other food crop.[11]

The years 1975 and 1976 also saw some other events that had a tremendous impact on both the CPB and the Wa. Apart from supporting the CPB, Kang Sheng had also been instrumental in building up Pol Pot's Khmer Rouge in Cambodia after its head of state, Prince Sihanouk, had been ousted in a coup in March 1970. Kang Sheng lived to see the Khmer Rouge march into Phnom Penh in April 1975, but died of bladder cancer on December 16 that year. The most extreme of China's radical leaders was gone. His death intensified an already existing power struggle between hard-liners and pragmatists within the Chinese leadership. The hard-liners were centered around Mao's closest followers, including his wife Jiang Qing, who along with Kang Sheng had played a leading role during the Cultural Revolution, while Deng Xiaoping was the most prominent among the pragmatists.

In April 1976, when the radical Left reasserted itself and ousted Deng, the CPB, unlike most other communist parties in the region, spoke out loudly in favor of the hard-liners. "The revisionist clique [with which Deng was linked] headed by [former president] Liu Shaoqi has been defeated,"[12] the CPB stated in a congratulatory message to the 55th anniversary of the CPC in June 1976. It went on: "The movement to repulse the Right deviationist attempt at reversing correct verdicts, and the decision of the Central Committee of the CPC on measures taken against rightist chieftain Deng Xiaoping are in full accord with Marxism-Leninism, Mao Zedong thought."[13]

Then, on September 9, Mao died. In a second message to the CPC, now mourning his death, the CPB stated:

> Guided by Chairman Mao Zedong's proletarian revolutionary line, the Chinese people seized great victories in the socialist revolution and socialist construction in the Great Proletarian Cultural Revolution, in criticising Liu Shaoqi's counter-revolutionary revisionist line, in criticising Lin Biao and Confucius and in criticising Deng Xiaoping and repulsing the Right deviationist attempt at reversing correct verdicts and consolidating the dictatorship of the proletariat, thus, consolidating the People's Republic of China—the reliable bulwark of the world proletarian revolution.[14]

The CPB had reason to reevaluate the reliability of that bulwark the following year when Deng reassumed power in Beijing. The CPB, which once had branded its own 'revisionists' *yebaw* Htay and H.

N. Ghoshal as 'Burma's Deng Xiaoping' and 'Burma's Liu Shaoqi,' respectively, fell silent. The *Beijing Review* and other official Chinese publications, which had previously published battle news and CPB statements, stopped reporting anything about the 'revolutionary struggle in Burma.' The CPB had been mentioned for the last time in November 1976 when Thakin Ba Thein Tin and vice chairman Thakin Pe Tint had called on Mao's successor, Hua Guofeng, in Beijing.[15]

All those intrigues and bombastic statements meant nothing to ordinary Wa, who could not care less about power struggles in distant Beijing. Deng's return to power, however, meant that Chinese aid to the CPB was significantly reduced. It was not completely cut off, but it was curtailed enough for the Wa to notice that something had changed. They were told to economize with the ammunition they had been allotted, and food, medicines, and other supplies from China did not come in the same quantities as before.

In January 1978, Deng Xiaoping, then vice premier, traveled to Rangoon to improve relations with Ne Win's government which had shown its goodwill towards China. In late November 1977, Ne Win had become the first and only head of state of a non-communist country to visit China's diplomatically isolated ally Cambodia when the Khmer Rouge was still in power. He spent several days in the country, hosted by Khieu Samphan and other Khmer Rouge leaders, who took him to see Angkor Wat and other cultural landmarks. Deng's visit to Burma two months later was another step towards improved relations between Beijing and Rangoon. China's interests were economic—to improve bilateral trade—as well as political. China wanted Burma on its side in the regional rivalry with Vietnam. Ne Win obliged, and China promised to scale down its support to the CPB even further.[16]

Within months of Deng's visit, the CPB had to vacate the offices it had maintained in Kunming and other towns in Yunnan. *The People's Voice of Burma*, which had been broadcasting from Mangshi in Yunnan since 1971, had to move to Panghsang, where a new studio was built for the radio station. The Chinese also recalled most of their volunteers. Only a few were left behind to maintain Chinese influence over the party and its army. Those who stayed were skilled operatives who, after spending years in the CPB's base areas, had become fluent in Burmese as well as minority languages such as Shan and Kachin. Wa, though, was not spoken by them. When communicating with the volunteers, the Wa had to speak Chinese, Shan, or Burmese

The CPB was plunged into crisis, and despite the strength of its army, the actual party organization remained weak. In the late 1970s, there were only 2,520 party members in the CPB's 'liberated area' of whom, significantly, only 888 came from the 23,000-strong army. The party's youth organization claimed a membership of 2,315, and various 'peasant unions'—the basis of the CPB's 'people's power' structure in the northeast—enlisted 87,608 members in 882 different local organizations.[17] But those 'mass organizations' existed only on paper. The CPB had, in effect, ceased to function as a properly organized communist party, and the administration of its territory was becoming dysfunctional. Petty party officials had to finds ways of making money to support themselves and began to spend less and less time in their offices.[18]

Faced with this new situation, the CPB's central committee met, first at Mong Ko and later at Panghsang, between November 1978 and June 1979. The mood was somber when the CPB celebrated its 40th anniversary on August 15. Thakin Ba Thein Tin gave a speech in which he emphasized that the party had to be "self-reliant" and, without being specific, said that the CPB "had made many mistakes" during its forty-year-long history. In other announcements from the meeting, "non-interference" was declared to be a major aspect of the CPB's relations with "fraternal communist parties."[19]

The Burmese government took full advantage of the situation. In November, a major offensive code-named Min Yan Aung-I ('King Conqueror-I') was launched with the aim of capturing Panghsang before Christmas. Thousands of troops, supported by heavy artillery and air strikes, took up positions in the Mawhpa area southwest of Panghsang. Heavy fighting raged for more than a month. The CPB put up fierce resistance and managed to defend Panghsang. It did not fall, and on January 6, 1980 the government called off the offensive. Although the operation fell short of its objective, the Burmese army managed to regain control over most of Mawhpa. A forward base was established at Loi Hsia-Kao Mountain, less than thirty kilometers southwest of Panghsang. The CPB claims that the government's forces suffered 2,085 dead and 3,537 wounded, and that the CPB captured 320 prisoners of war.[20] Even if exaggerated, these figures show that the Burmese military was willing to accept heavy casualties in order to make territorial gains against the CPB.

But the government in Rangoon was not averse to the thought of finding a solution to the civil war by political means. In 1980, it announced a general amnesty for all insurgents in the country. Though it was the first move of its kind since the 1963 peace talks, the insurgents were not particularly enthusiastic about the offer. Officially, 450 rebels from the CPB surrendered along with 400 KIA soldiers, 260 from the Karen rebel army, 160 from 'Kokang,' and over 450 'expatriates' returned from the Thai border and abroad.

Although this adds up to 1,720, the government claimed 2,257 rebels had surrendered.[21]

There was no way to cross-check those contradictory figures, but I am aware of surrenders only among the 'Kokang group,' or followers of the opium warlord Luo Xinghan, who had gone underground in 1973 and then stayed in camps near the Thai border, and 'expatriates' (the non-communist Burmese opposition led by former prime minister U Nu, who had also been encamped on the Thai border), and remnants of the CPB in the Pokaung range and Arakan (Rakhine) State. There were no surrenders in Kachin State and certainly none from the CPB in the northeast. To whom would any Wa have surrendered? Most of them could not even speak Burmese.

Nonetheless, both the CPB and the KIA entered into peace talks with the government. The Kachin held several rounds of negotiations with the regime, in Rangoon as well as in Kachin State, between August 1980 and May 1981. While in Rangoon, the Kachin rebel leader Brang Seng declared that his troops were willing to lay down arms only if the government granted autonomy to Kachin State, stressing that secession from the Union of Burma was no longer an issue.[22] The government's response was to offer rehabilitation for the KIA's fighters. They would have to surrender their arms and return to their home towns and villages where the government would give them some assistance to start new lives. No political concessions were forthcoming, and the talks eventually broke down.

In contrast, talks in May 1981 between government officials and the CPB lasted only one day. A three-man delegation led by vice chairman Thakin Pe Tint, along with Ye Tun (a veteran from Pyinmana) and Hpalang Gam Di (one of Naw Seng's men), went to Lashio and put forth three demands:

1. Recognition of the CPB as a legal political party;
2. Recognition of the CPB's base area as an 'autonomous entity';
3. Recognition of the CPB's army.[23]

Apparently, finding no room to negotiate, the Burmese officials ended the talks without further discussion.

As the years went by, some of the old leaders dropped out of the picture. Hard-liner Taik Aung, the butcher of the Pegu Yoma, suffered a stroke and became paralyzed after drinking homemade moonshine in 1983. He left Panghsang and was hospitalized in China. Thakin Pe Tint got throat cancer and also had to leave for China to get medical treatment. Hpalang Gam Di, because of old age and ill health, began to spend more and more time in Chinese hospitals as well. Than Shwe, the first political commissar of the northeastern base area, quit the party and retired in China because of disagreements with the party leadership. He had argued that the time was not ripe for armed struggle and it would be better, at least for the time being, to work within the political system in Burma, even if that meant accepting the rule of the military-dominated government in Rangoon.[24]

Meanwhile, relations between Burma and China continued to improve. In January 1981, China's new premier, Zhao Ziyang, a staunch supporter of Deng and an advocate for market economic reforms, visited Burma. That paved the way for an agreement on bilateral economic and technical cooperation, which was signed in June 1984. The following year, some more exchanges took place. In March, Chinese president Li Xiannian, one of the most important architects of the economic reforms that followed the disastrous Cultural Revolution, traveled to Burma. In May, Ne Win went to China where he held talks with Deng. During one of those meetings, Deng said that both China and Burma were initiators of the Five Principles of Co-Existence, which were first used in talks between China and India and then expanded at a summit of newly independent Asia and African states in Bandung in Indonesia in 1955. Two of the key principles were "mutual respect for each other's territorial integrity and sovereignty" and "mutual non-interference in each other's internal affairs."[25]

In order to restructure the CPB, a party congress was convened at Panghsang on September 9, 1985. It was only the third time since the party was founded that a congress was held. The first was in August 1939, when a group of young leftist nationalists met in Rangoon to set up the CPB, and the second when the party was reorganized after the fall of the Pegu Yoma in 1975. Some call it the 3rd congress while others do not consider the 1939 meeting a real congress and therefore refer to the one in 1985 as "the 2nd Congress of the CPB."

Whatever the designation, the congress, which lasted until October 2, was attended by more than 170 delegates from various parts of the northeastern base areas as well as a representative from the remnants in Tenasserim and two underground workers from Rangoon. A new central committee was elected and, officially, "taking the integration of Marxism-Leninism, Mao Zedong thought with the concrete practice of Burma as guidance, the 24-day congress was a congress of unity, a congress of victory."[26]

In reality, serious disagreements between the old CPB veterans and younger intellectuals, who had joined the struggle in the 1970s, surfaced during the congress. The central committee's report stated that on independence on January 4, 1948 "Burma became a semi-colonial and semi-feudal state which is politically independent but economically dependent upon various imperialist countries. Hence, the nature of the revolution in Burma is the people's democratic revolution aimed at overthrowing imperialism, feudalism and bureaucratic capitalism."[27] Therefore, "the tactical line for the present stage of the revolution [is that] armed struggle is the main form of struggle … [with the aim of] establishing bases in the rural areas surrounding the cities."[28]

The younger cadres argued that feudal lords and greedy moneylenders had passed into history long ago and that the old leaders were describing a society they had left more than thirty-five years before for the jungle, or for China. They also argued that the main problems now facing the peasantry were how to meet often unrealistic production quotas set by the government, and how to avoid selling rice to the government at rates well below market prices. The same younger critics also questioned the use of the term 'semi-colonial' and 'semi-feudal' to describe Burma and its xenophobic, atavistic regime. Rangoon's quest for self-reliance and its desire to keep outside influence, and outside trade, at an absolute minimum had created one of Asia's most thriving black-market economies on which not only private merchants but also many government officials and army officers had made fortunes. According to the younger cadres, it would be more appropriate to expose these things than to talk about 'colonial exploitation.' However, the opposition was defeated and some of the younger cadres were even warned not to raise such issues, or they would face disciplinary action.[29]

Ethnic issues were not discussed during the congress, and ethnic representation in the newly elected top leadership remained small. Only two Wa, Zhao Yilai and Bao Youxiang, along with Saw Ba Moe, a Karen who had joined the CPB in 1973, were among the eight alternate members of the central committee. Of the twenty-one regular central committee members there was one Shan, Sai Aung Win, and two came from the *Guizhou laobing*: Hpalang Gam Di and Zau Mai. The rest, and all five members of the politburo, were *Sichuan laobing*, or had a background in the old base areas in central Burma.[30]

The loss of much of the financial and material support from China that the party had enjoyed since the 1960s prompted the party leadership to turn to the potentially lucrative drug trade. It was certainly an unorthodox alternative for a party claiming to be communists, but the CPB already controlled most of Burma's poppy-growing areas. Some party members objected but were overruled by those who saw no other way out of the party's financial problems.

Thousands of *viss* (1.6 kilograms) of opium were collected from the farmers and stockpiled at Panghsang. From there, armed units transported the drugs via Mong Pawk south of Panghsang to the bank of the Nam Hka River, then on by bamboo raft down to the junction of the Salween and downriver to Ta-Kaw, where they were loaded onto mules and porters and carried to the Thai border. Once there, the raw opium was sold to local merchants who ran laboratories where it was refined into heroin. Thus, the CPB became involved with opium merchants associated with remnants of the old Kuomintang, and with Khun Sa, or Zhang Qifu, one of the most notorious warlords involved in the Golden Triangle narcotics trade.

The CPB also allowed merchants to operate laboratories in the northeastern base area. Those merchants belonged to the same syndicates as the ones on the Thai border, and they had to pay 'protection money' and 'taxes' to the CPB. Such laboratories were established at Pang Hpeung near Panghsang, at Wan Ho-tao east of Panghsang, and near the Salween River in the Kokang area in the north. But those laboratories were not capable of refining raw opium into heroin, only *pitzu*, a brownish-yellowish powder, which when it is further refined becomes pure white number 4 heroin. As a general rule, ten kilograms of raw opium, plus acetic anhydrite and other chemicals, are needed to produce one kilogram of heroin. But raw opium was bulky to move, and transportation of the drugs down to the Thai border was made a lot easier when only bags of *pitzu* had to be carried by porters or by mules.

Another important development took place shortly after the 1985 party congress. Following the failure of the peace talks from 1980 to 1981, the Kachin concluded that only a broader front of ethnic and political rebels would be able to force the government to concede their demands for constitutional change, which would be replacing the centralized system which the military had introduced after 1962, and with modifications would signal a return to the federal system that had existed before the coup. Representatives of the KIA, or rather of its political wing, the Kachin Independence Organisation (KIO), left their headquarters in the far north in early 1983 and trekked through Shan State down to the Thai border, where they made contacts with other ethnic rebel armies. The KIO rejoined the National Democratic Front (NDF), a gathering of then eight, mostly Thai border-based rebel outfits, and invited them to send delegates to KIA-controlled areas in the north.

A twenty-six-man team, escorted by several hundred Shan and Kachin guerrillas, set off from the Thai border in April 1985. The Burmese military tried to intercept and block them, but they finally reached Kachin State in November to a rousing welcome of dancing villagers, Kachin bagpipers, and salutes from 12.5mm anti-aircraft guns.

A conference was held at the KIO's Pa Jau headquarters, which lasted from December 16 , 1985 to January 20, 1986. The conclusion was that the NDF was a united front in name only. More coordination of the activities of its various members was needed. In late January, the NDF delegation marched south into areas controlled by the CPB, and in March a second conference was held at Panghsang. The meeting took place in the premises of the broadcasting station, a concrete building overlooking the Nam Hka River. On March 24, the NDF and CPB agreed to coordinate their military operations against the Burmese army. The purpose was not to escalate the war but to step up the pressure on the government in Rangoon so that the next time peace talks were held, the government would have to face a unified, militarily powerful opposition.[31]

After meeting the CPB, the NDF delegates made their way back to the Thai border. However, the broader alliance that had been envisaged at Pa Jau and Panghsang never materialized. The Karen leadership, headed by the staunchly anticommunist general Bo Mya, denounced the alliance, causing a split within the NDF from which the front never fully recovered. It was only in the north that a common command consisting of the KIA, the SSA, and the Palaung State Liberation Army was set up and reached out to the CPB.

That alliance was put to test on the battlefield in mid-November 1986. On the 16th, hundreds of heavily armed CPB troops attacked government positions on Hsi-Hsinwan, a mountain west of Mong Ko. Kachin, Shan, and Palaung rebels were enlisted to ambush reinforcements that the government sent up north from Mandalay and Lashio.

The attack on Hsi-Hsinwan was led by Zhang Zhiming, a Chinese volunteer who had come across the border from Yunnan in the late

1960s to join the CPB. He liked to style himself 'Kyi Myint,' which is how 'Zhiming' would sound in Burmese. When China had recalled their volunteers in 1978, he belonged to a small group that had been left behind, most probably to keep an eye on the CPB for China's intelligence services.

The battle continued for several days. The outposts on the top of the mountain were overrun, only to provoke a massive counteroffensive from the government's side. Airplanes were dispatched from Meiktila air base south of Mandalay and howitzers and other heavy artillery were positioned around Hsi-Hsinwan. On December 7, the CPB was forced to retreat from the mountain, and four weeks later government forces pushed on and captured not only Mong Paw, a bustling market village on the foot of Hsi-Hsinwan, but also the border town of Panghsai, which the CPB had captured in March 1970.[32] With those territories gone, it was easy for the Burmese army to cross the Shweli and retake, without resistance, the small enclaves of Khun Hai and Man Hio north of the river, or what the CPB used to call its 'Namkham District.'

In terms of territory those were not big losses. The areas which the government retook in late 1986 and early 1987 totaled not more than five hundred square kilometers out of the CPB's large twenty thousand-square-kilometer base area in the northeast. But it was a devastating blow to the morale of the CPB's soldiers. Moreover, the fall of Panghsai and the areas around it was more than just a question of the loss of a few hundred square kilometers. With several thousand inhabitants, Panghsai was the largest settlement within the CPB's northern base areas and the party's main commercial center. Tax on the cross-border trade with China had been one of the CPB's main sources of income, and now that now gone.

Shortly before the battle of Hsi-Hsinwan began, KIO chairman Brang Seng and some other Kachin leaders had left Pa Jau and trekked down to Thailand. When Burma's military intelligence services discovered that he was there holding talks with other rebel leaders, a massive offensive was mounted in Kachin State. Both Pa Jau and the KIA's military headquarters at Na Hpaw were captured by government forces in May 1987. The Burmese army appeared invincible, and the NDF was no closer to achieving its goal of autonomy for their respective areas than it had been before the meetings in Pa Jau and Panghsang.

At the same time, the ethnic rank-and-file of the CPB's army was becoming increasingly dissatisfied with the way the predominantly Burman leadership of the party and the army viewed them as dispensable cannon fodder.[33] When the NDF delegation trekked through the CPB's base areas, it included a young Wa called Ai Hkam Aik. He represented the Wa National Organisation (WNO) and army (WNA), a small outfit made up of Wa who had fled to the Thai border when the CPB took over the Wa Hills in the early 1970s. It was not a big group but it was a member of the NDF. Now, for the first time, the Wa saw one of their own in a uniform that was not communist. Moreover, they became aware of the existence of the WNO and the WNA. Ai Hkam Aik did not propagate a non-communist line, but it was enough that he was seen there. Many Wa began to wonder why they had to fight for Burmese communists instead of having their own army.

The WNO/WNA was led by the old warlord Mahasang, whose father Sao Maha had been the *saohpa* of Vingngun and participated in the Panglong conferences. In the 1950s, Mahasang's older brother, Maha Khong, had been recruited by the Kuomintang and was even sent to Taiwan for training but was killed by the communists when they took over Vingngun and the entire southern Wa Hills. Mahasang, who commanded a small tribal force in the area, allied himself with the Burmese army and became a home guard commander under a scheme the government called Ka Kwe Ye (KKY), or 'defense.' They were allowed to trade in opium to sustain themselves. Mahasang's partner in the business was Luo Xinghan, one of the most powerful of the KKY commanders and once dubbed 'the King of Opium' by the US narcotics bureau.[34]

However, the KKY militias grew too powerful for their own good, and in May 1973 they were disbanded by the government. Luo and Mahasang then went underground to join forces with the SSA. Luo, however, was arrested on the Thai border and extradited to Burma, where he was sentenced to death, not for opium trafficking, which he had the unofficial permission of the Burmese army to engage in, but for "treason" and "rebellion against the state" in reference to his brief alliance with the SSA.[35]

Mahasang remained on the Thai border after Luo's arrest, and in 1974, with the help of the SSA, converted his former KKY force into the WNA. Three years later, he broke with the SSA and joined forces with another Shan army, the Shan United Revolutionary Army (SURA), which was allied with the remnants of the Kuomintang. The WNO, the political wing of the WNA, joined the NDF in 1983. There was also an administrative arm of the non-communist Wa movement, the Wa National Council (WNC) but, in reality, it functioned as a separate organization. Its leader, Ai Kyaw Hso (Ai Xiao Sue), came from Yawnghpre in the northern Wa Hills and had, like Mahasang, also once been a KKY commander. Like SURA, which, in effect, had become the Kuomintang's operative arm inside Shan State after most of the Chinese nationalists had settled in northern Thai border villages, the Wa outfits in the south were heavily involved in the drug trade, and most of the opium that was refined into heroin originated in CPB-controlled areas such as Kokang, the Wa Hills, and the mountains north of Kengtung.

In line with the new policy of becoming 'self-reliant,' the CPB's official policy was to collect twenty percent of the raw opium harvested in its base areas. This was kept not only in Panghsang but also at local district offices. The CPB's 'trade and commerce department' then sold the opium to local traders from Tang-yan, Lashio, and other opium-trading centers in government-held towns west of the Salween. In addition, there was a ten percent 'trade tax' on opium that was sold in local markets and a five percent tax on any quantity of opium leaving the CPB's areas for other destinations.[36] The funds derived from these sources were viewed as legitimate, but several local commanders became increasingly involved in private trading activities as well as the production of *pitzu* heroin base.

That was when the CPB's once rather efficient civil administration began to break down. Schools and clinics had to close all over the Wa Hills and other base areas because of lack of funds, and party officials began to show almost no interest in their administrative duties. The main preoccupation of the civil administrators out in the districts became tax collection for the party, and enriching themselves and their families by trading in drugs. Ironically, the area controlled by the orthodox Maoists of the CPB became a haven for free trade in then socialist Burma. The economy remained thoroughly capitalistic, and the CPB gave up trying to implement a land reform in the northeast, in sharp contrast to the dramatic land-distributing schemes which the party had carried out in central Burma in the late 1940s and early

1950s. Communist ideology became a hollow concept without any real meaning to the Wa and other tribal peoples in the northeastern base area. But then, in the minds of the CPB leaders, those areas had never been anything more than launching pads from which they had hoped to push down to central Burma. Moreover, the people who lived there were not their constituency.

Nevertheless, shortly after the 1985 party congress, the CPB decided to launch a 'rectification campaign' with the aim of "improving discipline and political as well as military training of soldiers and cadres, rebuilding the civil administration, improving relations with other rebel armies and punishing cadres involved in illegal activities."[37] In directives related to the last item, the CPB leadership stated that any party member found to be involved in private opium trading would face severe punishment and anyone caught with two kilograms of more of heroin base would be executed.[38]

The CPB's involvement in the Golden Triangle drug trade had become an embarrassment to the party's aging, still ideologically motivated leadership. It is also plausible to assume that the 'campaign' had been launched under Chinese pressure. The spillover of drugs from the CPB's areas into China was becoming a huge social problem in Yunnan, and increasing amounts of drugs were also being smuggled via Kunming to Hong Kong and beyond. Subsequent to the decision in 1985 to clamp down on the drug trade, party agents were sent to check up on local cadres and report on wrongdoings to the center at Panghsang. While this did not affect the mostly illiterate rank-and-file of the CPB, it exacerbated already existing frictions between the top party leadership and several local commanders who had begun to act as warlords in their respective areas.

Then came the big prodemocracy uprising in central Burma in 1988. Across the country, millions of people took to the streets to vent decades of pent-up frustrations with a military-dominated government that had turned what was once one of Asia's most prosperous countries into an economic and social wreck. The CPB paid minimal interest to the movement. The 1985 congress had reiterated the Maoist doctrine of capturing the countryside first, then surrounding the cities and moving into urban areas later. Anything else was considered 'adventuristic' and not in accordance with Marxism-Leninism, Mao Zedong thought.

On May 19 and 20, 1988, the CPB's clandestine radio station had carried a surprisingly detailed and accurate account of the first outbreak of antigovernment demonstrations in March.[39] The sources for that account were most probably Tin Aung and Thet Khaing, the two party members from Rangoon who had participated in the 1985 congress and afterwards returned to the capital. Thet Khaing was married to Hla Kyaw Zaw, the daughter of Kyaw Zaw, one of the Thirty Comrades and a legendary Burmese army officer who had joined the CPB in 1976. Tin Aung was an underground party organizer who, in 1969, had been sent to the Coco Islands in the Andaman Sea where the government had established a penal colony for political prisoners. He and the other prisoners, most of them CPB members or sympathizers, were released in 1972.[40] Tin Aung and Thet Khaing had been active among students in Rangoon in 1988, but both were arrested in July 1989 and severely tortured.

That was almost the extent of the CPB's involvement in the 1988 uprising. The party's policy towards the prodemocracy movement was discussed at a politburo meeting in Mong Ko on September 10. The demonstrations in Rangoon and elsewhere were at their height, and some of the younger party members were encouraged by the urban rising and wanted to link up with it. But after discussing in general terms the movement's demand for the formation of an interim government in Rangoon, one of the aging Maoist leaders concluded: "The No. 1 point I would like to say is not to let them [i.e., the younger cadres] lose sight of the fact that we are fighting a longterm war. It is impossible for us to make attacks in the towns taking months and years. That is possible only in rural areas."[41]

When large numbers of students as well as other activists fled Rangoon after the military stepped in to reassert power on September 18, 1988, thousands arrived in areas controlled by various ethnic rebels along the Thai border and in Kachin State. Significantly, only fifty or sixty went to the CPB's territory.[42] The CPB's failure to link up with the biggest popular uprising in modern Burmese history annoyed the younger intellectuals in the party and some of the better-educated Burmese-speaking minority cadres who had heard about the uprising on the BBC's Burmese-language service. The vast majority of the CPB's hilltribe rank-and-file was, however, unaware of the fact that there was a mass uprising in central Burma in the first place.

There were also other rumblings within the party and its army. As early as December 20, 1988, Zhao Yilai and Bao Youxiang met for the first time to conspire against the CPB leadership. Plans were drawn up to form a political organization that would be exclusively Wa, and not communist.[43] Before they could make a move against the CPB leadership, however, the unit in Kokang led by Peng Jiasheng rebelled. On March 12, 1989, Peng announced that he and his troops had broken away from the CPB, and two days later they took over the party's northern bureau headquarters at Mong Ko.[44]

On April 13, Zhao and Bao met again and decided that they could not wait any longer. Four days later, seven hundred Wa troops marched into Panghsang and surrounded the headquarters area, where the top leaders were staying. The mutineers went on to seize the well-stocked armory, the broadcasting station, and other central buildings. While Wa soldiers were smashing portraits of communist icons Marx, Engels, Lenin, Stalin, and Mao and burning party literature in an outburst of antiparty feelings, the Burman Maoist leaders escaped across the Nam Hka River into China.

The Wa now had their own organization and called it the Burma National United Party (BNUP). On April 18, the mutineers broadcast the first denouncement of what they termed "the narrow racial policies of the Communist Party of Burma."[45] An even stronger broadcast followed on April 28:

Conditions were good before 1989. But what has the situation come to now? No progress whatsoever is being made. Why? In our opinion, it is because some leaders are clinging to power and are obstinately pursuing an erroneous line. They are divorced from reality, practising individualism and sectarianism, failing to study and analyse local and foreign conditions, and ignoring actual material conditions.... They have cheated the people of the Wa region, and through lies and propaganda have dragged us into their sham revolution. How can an enemy armed with modern weapons be defeated by empty ideology and through military methods that do not integrate theory with practice? We, the people of the Wa region, never kowtow before an aggressor army whether it be local or foreign. Although we are poor and backward in terms of culture and literature, we are very strong in our determination.

What became of the lives of people in the Wa region following the wrestling of power by an evil-minded individual within the CPB at a certain time in the past? It was a hard life for the people. The burden on the people became heavier with more taxes being levied. We faced grave hardships. Can the people avoid staging an uprising under such a condition?[46]

It is uncertain who that "evil-minded individual" could have been. But while all of the most important CPB leaders escaped to China unharmed, two especially disliked figures were captured alive: Mya Thaung, the political commissar of the Northern Wa District, and Soe Thein, the overall political commissar of the northeastern region. Both were notorious for having manipulated the ethnic minorities, A third high-ranking CPB leader who was earmarked for arrest, and possible execution, was the chief of staff of the army, Tin Yee, who had been responsible for sending many young Wa to die in human-wave attacks on government positions. Tin Yee managed to cross the Nam Hka before he could be captured, while Mya Thaung and Soe Thein were kept in custody until the Chinese told the Wa to release them.

The role China might have played behind the scenes is still a matter of conjecture. By the time the mutiny broke out, the Chinese had signed several trade agreements with the Burmese authorities, and Chinese pressure on the CPB to reconsider its old policies had become more persistent. Already in 1981, as Deng Xiaoping was beginning to put his first promarket reforms into practice, the Chinese had offered asylum to party leaders and high-ranking cadres. This offer included a modest government pension—250 renminbi a month for a politburo member, 200 renminbi for a member of the central committee, 180 renminbi for any other leading cadre, and 100 renminbi for ordinary party members—and a house with a plot of land. However, this was on condition that the retired CPB cadres refrained from political activity of any kind in China. The old guard, especially the *Sichuan laobing* who had lived in China during the Cultural Revolution and been close to Mao, saw the offer as treachery, although they, at first, did not criticize China's new policies openly. The offer was repeated in 1985 and again in 1988. Some of the younger low-ranking CPB cadres accepted the offer to give up and retire in China. The senior members simply ignored it.

Then, in early 1989, the Chinese once again approached the CPB and tried to persuade the leadership to give up. A crisis meeting was convened at Panghsang on February 20, and for the first time Thakin Ba Thein Tin lashed out against the Chinese. In an address to the secret meeting, he referred to "misunderstandings in our relations with a sister party. Even if there are differences between us, we have to coexist and adhere to the principles of non-interference in each other's affairs. This is the same as in 1981, 1985 and 1988. We have no desire to become revisionists."[47] The minutes of the secret meeting were leaked, and this may have encouraged disgruntled local commanders to rise up against the old leadership. A major reason it did not happen earlier was that the ordinary soldiers and their officers were uncertain of China's reaction to such a move. After all, the CPB leaders still went to China every now and then, and they were always picked up at the border by Chinese officials in limousines.[48]

After the February meeting, it is plausible to assume that the Chinese gave some local commanders the green light to rebel, and the reason the mutiny broke out prematurely in Kokang instead of in the Wa Hills could well have been that the Chinese had closer fraternal relations with the ethnic Chinese in Kokang than with the potentially more unruly Wa. Whatever the case, the more than three hundred party members and their families were first trucked through China north to Pangva in the area in Kachin State which was controlled by the CPB. Some remained there while most of them were later moved to Kunming.

Julia Lovell, a professor of modern China at Birkbeck College, University of London, quoting a Chinese-language Hong Kong publication, writes in her book *Maoism: A Global History* that the CPB veterans in China "were marginal, impoverished figures, who could occasionally be glimpsed in the cities of south and west China, their Mao jackets tattered, their toes poking through their old cloth shoes."[49]

Nothing could be more wrong. I visited the ex-CPB exiles in Kunming several times after the mutiny, and they had been given the pensions and the housing the Chinese had promised them. A few had also settled in Ruili, Tengchong, and other border towns.

The only exceptions were the party's two oldest members, Thakin Ba Thein Tin and the Pyinmana veteran Ye Tun, the CPB's delegate to the 1981 peace talks with the government, who were sent to Changsha in Hunan Province where they were kept in isolation so they would not try to rebuild the CPB. Mao had begun his political career in Changsha in the 1910s, and it was there that the Malayan communists had had their broadcasting station, so the location was deemed suitable for the two communist veterans from Burma. They were treated well until they died there, first Thakin Ba Thein Tin in 1995 and then Ye Tun in 1998. But one thing was certain. The CPB insurrection was over forty-one years after the first shots were fired in a small village near Pegu and twenty-one years since Naw Seng and his men had come across the border from Yunnan and captured Mong Ko. Now, the Wa were masters of their own destiny. Or, at least, to some extent.

4

The Growth of the United Wa State Army

The tumultuous events in the Wa Hills and other parts of the former base areas of the Communist Party of Burma (CPB) in the late 1980s altered dramatically the military map of Burma in a way that no offensive by the government's army could ever have done. Many outsiders had initially expected that the Wa and other CPB mutineers would link up with Burma's other ethnic minority armies, and perhaps even the urban dissidents who had fled to rebel-controlled areas after the bloody crackdown on the prodemocracy movement in September 1988, but that did not happen.

The National Democratic Front (NDF) did indeed send a delegation to Panghsang after the mutiny. Mahasang from the Wa National Organisation (WNO) led the group, and his ethnic allies expected that he would be able to win the Wa and other former CPB forces over to the NDF and thus forge a broad alliance against the government. Sensing what was about to happen, the new military junta acted faster and with much more to offer than the ethnic rebels. The generals now in power in Rangoon were determined to prevent such a linkup that could have potentially disastrous consequences for the new regime, and the strategy they employed was to neutralize the ex-CPB forces with ceasefire deals and promises of lucrative business opportunities.

The first surprise came within days of the mutiny and before Mahasang had arrived in Panghsang. He was arrested by his Wa brethren, but managed to escape and make it back to Thailand. What had happened in the meantime was that General Khin Nyunt, the powerful chief of Burma's military intelligence service, had called in the old Kokang warlord Luo Xinghan to act as an intermediary with the mutineers. Luo's death sentence, passed in 1976 after a lengthy trial, had not been carried out. He had been released during the 1980 amnesty when most of his men also returned from the Thai border. Luo had also been given two million Burmese kyat by the government to build a military camp southeast of Lashio. Called 'the Salween Village,' it became the base for a new home guard unit, this time under the government's new *pyi thu sit* ('people's militia') program, which was launched after the disbandment of the old Ka Kwe Ye (KKY) seven years before. The new agreement was effectively the same as the former accord between Rangoon and the local militias: fight the rebels and gain, in return, access to government-controlled roads and towns for smuggling.

However, it was not until the CPB mutiny that Luo was able to regain his former strength and prominence. On March 20–21, only a week after the first uprising in Kokang and Mong Ko, Luo was dispatched to the area, and this time his former enemies Peng Jiasheng and Peng Jiafu arranged a dinner party for him. Luo's message to the northern mutineers was clear: the government is willing to let you keep your guns and control of your area in exchange for a ceasefire and a pledge not to share your guns with other ethnic rebels or the urban dissidents.[1]

Luo's meeting with the mutineers in Kokang was followed by a trip to the north by Aung Gyi, a Sino-Burmese former brigadier general in the Burmese army who became a politician during the 1988 uprising, and Olive Yang, a colorful and well-known Kokang Chinese warlady.[2] She belonged to the old ruling family of Kokang, and had become famous when she linked up with the Kuomintang in the 1950s and early 1960s and became the first drug trafficker to send opium in lorry convoys down to the Thai border.[3] Aung Gyi and Olive Yang met the Peng brothers under the watchful eye of Burma's military intelligence in the garrison town of Lashio.

In late April, shortly after the Wa had taken over Panghsang and Aung Gyi and Olive Yang had visited the north, Khin Nyunt himself and Colonel Maung Tint, the chief of the Burmese army's Lashio-based northeastern command, flew by helicopter to Kunlong on the Salween River, the site of the forty-two-day battle in 1971–72. They met Peng Jiafu and agreed on a temporary ceasefire. After this initial meeting in Kunlong, Khin Nyunt paid several visits to Kokang, which received wide coverage in Burma's government-controlled media.[4]

The time was ripe to invite Zhao Yilai and other Wa leaders, who controlled nearly eighty percent of the CPB's old army. A helicopter was sent to the Wa Hills to pick them up, and meetings were held in Lashio between them and Khin Nyunt, Maung Tint, and other officers from Burma's regular army as well as its military intelligence services. The junta in Rangoon pledged to spend seventy million kyat on a 'border development program' under which roads, bridges, schools, and hospitals were going to be built in the Wa Hills. Diesel, petrol, kerosene, and rice would also be distributed in former CPB areas.[5]

Luo's importance grew as he was able to strike business deals with the mutineers in Kokang. A company called Asia World was founded, and within years of the mutiny became one of Burma's most powerful conglomerates. Former CPB commanders, who only months before had been denounced in the government-controlled media as 'drug traffickers,' 'drunkards,' 'womanisers,' and 'bandits,' suddenly became respectable citizens, now described as 'village elders' and 'leaders of the national races.'[6] In what could have been an oversight by the editor of *The Working People's Daily*, its December 5, 1989 issue published a vitriolic attack on the former CPB commander Zhang Zhiming (Kyi Myint), who was described as a "bull on heat when it comes to female matters."[7] On the day the article appeared in the official newspaper, Zhang Zhiming was in Rangoon, engaged in unofficial talks to hammer out the details of a ceasefire deal with the military authorities.

The former CPB army, meanwhile, had split up into four different forces based along ethnic lines. What used to be called the 101 Warzone in Kachin State, a sliver of land along the Chinese border stretching from Chimeli pass to Kambaiti, became the New Democratic Army, sometimes with 'Kachin' added after it, and so abbreviated to NDA-K. It was led by Sakhon Ting Ying and Zalum who had defected from the Kachin Independence Army (KIA) in 1968. The population there, only a few thousand, was almost exclusively Kachin. In Kokang, the Peng brothers set up the Myanmar National Democratic Alliance Army (MNDAA), while Peng Jiasheng's son-in-law, Lin Mingxian, or Sai Leun, in Mong La and the former 815 War Zone became the National Democratic Alliance Army (Eastern Shan State), or NDAA(ESS).

On November 30, 1989, the newly formed Burma National United Party (BNUP) merged with, or rather absorbed, the much smaller Wa National Council (WNC), officially the administrative arm of the WNO but, in reality, a separate entity. The links between the two groups that existed before 1989 were formalized and the new unified organization was named the United Wa State Party (UWSP). Its forces, by far the largest non-governmental army in Burma, became the United Wa State Army (UWSA). Zhao Yilai headed the civilian side of the movement while Bao Youxiang was appointed chief of the military. Headquartered at Panghsang, which was renamed Pangkham, the UWSA took over the CPB's old stocks of Chinese-supplied weapons, which were kept in warehouses near the homes of the former party leaders.

After concluding a ceasefire agreement with the MNDAA in Kokang, the government offered the Wa and the other former CPB forces the same deal. Western media and even academics usually state that the UWSA and the other groups "signed ceasefire agreements with the government in 1989."[8] But, at that stage, nothing was signed. All agreements were mere verbal understandings. It was not until October 1, 2011 that the UWSA actually signed a document, followed by another agreement on December 26, 2012 and a third on July 13, 2013.[9] Those agreements said little more than that the Wa had no intention of breaking away from the union. The Wa area was also designated 'Special Region (2)' because their organization was the second to enter into a pact with the central government. Kokang, the first ex-CPB force to enter into an agreement with the government, became 'Special Region (1),' while the NDAA (ESS)'s area was designated 'Special Region (4)'. The Shan State Army (SSA), which had been a close CPB ally since the mid-1970s, concluded a ceasefire agreement with the government on September 2, 1989, and its area in central Shan State became 'Special Region (3).'

The 1989 agreements meant that there was no chance of a linkup between the CPB mutineers and the country's many ethnic and political rebels. Moreover, shortly after deals had been struck between the former CPB forces and the government in Rangoon, other ethnic armies that had depended on the communists for arms supplies entered into similar agreement with central authorities. Once the SSA had made peace with the government, other smaller groups in Shan State, such as some Palaung and Pa-O armies, followed suit.

A major blow to old alliances in the north came when, in January 1991, the 4th Brigade of the KIA in northeastern Shan State broke away to become the Kachin Democratic Army (KDA), and made peace with the government. The next big setback for the NDF came when the main KIA gave up its armed struggle in September 1993. On February 24, 1994, the KIA's political wing, the Kachin Independence Organisation (KIO), signed an official ceasefire agreement at a grand ceremony in Myitkyina, the capital of Kachin State. The KIO was the only ethnic armed organization that insisted on such a written agreement and got it.

The crackdown on the prodemocracy uprising in 1988 had been extremely bloody. Thousands of demonstrators and activists had been gunned down and even more put in jail. But the military had made some changes to the old system and abolished the old one-party system under Ne Win's Burma Socialist Programme Party (BSPP). It was now permitted to form other parties, and so the prodemocracy movement set up the National League for Democracy (NLD). These developments did not signify that the country was becoming any more democratic than before. In another crackdown in July 1989, the NLD's entire leadership was detained. Most of them ended up in Rangoon's notorious Insein Jail while the main leader, Aung San's daughter, Aung San Suu Kyi, was placed under house arrest in her home in Rangoon.

Ironically, at a time when almost the entire population of Burma had turned against the regime, thousands of former insurgents who had been fighting against the central government made deals with the ruling military. The threat from the border areas was thwarted and the regime was safe, but the consequences for the country and the outside world were disastrous. Freedom to engage in 'business' in the northeast meant that no authority would stop the production of opium and its derivative heroin. In 1987, the US State Department estimated that the area under poppy cultivation in Burma was 92,300 hectares. In 1989, that rose to 142,742 hectares, and in 1991, 161,012 hectares with a potential production of 185 metric tons of heroin, up from 53 tons in 1987.[10] The US Drug Enforcement Administration (DEA) has slightly different figures, but those also show a sharp increase in opium and heroin production after the UWSA entered into a ceasefire agreement with the military government in Rangoon. In 1986, the DEA states, Burma produced 900 tons of opium and 75 tons of heroin. It rose to 2,430 tons of opium and 203 tons of heroin in 1989 to reach a peak of 2,575 tons of opium and 215 tons of heroin in 1993.[11]

The ceasefire agreements with the government made it possible for the CPB mutineers to travel more freely, and thus to import acetic anhydrite and other chemicals from China, India, and Thailand. For the first time, pure white number 4 heroin was produced in the former CPB areas. In the early 1990s, there were at least seventeen heroin laboratories at locations stretching from Mong Ko and Kokang in the north through the Wa Hills in the middle, and to the NDAA (ESS)'s area in eastern Shan State.[12]

The Wa mutineers' merger with the WNC, and the Wa who had fled the Wa Hills in the early 1970s and then encamped themselves on the Thai border, also made it possible for the UWSA to establish an entirely new base area far from their traditional homeland along the Chinese frontier. Beginning in the mid-1990s, tens of thousands of Wa, and some Lahu as well from the north, were relocated to the south. Entire new towns sprung up just across the border from Thailand, and the inhabitants of the area, mostly ethnic Shan, were driven out and became refugees in Thailand.

The Wa leadership motivated the Wa to move south by claiming that they wanted to get the peasants in the north away from growing poppies. The Wa also said that those areas along the Thai border were theirs because the first inhabitants there were the closely related Lawa, to whom the rulers of Chiang Mai as well as Kengtung had had to pay tribute as the "original owners of the land."[13] The first claim was not convincing, as drug production flourished in the Thai border areas after the move. The second argument may have been historically correct, but the Lawa population of northern Thailand is negligible and thousands of Shan had lived there for centuries. But with their superior firepower, the UWSA wrested control over a new area in the south almost as large as the northern Wa Hills.

The leader of the now defunct WNC, Ai Kyaw Hso (Ai Xiao Sue), a former KKY commander from Yawnghpre in the northern Wa Hills and one-time ally of Mahasang, had opened the southern areas for the Wa, but he was far from the most important player along the Thai border. His organization was, in effect, controlled by the Weis, three brothers of Yunnanese extraction who had spent years in the

Wa Hills. Their family had fled across the border after the communist victory in the Chinese civil war and settled in Vingngun, where they became involved with the local Wa *saohpa* as well as the Kuomintang and the US Central Intelligence Agency (CIA).[14]

The Wei brothers withdrew with Mahasang's Wa to the Thai border after the CPB had taken over the Wa Hills. The middle brother, Wei Xuegang, first joined opium warlord Khun Sa's Shanland United Army (SUA) and served for several years as its treasurer. During that time, he traveled extensively to Taiwan, West Germany, and other countries. Through contacts in Thailand, he had acquired Thai citizenship and used Thai passports when he traveled abroad. His Thai passport name was Prasit Chiwinitipanya, sometimes Charnchai Chiwinitipanya, while the elder brother, Wei Xuelong, also a Thai citizen, became Apichart Chiwinprapasri, and the younger brother, Wei Xueyin, was given the Thai name Pairot Sameur Jayneuk.[15] The wily warlord Khun Sa, whose Chinese name was Zhang Qifu, had also become a Thai citizen with the name Chan Changtrakul, yet another outcome of the close relationship that once existed between Burma's druglords and Thailand's security services.

Wei Xuegang fell out with Khun Sa after allegedly having embezzled a large sum of money and was imprisoned at the warlord's headquarters at Ban Hin Taek in the mountains northwest of Chiang Rai. Wei managed to escape, however, and in 1982 and 1983 took refuge in Taiwan before returning to the Thai-Burmese border areas where he built up his own drug empire. Lacking an army inside Burma, he and his brothers made use of their old contacts with the Wa and bankrolled the buildup of the WNO, WNA, and WNC. When the WNC merged with the northern Wa and the UWSA was established in 1989, the Wei brothers gained access to the vast poppy fields in the Wa Hills as well as areas where raw opium could be refined into heroin.

The WNC leader Ai Kyaw Hso (Ai Xiao Sue) soon faded into the background as the Wei brothers assumed almost total control of the UWSA's southern forces. The Weis also introduced a new drug: methamphetamine. Unlike heroin, which could only be produced after months of laborious work in the poppy fields and then cumbersome refining procedures, methamphetamine could be manufactured synthetically. Bags with small methamphetamine pills were also easier to smuggle across the border. The main market was right there, in Thailand and other Southeast Asian countries. Heroin, on the other hand, had to be smuggled to China and Western countries, which was far riskier and involved a number of local middlemen who could not always be trusted.

Khun Sa, whose army was now called the Mong Tai Army (MTA), was the main rival in the trade, vying for control of lucrative trading routes to Thailand and the outside world. Throughout the early 1990s, fierce battles were fought between the UWSA and the MTA. Following the 1989 ceasefire agreement with the Burmese government, the UWSA was able to send thousands of troops down to the Thai border. Khun Sa was cornered, and in January 1996 he decided, to the surprise of many, to surrender to the Burmese authorities. His once mighty MTA was disbanded, Khun Sa moved to Rangoon, and his top lieutenants established themselves as perfectly legitimate businessmen in the Burmese capital, in Mandalay and in Lashio.

It was the deal of the century, but it also inadvertently meant that the UWSA became the strongest and most important player in the northern Thai-Burmese border areas. However, a few of Khun Sa's men led by a junior officer called Yawt Serk, who had refused to surrender, built up a new rebel outfit called the Restoration Council of Shan State (RCSS). The Thais probably needed someone to counterbalance the UWSA so that the RCSS was able to obtain guns, uniforms, and other equipment from the Thai side of the border. Among the Shan, Yawt Serk managed to cause some confusion by naming his army the Shan State Army. To distinguish it from the old SSA, Yawt Serk's army became known as 'SSA-South.' The real SSA and its political wing, the Shan State Progress Party (SSPP), was subsequently referred to in foreign reports and literature as 'SSA-North.'

In 2007, the East-West Center in Washington published a booklet called *The United Wa State Army: Narco-Army or Ethnic Nationalist Party*? It was well-written and informative, but the mistake was to put a question mark in the title. An ethnic or politically motivated nongovernmental army can be both, like *Fuerzas Armadas Revolucionarias de Colombia*, or Farc, the Revolutionary Armed Forces of Colombia, which used to trade in cocaine at the same time as adhering to Marxist ideologies and principles. Likewise, the UWSA's political wing, the UWSP, used income from the drug trade to promote Wa nationalism and develop the area under its control.

Within years of the mutiny, Panghsang had been transformed into a modern town with marketplaces, retail stores, workshops, multistory houses, and paved streets with streetlights powered by solar panels. During the CPB days, there were only some old Chinese army trucks and jeeps in Panghsang. Now, new cars, buses, and trucks began to ply the streets in town and the roads between the various settlements. A new concrete bridge was built to connect Panghsang with the town of Meng A on the Chinese side of the Nam Hka River.

The diversity of the population was reflected in the new religious buildings that were erected: a new Buddhist pagoda, Christian churches, and a big mosque with a dome. Restaurants serving Chinese and Shan food opened up, along with hotels, smaller guest houses, and a casino, which attracted high rollers from Yunnan and elsewhere in China. Chinese companies were hired to build roads between villages that had previously been reachable only on foot along slippery mountain paths.

Above all, the creation of an indigenous authority saw the revival of Wa culture, something that the CPB had paid little or no interest in preserving. The schools began to teach in Wa, Chinese, Shan, Lahu, and other local languages as well as, for good measure, Burmese. Chinese and Shan are most widely spoken as a second language among the Wa while Burmese, despite the pacts with the central government, is still considered an alien tongue to most inhabitants of the border areas. Books and journals were printed in romanized Wa, using the old system Vincent Young and the missionaries had developed before World War II, not the one the Chinese introduced in southern Yunnan in the 1950s. Statues of Wa heroes and the national symbol, the buffalo, were placed at major intersections in Panghsang to serve as reminders of Wa culture and heritage.

For the Wa, their mountains are not, as they had been for the CPB, a 'springboard' from where they were going to move somewhere else. This is their homeland. In 1995, the government referred to as 'the Wa Central Authority' (WCA) was established at Panghsang, or Pangkham as they sometimes prefer to call it. It has twelve bureaus responsible for finance, political work, agriculture and forestry, public relations, law enforcement, logistics, health and education, construction, military matters, foreign relations, and even a unit for women's affairs. Before 1989, there were only twenty schools with 480 pupils and a hundred teachers in the Wa Hills. Now there are 409 with more than 60,000 pupils and 2,400 teachers. Today, nearly every village has its own primary school and there is a high school in every township. When the CPB ruled the area, there were only four poorly equipped hospitals. In 2019, there were 26 better equipped facilities, including smaller clinics with doctors and nurses who have been educated in China.[16]

Where in the past mule tracks were the most advanced lines of communication, new roads have been built by Chinese contractors to connect major settlements. The roads in the Wa Hills are even in a much better condition than those in government-controlled areas.[17] The initial capital to pay for all this may have come from the drug trade, but in recent years the Wa economy has been diversified to include income from tin mining and investments in Burma, China, and Thailand. Poppy fields have given way to rubber plantations and tea gardens. But it is a capitalism with many distinct Chinese characteristics, as researcher Hans Steinmüller points out in a study: "The kind of authoritarian capitalism that has developed in the Wa State has similar effects as in China. Even though relative inequality has risen exponentially, living standards are higher and absolute poverty is lower than in the past."[18]

Large-scale construction projects are managed directly by the top authority but the payment of salaries has created a cash economy where, in the past, barter was the norm, and the only hard currencies that people in the Wa Hills accepted were opium and old Indian silver coins. But it is the Chinese yuan, not the Burmese kyat, that is used for business and in markets and shops in Wa areas. Mobile phones and the Internet are also connected to Chinese, not Burmese, servers.

Moreover, as Steinmüller points out, many young Wa go across the border to find work, generally without permits or identity cards, but they are taken to Chinese factories by Chinese and Wa middlemen.[19]

The Wa authority has its own set of laws, which were passed on December 24, 2003 and printed in the Wa language as well as in Chinese and Burmese. A court system is in place, and while local courts can sentence offenders to imprisonment and the payment of fines, the death penalty, which is on the books, can be meted out only by the top leadership.[20] Administratively, the WCA, which is headed by a chairman, has a 'political advisory committee' that serves as an unofficial parliament. The head of the UWSP is a secretary general, and the UWSA is led by its commander-in-chief.

Each township—and there are three in the north plus two 'special townships'—has its own local government, and a 'local administrative committee' is in charge of the southern areas along the Thai border. In addition, the WCA maintains liaison offices in the government-controlled cities and towns of Rangoon, Lashio, Mandalay, Tachilek, and Kengtung.[21]

Despite its well-organized administrative structure, new 'Wa State,' as it became known although it was recognized officially only as a 'special region' within the Union of Burma, is no democracy. It is a one-party state under the UWSP, and the UWSP controls the 'Wa government' as well as the UWSA. The basic setup that has emerged since the mutiny is, in essence, Leninist, and apart from the ideology its organizational structure is more or less the same as that of the old CPB. The UWSP remains a Leninist-style vanguard party with only 10,000 of the approximately 500,000 inhabitants in the area it controls being members. It is not a mass organization.

Zhao Yilai's authority as chairman of the government and secretary general of the party was formalized at the UWSP's first congress in January 1992. But Zhao's health was failing, and in February 1995 he suffered a stroke and had to be hospitalized, first in Cangyuan across the border in Yunnan and later in Shanghai. He continued to attend meetings after his return to Panghsang, often sitting in a wheelchair. He was soon hospitalized again, this time in Lancang in Yunnan, following another stroke. He died there on the morning of September 8, 2009. Four days later, more than a thousand people gathered for his funeral at Saohpa, a small town near the Chinese border where he was born. Speakers at the ceremony pointed out that it was Zhao who had unified the Wa people and lifted them out of poverty, humiliation, and oppression. Even today, Zhao Yilai, or Ta Lai as he is called in his own language, is seen as the father of the modern Wa nation. After the 1989 mutiny, he converted to Christianity to honor his stepfather, a Wa Christian who had taken care of the young boy when his own poor parents had been unable to do so.

While Zhao remained the father of the nation until his death, the new leader, Bao Youxiang, had actually been acting general secretary of the UWSP since 2004, serving concurrently as commander-in-chief of the UWSA and chairman of the Wa administration, thus holding all three key positions in the leadership of the unofficial 'Wa State.' After the death of Zhao, Bao Youxiang and his brothers—the elder Bao Youri and the younger Bao Youliang—became the undisputed triumvirate ruling the Wa region. A fourth brother, Bao Youhua, died of a massive stroke in 2007. Bao Youri was put in charge of managing the movement's finances while Bao Youliang became the head of Mong Mau, a district which includes a financially important tin mining area.

The Bao brothers, and especially Bao Youxiang himself, made sure they and trusted Wa associates controlled the UWSA. The number two in the military setup, Zhao Zhongdan, was one of them, and when Bao's health began to fail in the 2000s, he was entrusted to run the day-to-day affairs of the army. Bao had contracted chronic trichinosis after eating poorly prepared pickled pork, called *neu som* in Shan and *naem* in Thai, and that illness makes any physical or mental activity extremely strenuous.

The civil administration that emerged in the 1990s and early 2000s, though, shows a different, less cohesive pattern. Chin Ko-lin, a Burma-born ethnic Chinese-American criminologist, describes it this way:

> Within the Wa administration, Wa leaders are viewed as the muscle and the Chinese are the brains. Ethnic Wa are respected for their fighting skills and, because of their ethnicity, they are the masters of the Wa area, despite the fact that some of them were born in China and came to the Wa area only recently. Ethnic Chinese are considered to be smart people with good business and organisational skills, but because they are not ethnic Wa, they can only work for the Wa people, even though some of the Chinese were born in the Wa area. As a result, many Wa government units are headed by ethnic Wa, but day-to-day operations of these units are conducted by ethnic Chinese who are usually deputy chiefs.[22]

That is where the Wei brothers come into the picture. As smart business people, they took charge of Wa enterprises, and not only the drug trade. Profits were reinvested in hotels and real estate in

Rangoon and Mandalay, and using proxies the Weis even took over Yangon Airlines, a domestic carrier.

Xiao Minliang, second in command of civil administration and entrusted with clerical and organizational work for the WCA, belongs to the other category, that of a China-born Wa. He hails from a small Wa village near Cangyuan in Yunnan and was educated there. At twenty he was sent to join the CPB and later came to serve under Bao Youxiang and Li Ziru in central Shan State. Li Ziru, an ethnic Chinese from Baoshan in Yunnan and one of the old Red Guard volunteers, actually rose to be deputy commander-in-chief of the UWSA after 1989, while simultaneously running various kinds of businesses from his base at Nalawt, a few kilometers west of Panghsang. Li suffered a stroke and died in 2005 and since then the only Chinese ex-volunteer who has remained in a high position within the Wa administration is Zhao Guoan. Born in Nansan near Yunnan's border with Kokang, he is in charge of foreign affairs and has represented the UWSA at peace talks with the Myanmar government. Li Ziru's two sons, Li Zuhua and Li Ching, have taken over their father's various business enterprises, which, at least in the beginning, included investment in the drug trade.

The other former CPB areas also saw rapid economic and social development after the 1989 mutiny. The Kokang Chinese built a new fortune based on drugs, but rival gangs soon fell out over who should be controlling the trade. In 1992, open warfare broke out as Yang Maolian, a former CPB military officer, drove Peng Jiasheng out of Kokang. Yang became the new chieftain, but his relations with China suffered a severe blow in 1994 when his younger brother, Yang Maoxian, was arrested by the Chinese, convicted of drug trafficking, and executed in Kunming.

In the former 815 War Zone, which had become the NDAA (ESS), Lin Mingxian, or Sai Leun, transformed his Mong La headquarters into a center for all kinds of vice, including gambling, prostitution, and transvestite shows. This entertainment industry, rather unorthodox in a former communist stronghold, catered to a mainly Chinese clientele, and buses from China became a common sight in Mong La. New buildings, including fancy hotels, casinos, karaoke, bars and nightclubs, sprung up in and around Mong La. A new hydroelectric power station was built on the Nam Loi River to provide those establishment with round-the-clock electricity.

As in other former CPB areas, income from the drug trade provided the financial basis for that development. Shortly after the 1989 mutiny, heroin laboratories were set up near Mong La and in the mountains closer to the Mekong River. Drug production activities in those areas were controlled by the top leadership of the NDAA (ESS) as a highly centralized committee headed by Lin and including twelve other local functionaries. They decided which operators were going to operate where and how much they should pay in taxes and duties to the center at Mong La. The profits were then equally divided between Lin and other shareholders in the enterprise.

However, as one would expect when drugs are involved, all was not well in Mong La. In November 1993, three men were dragged out into the central market and executed by firing squad in front of a big audience. They were accused of having tried to assassinate Lin. The plot, Lin suspected, had been masterminded by his then main rival in the drug trade, Khun Sa.[23]

Most of the NDAA (ESS)'s troops, a few thousand, were Shan, Akha, and eastern Palaung but many of its officers were Chinese or, as in the case of Lin, Sino-Shan. His second in command, Zhang

Zhiming, or Kyi Myint, is an old childhood friend. Zhang was born in Wanding on the Chinese side of the border opposite Lin's native place Panghsai. Like Li Ziru and Zhao Guoan, Zhang also came as a Red Guard volunteer to fight alongside the CPB in the late 1960s and stayed on when the others were recalled to China in the late 1970s.

Mong La grew to become one of the most prosperous towns on the Burma-China frontier, and some of the proceeds from there were also reinvested in real estate in Rangoon and Mandalay, in Yunnan, in northern Thailand, and even in Hong Kong and Taiwan.[24] As the tourism industry grew, especially the lucrative casino business, drugs became a minor income for Lin and his NDAA (ESS), and today their contribution is believed to be negligible. There may be private dealers in Mong La, but it is no longer an official 'government' business.

In Kachin State, the area controlled by Ting Ying's and Zalum's NDA-K was too remote to attract large numbers of Chinese visitors. However, it had one resource that turned out to be a boon for the former Kachin communists: timber. The World Resources Institute reported as early as 1998 that "high-resolution satellite data show that this frontier is now being threatened by logging. Evidence elsewhere in the region suggests that Kachin State may be in the early stages of a period of intense deforestation that could culminate in the clearing of all accessible timber, leaving just a patchwork of severely damaged forest fragments."[25] In October 2005, Global Witness published a damaging report on deforestation in northern Burma, as well as legal and illegal exports of timber to China.[26] That report caused quite an uproar among official circles in China, as it revealed that thousands of tons of teak, other hardwood, and assorted forestry products were being transported across the border to Yunnan. The Chinese foreign ministry claimed in a statement that the Global

Witness report contained a lot of "untruthful information," and went on to say that China does not allow its citizens "to conduct illegal deforestation activities and trade across the border."[27] That, of course, was a ludicrous claim as convoys of heavily laden timber trucks could be seen leaving the NDA-K area for Tengchong and other towns in Yunnan every day. But the exposure led to a partial clampdown on the trade, which, however, came too late. By the mid-2010s, most of the forest was gone, leaving opium poppies to be planted on the denuded mountains.

While the UWSA and the NDAA (ESS) managed to survive and prosper, the NDA-K soon fell apart because of infighting and personal rivalries. Zalum was ousted after trying to stage a coup, and Ting Ying moved even closer to the ruling military by agreeing to be the leader of a so-called Border Guard Force under Burmese command. Other units remained at Kambaiti and Pangva on the Chinese border where they soon became engaged in drug trafficking and the production of weapons in clandestine arms factories.

Some of the younger former CPB cadres who had been sent to Pangva along with the party leadership after the 1989 mutiny had decided to stay on when the top leaders and their families were transferred to retirement homes in Kunming. For some reason, Ting Yang and his men thought those younger former CPB members were going to resurrect the party and had several of them arrested and executed. By 2020, the fragmentation of the NDA-K was almost complete. Only small bands of armed militiamen remained in the area.

In the beginning, China's reaction to all these developments did not appear to be particularly clear, and there did not seem to be any kind of coordinated policy apart from denial of any 'interference' in

Burma's internal affairs, as Song Qingrun, an associate professor at China's Institute of South Asia, wrote in March 2015: "The truth … is that China has never intervened in Myanmar's internal affairs."[28] Such nonsense has been repeated by a number of China-associated scholars, among them Yun Sun at the Stimson Center in the US, who frequently refers to China's "principle of non-interference in other countries' internal affairs."[29]

The truth is that China has always interfered in Myanmar's internal affairs and done so blatantly, and that policy has not changed since hard-line communism was abandoned in the 1980s. But with the promotion of free trade, and with drug production across the border in Burma skyrocketing in the 1990s, China's priorities changed at the same time as it became almost impossible to curtail corruption within the less ideologically motivated post-Mao administration. Officially, many of the former CPB commanders who had become drug dealers, especially those from Mong Ko and Kokang, were barred from entering China. The fact that all of them had been operating for years along the Sino-Burmese border meant, however, that they had long-standing working relationships with Chinese security authorities. This personal relationship enabled them to visit China regularly and to own property, including hotels and private houses, across the border. They were often also seen being driven around in cars owned by local Chinese security officials.[30]

Before the communist takeover in 1949, China had vast poppy fields and millions of opium smokers. Addiction was considered one of the country's most serious social problems and that was why the communists decided to put an end to it. The methods were brutal, but they worked. Hundreds, if not thousands, of gangsters, dealers, and even addicts were rounded up and shot after summary trials. Addicts who were considered curable were sent to rehabilitation camps, and the vast poppy fields in China's interior, mainly in Sichuan and Yunnan, were cut down.

Then came China's new economic policies in the 1980s. As private enterprise was encouraged, people became more mobile and borders were not as closely guarded as they had been during the Mao regime. Those developments, combined with the surge in drug production across the border in Burma, led to the return of drug abuse all over China. Heroin became the drug of choice, and it was readily available not only in Yunnanese towns such as Kunming, Ruili, and Baoshan but in all major Chinese cities.

The degree to which drugs and drug money had affected local politics and corrupted society became clear when, in the evening of August 30, 1992, a motorcade of over a hundred military vehicles carrying 2,000 police and paramilitary policemen left Kunming and headed south towards the border with Vietnam. Their target was the town of Pingyuan, which for years had served as a transit point for the trade in contraband with Vietnam and Laos. Taking advantage of the new economic opening, Pingyuan had also become a center for the collection and distribution of opium, heroin, and guns. From Pingyuan, drugs brought in from Burma, either directly or via Laos, were shipped on to more than twenty-four provinces throughout China.[31] The armed task force that was dispatched from Kunming had been instructed to recapture the town from the traffickers.

It was deemed a sensitive operation because the vast majority of Pingyuan's population was Hui, or Yunnanese Muslims (who the Burmese refer to as Panthay). They had rebelled during the Cultural Revolution, which had led to a bloody crackdown resulting in more than 1,600 of them being killed by the People's Liberation

Army (PLA). Hardly surprisingly, distrust of the authorities was deeply rooted among the Hui in Pingyuan, and the massacre in the mid-1970s was probably why the provincial government this time deployed paramilitary units rather than the regular military.

The operation began on August 31 and lasted for eighty days, first as a siege and then as armed confrontation. The Hui in the town had guns. They fought back, but eventually surrendered to the superior force from Kunming. When it was over, the Chinese commanders found luxury villas, bars, and dance halls run by the traffickers. Among the traffickers was Ma Siling, who was found living in a fortified villa in Pingyuan despite having been sentenced to death by a local court for drug trafficking. The net haul after the operation: 854 people arrested and 981 kilograms of drugs seized along with 353 assorted weapons.[32]

A public trial attended by more than 8,000 people was held on October 14. Two traffickers who had been apprehended during the operation were sentenced to death and immediately executed, and twenty-two were given prison sentences. At a second public trial on November 12, which was attended by 12,000 people, five were given the death penalty. Among them were the vice director of Pingyuan township and the general steward of the local mosque.[33]

Significantly, low-level officials in Yunnan were kept in the dark when the operation was planned in Kunming. Now, as researcher Zhou Yongming points out in his study of antidrug campaigns in China, the old power structure that had made Pingyuan uncontrollable was dismantled and replaced by a new one: "The authority of the government and regaining control of the local government materialized in the process of the drug crackdown. The Resident Committee, Village Council, Security Committee, and

Women's Association—organisations that had not been able to be establish before—were set up."[34]

Seen in a broader perspective, the Pingyuan operation shattered a network of contacts that had been in charge of drug distribution in the entire region. It is always sensitive, and often misleading, to talk about 'ethnic organized crime' because such labels tend to demonize an entire group of people rather than a few 'bad apples,' but members of the Hui community had long been some of the most important players in cross-border trade in the Golden Triangle. Called Panthay in Burmese and Jin Haw in Thai, they see themselves as descendants of Kublai Khan's horsemen. Many have the family name Ma, or horse, and have for centuries been the region's best muleteers. In the past, they had not only been the main buyers of Wa opium but had also conducted mule caravans that carried all kinds of contraband between the Wa Hills, northern Shan State, southern Yunnan, and even northern Laos and Vietnam.[35] In more recent times, they have turned to modern means of transport, such as lorries and other motor vehicles. But the network of contacts throughout the region has remained more or less intact.

The Pingyuan operation became a turning point in China's policies towards the ex-CPB forces in northeastern Burma. Bao Youxiang and other UWSA, MNDAA, and NDAA (ESS) leaders were summoned to Kunming and read the riot act. No drugs were to enter China. The central authorities in Beijing also began to take a more direct interest in the former CPB forces on the other side of the border. It was an issue that could not be left to local authorities in Yunnan's border counties or even the provincial government in Kunming. It was not only because of the drug issue but was also a question of national security. China's southern border had to be secured. Beijing's security planners also knew perfectly well that Burma was an important outlet for trade with South and Southeast Asia as well as the only country that could provide China with safe and relatively easy access to the Indian Ocean.

That policy had first been articulated by Pan Qi in his article in the *Beijing Review* of September 2, 1985.[36] The first border trade agreement between Burma and China was signed on August 6, 1988, at a time when Burma was in turmoil and almost the entire border was controlled by various rebel groups. The 1989 mutiny and the subsequent ceasefire agreements had changed all that, and China soon began to penetrate the Burmese market in a very systematic manner. A network of economic intelligence operatives collected data about the prices and availability of more than 2,000 locally manufactured as well as imported items—medicines, beer, soft drinks, sports shoes, rice cookers, motorbikes, cigarettes, crockery and so on—and then the same goods were produced much cheaper in China's own state-owned or private factories.

Chinese businessmen moved down to Lashio and Mandalay to supervise the trade, and some of them even managed to buy Burmese identity documents from corrupt local officials. As 'Burmese citizens' they could buy property and engage in other activities that are barred to foreigners.[37] UWSA and MNDAA soldiers in full uniform could also be seen in Mandalay and other towns, loading their Chinese-made army trucks with goods destined for the Chinese market, and paid for with laundered drug money.

Regardless of the financial basis for those transactions, their involvement in 'normal' commercial activities suited the Chinese. They were also able to maintain contacts with the UWSA and other former CPB forces through China's peculiar foreign policy of differentiating between 'government-to-government' and 'party-to-party' relations, an entirely artificial concept as the communist party is China's only legal political party and as such controls the government. But it means that it became possible for the UWSA to acquire weapons from China at the same time as Beijing maintained cordial relations with Burma's central government.

Over the years, transfers of Chinese weapons to the UWSA have included HN-5A Man-Portable Air Defence Systems, or MANPADS, heavy machine-guns, automatic rifles, mortars, artillery, armored fighting vehicles, and other sophisticated military equipment. Among the most recent deliveries are FN-6 MANPADS, 105mm recoilless guns, 122mm howitzers, 107mm surface-to-surface free-flights missiles, Xinxing ('New Star') wheeled armored personnel carriers, and weaponized drones.[38] This is not the kind of kit that falls off the back of a truck or could be supplied by some local PLA unit in Yunnan. The deliveries were almost certainly directed from the highest level in Beijing, and to disguise the origin often shipped into the UWSA's area via Laos.[39]

In 2007, advisers from the PLA provided training in the use of 122mm howitzers and 130mm field guns in the Lu Fang mountain range west of Panghsang. The UWSA's artillery regiment had been equipped with those weapons along with 12.7mm and 14.5mm anti-aircraft guns. Soldiers were mobilized to dig a complex of underground command centers near Panghsang, clearly intended for protection against aerial attacks by the Burmese air force in the event hostilities were to break out.

With new Chinese weapons came smart uniforms, not the baggy, old-fashioned clothes the fighters in the CPB had worn, and discipline within the UWSA was improved. Given the fact that the

UWSA had had a ceasefire agreement with the government since 1989, the average age of the soldier was also much higher than in the CPB's erstwhile army, which towards the end was made up of forcibly recruited teenagers because the majority of able-bodied men were either cripples or dead. Most soldiers are conscripted, but that practice is not universal and children of those who have good relations with the elite might avoid being recruited altogether or end up in more comfortable positions in the army.[40]

The army has been divided into the northern forces—four brigades and an artillery regiment—and those along the Thai border in the south, which consist of five brigades. The total number of troops is a well-guarded secret, but most outside observers put the figure at between 20,000 and 25,000, or possibly as many as 30,000. Those figures do not include reserves and local village militia forces. In addition, there is a police force with 2,500 men which is responsible for maintaining law and order in the Wa-administered area.[41] There are no Burmese government troops anywhere in territory that is governed by the WCA, and representatives of the central government come only for special occasions, such as in April 2019 when the Wa celebrated the 30th anniversary of the 1989 uprising.

The UWSA has become stronger and much better equipped that the CPB ever was. When Aung Min, then a minister in the Burmese president's office, visited Monywa, a town northwest of Mandalay, in November 2012 to meet local people protesting a controversial Chinese-backed copper mining project in the area, he openly admitted: "We are afraid of China ... we don't dare to have a row with [them]. If they feel annoyed with the shutdown of their projects and resume their support to the communists, the economy in the border areas would backslide. So you'd better think seriously."[42]

By 'the communists' he clearly meant the UWSA and its allies. And he was right. It may not be in China's interest to see fighting and unrest along its southwestern border, which could lead to a massive influx of refugees into China. That happened in 2015 when the MNDAA broke its ceasefire agreement with the government and attacked Burmese army positions in Kokang. It led to a massive counteroffensive, and 40,000–50,000 people sought refuge across the border in Yunnan. But a strong UWSA that sometimes shares its Chinese-made arsenal, which it has acquired through 'party-to-party' relations with China, with other ethnic armies serves as a stick in Beijing's relationship with Burma. Diplomacy and promises of aid to Burma's central authorities come under 'government-to-government relations.' That fictitious division of duties came in handy when China became involved in the Burmese government's peace process, which was initiated by then president Thein Sein in 2012. The Chinese could show that they, and only they, would be able to help the Burmese government solve its internal ethnic problems.

The Wa maintain close links with the other former CPB forces in Kokang and Mong La as well as with the KIA, the SSA, and two new ethnic armies, the Ta'ang National Liberation Army (TNLA), a Palaung group, and the Arakan Army (AA), which were formed after the central government launched its peace process. The TNLA as well as the AA were initially trained by the KIA, and later moved to other areas—the TNLA into the Palaung-inhabited hills of northern Shan State and the AA to Rakhine State. Both groups saw action in Kokang in 2015 when the MNDAA resorted to armed struggle against the Burmese army.

The TNLA has grown from a handful of soldiers a few years ago to the formidable 5,000-strong fighting force it is today. The AA, meanwhile, has grown also from a handful of fighters recruited from among Rakhine migrant workers in Kachin State to an army of between 2,000 and 3,000 today. It has launched a war in Rakhine State, an entirely new front in Burma's civil war. While the UWSA is not involved in any fighting with the Burmese army, it has supplied the TNLA, MNDAA, and AA with guns, either as gifts or sold at 'friendship' prices.[43]

The UWSA also supplied the SSA with weapons, which enabled it to defend its Wan Hai headquarters in central Shan State when the Burmese army attacked it in 2015. That help was strategic, as the SSA's areas west of the Salween River is the UWSA's buffer zone between them and the Burmese army. Were the SSA forced out of its strongholds, it would be easier for the Burmese army to attack the Wa areas east of the river, should the government decide to launch such as offensive.

The attack on the SSA and renewed fighting in Kokang are only two examples of how the government, and some of the ethnic armies as well, consider the ceasefire agreements that were reached in the late 1980s and early 1990s obsolete. The first sign of that came when the Burmese army launched an all-out attack on the KIA in June 2011, just as the Thein Sein government began talking about negotiations with the ethnic armies in order to find a peaceful solution to the country's decades-long civil war. Fierce fighting raged for several months in Kachin State. Although the Burmese army suffered huge casualties, it did manage to capture some KIA bases near the Chinese border, in western Kachin State, and in northern Shan State.

The KIA, however, has not benefited as much as some of the UWSA's other allies from Wa arms supplies. It got some 0.50-caliber machine-guns, ammunition, and two Humvees, but little more than that. The reason could be that the Chinese remain somewhat suspicious of the Kachin, a predominantly Christian people who in the past have reached out to the West, especially the United States, more than most other ethnic armies in Burma. Moreover, in the early 1990s, before the KIA signed its failed ceasefire agreement with the government, it received some support from India, and that could also help explain Chinese attitudes towards the group. There is also no way the UWSA can share its weaponry with other groups without at least the tacit approval of China's security services.

Relations with the NDAA (ESS), somewhat strangely considering their shared past, became tense in 2016. The UWSA even sent in troops to take over some of the NDAA (ESS)'s positions along what had been a common border. The problems arose after NDAA (ESS) leaders attended peace talks with the government in August of that year, and the Wa leaders feared that their allies were on the verge of reaching an agreement with the central authorities that would adversely affect the UWSA's interests. If a peace deal had been struck, the UWSA would have been cut off from roads leading through the NDAA (ESS)'s area to the Mekong River, which forms the border between Burma and Laos. Since the supplies of Chinese weapons usually transit through Laos, that would have been disastrous for the Wa. Since then, UWSA troops have also formed a defensive string of bases around the NDAA (ESS)'s area to make sure the group does not step out of line.

The Wa have also continued to flex their muscles in Burma's legitimate business environment. Researcher Andrew Ong of the National University of Singapore points out in an August 2018 article that the UWSA has business dealings not only with Chinese counterparts, but it has "since the 1990s demonstrated a creativity and ability to navigate different routes, markets and investments to buttress its self-reliance. Collaborations between Wa-owned companies and other Myanmar (Burmese) conglomerates point to strong business ties with elites in Yangon (Rangoon) and Mandalay."[44]

Because any armed conflict with the Burmese military would put such investment in jeopardy, the UWSA is interested in maintaining the status quo rather than actively joining its allies in their fight against the central government. It is a paradoxical situation, but from a Wa point of view perhaps the best solution, at least for the time being. They have their own government running their affairs. Their economy is strong and their army sufficiently well-equipped to dissuade the Burmese army from taking action against them. Fighting on other fronts also keeps the Burmese army from even contemplating attacking Wa areas. The Wa, for the first time in history, have become a unified nation with their own de facto state. That is no mean achievement by a people who until only a few decades ago were head-hunters, and then used as little more than cannon fodder for fulfilling the dream of a group of Burmese communists whose language they do not even speak.

5

The United Wa State Army and Drugs: A Chinese Dilemma

A major setback to the United Wa State Army's efforts to become legitimate, a goal the organization had held since it entered into a ceasefire agreement with the Burmese army in 1989, came on January 25, 2005. Roslynn R. Mauskopf, US attorney for the Eastern District of New York, and Anthony P. Placido, the special-agent-in-charge for the New York Field Division of the Drug Enforcement Administration (DEA), announced the unsealing of an indictment against eight high-ranking UWSA leaders on drug-trafficking related charges. The eight on the list were the four Wa brothers, Bao Youxiang, Bao Youri, Bao Bao Youliang, and Bao Youhua; the three Wa brothers, Wei Xuegang, Wei Xuelong, and Wei Xueyin; and Bao Huachiang, an unrelated Wa officer.[1]

The indictment, the US officials said, was the outcome of an investigation code-named 'Operation Warlord' which "focused on stemming the flow of illegal drugs at their source, and is the latest chapter in a long history of collaboration between the DEA and other law enforcement agencies to combat heroin trafficking in Southeast Asia."[2] No specific case involving smuggling to the United States was mentioned in the announcement, only vague references to trafficking beyond the immediate region:

The indictment alleges that through the UWSA, the defendants control all decision making relative to the cultivation, collection and transportation of opium in the territory under UWSA control. This includes taxing of narcotics shipments and drug refineries, and the collection of lucrative narcotics proceeds. In return, the defendants and the UWSA provide security for heroin and methamphetamine laboratories in Wa territory, as well as for drug caravans smuggling heroin and methamphetamine from Eastern Burma to Thailand, China, and Laos where independent brokers smuggle shipments to international distribution organizations in Asia, Europe and the United States.[3]

The announcement did not identify those "international distribution organizations," so it is unclear how the drugs allegedly from UWSA-controlled areas ended up in the United States. But the DEA went on to state that the UWSA is "one of the largest heroin producing and trafficking organizations in the world and was responsible for the production of more than 180 metric tons of opium in 2004."[4] The UWSA as well as Wei Xuegang "have been designated 'Drug Kingpins' by the United States government."[5]

There was, however, an additional sealed list which included the names of thirteen people with UWSA connections who had also been indicted—and the names on the two lists, one unsealed and the other sealed, reveal an important feature in drug production under the aegis of the UWSA. Although the three Bao brothers are on the unsealed list along with another Wa, Bao Huachiang, who is not a relative, the rest are Sino-Burmese or Sino-Thai. All of them are connected with Wei Xuegang's network. The sealed list, which contains thirteen names, includes the names of twelve Sino-Burmese and Sino-Thais. The thirteenth name on that list is Li Ziru, the Red Guard volunteer from China who joined the Communist Party of Burma (CPB) in the late 1960s.[6]

The refineries in the Wa area were set up by ethnic Chinese syndicates and taxed by the UWSA which, in return, provided protection and then arranged for the drugs to be smuggled out of the area, mostly down to Thailand but also across the border to China. Buyers would also send drugs to India and Bangladesh, where the UWSA was not present, so other armed factions, some of them government-recognized militias, would have to take care of transportation. That raises the question of how widely the UWSA's network of contacts actually reached. Although the US indictment also gave a long list of Wei-associated companies in Burma, it seems highly unlikely that he, the Bao brothers, or any other Wa, would have contacts in New York, or for that matter in Sydney, Amsterdam, or even a nearby drug market such as Hong Kong.

There is no doubt that the UWSA made a fortune from the drug trade, which enabled it to transform Panghsang from a spartan communist headquarters into a modern city, run its administration, and provide the villagers with basic social services. The new paved roads in the Wa Hills are better than those in government-controlled areas of Shan State, and even remote villages now have electricity and piped water, and most houses have been provided with corrugated iron roofs instead of thatch, all unknown luxuries during the CPB era and before. The Wa administration now runs 409 schools compared with only 20 in 1989, and 26 hospitals, up from four at the time of the mutiny.[7] Young Wa, whose parents were mostly illiterate and wore baggy fatigues and caps with a red star, now have mobile phones, are on email, and surf the Internet using Virtual Private Network (VPN) to get around Chinese restrictions. The ceasefire agreement with the government has enabled them to travel to cities like Mandalay and Rangoon. Some have even been to Chiang Mai and Bangkok.

While the UWSA and the people living under its control have benefited from the drug trade, a 1998 study of drug prices from producer to consumer shows that the biggest profits were not made in the mountains of northern Burma but where the drugs were actually sold. At that time, a hilltribe poppy farmer in the Burmese sector of the Golden Triangle could sell his raw opium to a local merchant for 20,000 Burmese kyat, then the equivalent of US$75, per *viss* or *joi*, the equivalent of 1.6 kilograms. The refinery operators would cook the opium, and although ten kilograms of it plus chemicals such as acetic anhydrite would make one kilogram of pure white number 4 heroin, the bricks that were produced would not be counted in kilograms but in bricks, each weighing 700 grams. The wholesale price for such a brick at the refineries in Burma also varied at that time between US$3,750 and US$4,250. In other words, 700 grams of heroin equaled US$330 worth of raw opium for the farmer.[8]

Once smuggled across the border into northern Thailand, a buyer would pay up to US$4,750–5,000 for the same 700-gram brick. Brought from the border to the city of Chiang Mai in northern Thailand, the price would have increased to US$5,625. Then, when the heroin had been transported down to Bangkok, the price per brick would be US$6,250–7,500. In Hong Kong, the same brick would have fetched US$21,000, and in Taiwan as much as US$37,500. The wholesale price in Sydney was AUS$75,000–85,000, or US$46,000–52,000 at the time, if sold from an Asian to an Asian. The importer would then sell the same unit to a retailer for AUS$180,000, or US$110,000. In Australia, the heroin would be broken up into 0.02-gram capsules, which were sold in the streets for AUS\$30, or US\$18.50 each—or AUS\$1.05 million, or US\$617,000 for the equivalent of the price for a 700-gram brick in the Golden Triangle.

In New York, the wholesale price at the time was US\$80,000 per brick, which would be adulterated and packed into bags containing 25 milligrams of heroin and 25 grams of lactose. Thus, 700 grams of heroin would make 28,000 such bags, which were sold to addicts for US\$10 each. The value of the same heroin that cost US\$3,750-4,250 at the refinery in Burma—and the opium equivalent of which was priced at US\$330 for the Golden Triangle poppy farmer—had increased to gross sales of at least US\$280,000.

It is not hard to draw the conclusion that opium was not cultivated by "hostile poppy farmers," as the international press sometimes calls them. That is a gross distortion of reality. The main profiteers were not even refinery operators in the Golden Triangle, but rather the importers and retailers in cities in the West. Few of them would have even heard of the Wa and the UWSA. But when drug seizures are made in countries such as Burma, the value of the catch is always counted as if New York street prices would be applicable even there.

The other myth is the kingpin theory, which is little more than a Hollywood-like portrayal of Asia's drug trade. In reality, the trade is, and has always been, run by loosely and informally organized networks, and not by some overarching, all-powerful 'kingpins.' Ko-lin Chin and Sheldon X. Zhang, two of America's most accomplished criminologists, have shown in seminal books, including *The Chinese Heroin Trade* and *The Golden Triangle: Inside Southeast Asia's Drug Trade*, as well as numerous papers and articles that Chinese drug and crime networks "are horizontally structured, fluid, and opportunistic."[9] They have also argued that, in private conversations, "even US drug enforcement officials in the field have acknowledged that there are no kingpins, or at least they have not seen any in China and Southeast Asia."[10]

Chin and Zhang state categorically in their studies that they have never encountered any significant involvement in the drug trade of the notorious, organized crime groups in Hong Kong, Taiwan, and mainland China that are known as Triads. Those gangs are often depicted in the press as the main players but, as Chin and Zhang argue, some Triad members may deal in drugs but their income derives chiefly from enterprises such as construction, extortion, gambling, prostitution, and fraud.

Indeed, the use of the term 'kingpin' is misleading when referring to narcotics suppression in Southeast Asia. A 'kingpin' by definition is the pin at the center in bowling and if toppled all the other pins will fall as well. But history has shown time and time again that this is not how the Golden Triangle drug trade is structured: as one alleged 'kingpin' has fallen, others have been left standing, conveniently in place to take on the misnomer mantle.

The notion of a drug 'kingpin' is often produced as a diversionary focal point while other actors, including supposedly legitimate businessmen and even state officials, deal in narcotics under the radar. But naming and shaming those individuals could have diplomatic as well as legal consequences.

In the early 1970s, as Kokang warlord Luo Xinghan was crowned 'king' of the Golden Triangle, two relatively unknown opium merchants in Kengtung, Shi Kya Chui and Yang Sang aka Yang Shi-li, were in fact trading in much larger quantities than Luo. Because they were more conveniently located at Kengtung, only 168 kilometers north of the border town of Tachilek, opposite Mae Sai in Thailand, they were able to make ten drug-running trips or more a year. In Tachilek, other traders took over the drugs and it is doubtful whether Shi and Yang, or even Luo, knew much about those networks and how they operated.

Luo, who was based in Lashio in northern Shan State, could organize only one trip to Tachilek a year. But he was a convenient target because he had a formidable fighting force, which he needed to protect his convoys when they moved through almost the entire length of Shan State. It was also forgotten by international narcotics suppression agencies that Luo began his career as a government-recognized militia commander and was informally allowed to traffic in opium in exchange for fighting ethnic and political insurgents in Burma's Shan State. Moreover, most of the opium that Luo and his army transported down to the Thai border did not actually belong to him. Because he was a militia commander, he was also able to provide protection for individual opium traders who lacked their own armed forces. Even so, senior US narcotics adviser Nelson Gross at the time, said that Luo "is an international bandit and responsible for a growing proportion of Asia's and America's drug-caused miseries."[11]

Hardly surprisingly, Luo's arrest in Thailand in 1973 and his death sentence for "rebellion against the state" did not have any impact on drug production in the Golden Triangle. Another 'kingpin' emerged on the scene: Zhang Qifu alias Khun Sa who, like Luo before him, had a huge army and was therefore highly visible in the area. Like Luo, Khun Sa had started off as a government-recognized militia commander and only later went underground. Meanwhile, the death sentence against Luo was never carried out. He was pardoned during the general amnesty in 1980 and he returned to his old home in Lashio. There, he formed a new militia unit and built a base called the Salween village, south of the town. He also established Asia World, a private company that became one of Burma's most powerful conglomerates with interests in construction, trade, and ports. Likewise, Khun Sa's surrender in 1996 did not change anything. Although he lived out his life—he died in 2007—in quiet retirement in Rangoon, his family and top officers became 'legitimate businessmen' and invested their fortunes in construction, transport companies, a beer brewery, and similar businesses.

Next in the line-up of the region's alleged 'kingpins' is not only Wei Xuegang but, as the 2005 US indictment shows, also other top leaders of the UWSA. Like Luo and Khun Sa before him, Wei and his UWSA associates have significant investments in different types of businesses, including jade mining, retail trade, and other enterprises in Burma. How much, if at all, those businesses are used to launder funds derived from drug dealing is unclear. Nor has it ever been clear that he actually monopolized the Golden Triangle drug trade, as the DEA indictment suggests.

Whatever the case, in late 2019 the Asia-Pacific drug trade had a new kingpin according to the United Nations Office on Drugs and Crime (UNODC) and some Western narcotics officials. Tse Chi Lop, a Chinese-born Canadian, was supposedly the leader of a gang that controlled most of the region's illegal trade in methamphetamine. Jeremy Douglas, Southeast Asia and Pacific representative for UNODC, told Reuters, "Tse Chi Lop is in the league of El Chapo or maybe Pablo Escobar. The word kingpin often gets around, but there is no doubt it applies here."[12] The Reuters report referred to Tse Chi Lop as "Asia's most wanted man" who "runs a vast multinational drug trafficking syndicate" in alliance with "five of Asia's Triad groups."[13] Despite all those connections, his whereabouts seemed to be unknown. When and how that mysterious and elusive Chinese-Canadian 'kingpin' took over the Golden Triangle drug trade was also unclear. Sadly, it seemed to be just another Hollywoodesque misrepresentation of who is who in the drug trade and how the business works.

The UWSA's response to the January 2005 indictments in the US came a few months after the names of the alleged 'kingpins' had been made public. On June 24, 2005, the UWSA took the drastic step of banning all poppy cultivation within its area. There was some alarm within the international donor community, which became involved in developing the Wa area shortly after the 1989 CPB mutiny. The UNODC estimated in December that year that "350,000 households, or about two million people in Shan State alone, will lose their primary income as a result of bans on cultivation opium." (*sic*)[14]

"Two million people" was, of course, a gross exaggeration as that many people did not live in UWSA-controlled areas, but the fear that poor farmers would lose their income was real. The Netherlands-based Translational Institute warned in December 2005 that the proposed opium ban could spark a "humanitarian crisis ... the implementation of these opium bans in one of the world's largest opium-producing areas may sound promising to international anti-narcotics officials, but for the opium farmers living there it could spell disaster."[15]

But within a couple of years, the slopes of the Wa Hills were covered in rubber and tea plantations, and that was the doing of the Wa authorities, not because of any of the UNODC's programs, which could be described as general development schemes rather than drug-eradication efforts. Most of the produce was exported across the border to China.

It was also not the first time the Wa in the post-CPB era had tried to rid their area of opium production. That began with the arrest of Saw Lu, a prominent Wa community leader, in Lashio in January 1992. He had never been in the underground. It was also well known that Saw Lu had been a militia commander whose force fought against Zhao Yilai when he and the CPB had entered the Wa Hills in December 1969. He had also served loyally as an official of the Burma Socialist Programme Party (BSPP), the ruling party led by general Ne Win after the 1962 coup. After the 1988 prodemocracy uprising and the collapse of the BSPP, Saw Lu founded both the Wa National Development Party and, together with his Lahu wife Mary, the Lahu National Development Party.

Unbeknown to most people, however, Saw Lu was also an important source for the DEA in Rangoon. His codename in internal DEA communications was 'Superstar,' indicating his status as one of the agency's best informants. His arrest was prompted by a detailed report he had compiled about the involvement in the drug trade of the local military intelligence chief in Lashio. Somehow, it is not clear how, the report was intercepted as it was being sent down to Rangoon. Saw Lu, Mary, their two sons as well as two adopted sons were all thrown in jail in Lashio. Saw Lu himself was hung upside down and given electric shock treatment in the presence of the local intelligence chief.[16]

On hearing about the arrest, Zhao and the UWSA issued an ultimatum: if Saw Lu were not released before March 26, the ceasefire with Rangoon would be over. Zhao and Saw Lu might have fought each other in the late 1960s, but for Zhao it meant more that he was also a fellow Wa. On the 16th, Saw Lu was set free. Almost immediately he escaped to the Wa Hills, where the UWSA appointed him "official spokesman for international affairs."[17]

Saw Lu's first initiative was to persuade the Wa to accept an opium eradication program that he had worked out while still in Lashio. The Burmese military's 'Border Development Programme,' which was launched after the 1989 ceasefire agreement, and a similar UNODC scheme had not produced any tangible improvements in the Wa Hills. The UWSA now appealed to the international community for direct assistance.

Saw Lu and his Lahu assistant Benjamin Min were escorted by UWSA troops down to the Thai border. Once in Chiang Mai, they looked up William Young, the nephew of Vincent Young who had romanized the Wa language in the 1930s. Young was also a former agent of the US Central Intelligence Agency (CIA) and had, as such, played a crucial role in raising hilltribe armies to fight the communists in Laos during the Indochina wars of the 1960s. Now living in semiretirement in Chiang Mai, Young served as a part-time local analyst for the DEA.

Together, Saw Lu, Benjamin, and Young drafted a document titled 'The Bondage of Opium: The Agony of the Wa People, a Proposal and a Plea.'[18] It stated that "like the heroin addicts that result from the opium we grow, we, too, are in bondage. We are searching for help to break that bondage … we want to free ourselves from the slavery of an opium economy … [but] our people are already so poor that to take away opium production without giving them food would mean starvation." It concluded that crop substitution has worked in Thailand, and "it can work in the Wa area."[19]

Saw Lu handed over the document to DEA special agent Richard Horn, but as journalists Dennis Bernstein and Leslie Kean wrote in the *Baltimore Sun* three years after the events, "Communications between the DEA's Rangoon office and higher officials in Washington reveal that agent Horn had every intention of working with the Wa people to implement Saw Lu's proposal. But for reasons that remain unclear, the Central Intelligence Agency and the State Department had other ideas."[20]

The Wa had prepared bamboo arches and signboards to welcome the foreign visitors. When no one came and the proposal was, in effect, rejected, Saw Lu lost his credibility among the Wa. He retired to his home in the Saohpa area, while Benjamin remained in Chiang Mai, where he died in January 2000.

Despite possible goodwill, there was an important issue that the Wa-initiated crop substitution proposals and programs did not address: methamphetamine. The production of that drug in UWSA-controlled areas was initiated by the Wei brothers in the 1990s, and by the end of the decade it had become a more lucrative source of income for the local gangs than opium and heroin had ever been. In Thailand the pills—the laboratories in Burma produced pills rather than crystal methamphetamine which is more common in other parts of the world—became known as *ya ba*, 'madness drug' or 'madness medicine.' The most famous *ya ba* brand was called WY, and although it is not clear what it stands for, pills marked 'WY' have been found in Thailand, Burma, Laos, northeastern India, and Bangladesh, but seldom outside the region.

The new drug soon became an even more serious threat to Thai society than heroin had ever been because the consumers were not only 'traditional' drug users—young men and some women in the slums of Bangkok, juvenile delinquents, and other outcasts—but also high school and university students, workers in factories and on construction sites, long-distance bus and truck drivers, and ordinary partygoers. Millions of people became regular or occasional users. Unlike heroin, *ya ba* successfully transcended socioeconomic barriers, creating a new wave of drug addiction on an unprecedented scale in Thailand, and before long also in neighboring Laos and as far from the Wa Hills as northeastern India and Bangladesh.

While heroin was first marketed by the German pharmaceutical company Bayer in 1898 as a sedative for coughs[21] and only later found to have some undesirable side effects, amphetamine was sold in the 1930s as an over-the-counter inhaler to treat nasal congestion. The chemical structure of methamphetamine is similar to that of amphetamine, but it has more pronounced effects on the central nervous system. These drugs became known collectively as ATS, or amphetamine-type stimulants. In the beginning, they were synthesized from a series of compounds related to the derivative of the ephedra plant but were later produced chemically.

During World War II, ATS was widely used to keep fighting men of various armies awake so they could endure prolonged combat duties. Pilots in the German Luftwaffe were given chocolate dosed with methamphetamine, which became known as *fliegerschokolade*, or 'flyer's chocolate.' It was also rumored that Adolf Hitler himself received daily doses of a mixture that contained certain essential vitamins and amphetamine. Ordinary soldiers had to be content with a more common variety of methamphetamine, dispensed under the trade name Pervitin.

The use of this kind of drug was not confined to the German armed forces, however. Methamphetamine was also used by the US and

Japanese forces fighting each other in rough and harsh conditions in Asia's war zones.

When the war was over, large quantities of amphetamine and methamphetamine, which the Japanese army had stockpiled for its troops, became available in Tokyo and other cities under the common street name *shabu*. It was banned in 1951, but the *yakuza*, Japan's well-organized and infamous crime gangs, continued to produce it in clandestine laboratories. Following crackdowns in Japan, the *yakuza* moved their laboratories to South Korea and Taiwan, and later the Philippines and mainland China.

The demand was high in Japan, as the country was being rebuilt after the war. Construction workers took it to be able to work harder and longer hours. For the same reason, methamphetamine use spread to many other countries in the region which were going through similar economic developments. Use became widespread among factory workers even in the Soviet Union. In the United States, pharmaceutical companies urged doctors to prescribe the drug for depressed housewives and people with weight problems.

In Thailand, the new 'speed' drug was first marketed as an over-the-counter stimulant. It was first brought to the country by a South Korean company and became very popular in the 1950s. At the time, the tablets had a horse's head and the word 'London' on them. Consequently, they became known as *ya ma*, or 'horse drug.' The drug was used to treat narcolepsy and obesity, but was withdrawn when it became obvious that it had serious side effects such as nausea, hyperactivity, increased aggressiveness and, in some cases, total mental breakdown.

That did not prevent long-distance bus and truck drivers as well as unskilled laborers from using it. Crystal *ya ma* was produced clandestinely and sold through petrol stations and truck stops. It was when *ya ma* became *ya ba*, in the form of pills, that usage was no longer confined to those categories of people. Even teenagers began using it. It was cheaper than beer and easier to conceal than other drugs. No syringes were necessary and it was easy to keep a few pills in one's pockets.

The shift from opium and heroin to *ya ba* began shortly before Khun Sa's surrender in 1996, and then as an emergency solution to the financial troubles of his Mong Tai Army (MTA). The UWSA has fought bitter battles against the MTA over control of trade routes to Thailand. Deprived of the supply of raw opium from the north, Khun Sa's men found an alternative in easy-to-produce methamphetamine, but that did not save his organization and he was left with no other choice but to strike a deal with the Burmese military.

Around 1998, a Thai drug lord called Bang Ron, or Surachai Ngernthongfoo, arrived at the UWSA's new southern bases around Mong Yawn on the Thai border. Before escaping justice in Thailand, he had run one of that country's largest *ya ba* dealing networks and brought with him the expertise that was needed to produce and distribute methamphetamine. He and Wei Xuegang, who was in charge of the UWSA's new southern base area on the Thai border, were a perfect match. The duo established new *ya ba* laboratories around Mong Yawn and began flooding Thailand with pills. Seizures on the Thai side were always in the thousands of pills, but no police action seemed strong and effective enough to stem the tide. By 2011, the authorities estimated that nearly one in sixty Thais was a methamphetamine user.[22] Like the German *fliegerschokolade*, some pills were laced with chocolate to make them more appealing to youngsters.

In 2002, *Time* magazine published a cover story about the Wa and the *ya ba* trade which had the rather provocative title 'Speed Tribe: Inside the world of the Wa: Asia's deadliest drug cartel,' and, inside the magazine, 'Soldiers of fortune.'[23] It may have been an exaggeration to brand the UWSA as a 'drug cartel,' but the article did contain a wealth of information about the Wa as well as eyewitness reports from the area, which the authors had visited.

The portrayal of the UWSA as a 'drug cartel' did not go down well with the UNODC, which had a number of projects in the Wa Hills and other areas adjacent to the Chinese border. Jean-Luc Lemahieu, the UNODC's Rangoon representative, authored an open letter refuting *Time*'s findings and defending his agency's work inside the UWSA-controlled area.[24] But the letter was riddled with so many factual errors that he could not have done his homework before writing it, or he was simply blissfully ignorant of the history of the Golden Triangle drug trade. For instance, he writes this about Wei Xuegang: "To refresh our memory, born in China, his family fled to Shan State with the KMT (Kuomintang) but later joined Khun Sa's organization." Thus far, it is correct if ungrammatical, although he refers to Khun Sa's group as "the Mong Tai Army." When Wei joined Khun Sa, the organization was called the Shanland United Army and became the MTA only in 1987, after it had merged with another army and long after Wei had left it.

Lemahieu then went on to say that Wei fell "in disgrace with Khun Sa in 1974" and switched sides to the Communist Party of Burma, and further, "when the CPB fell in 1996, he moved along with the UWSA." It is unclear how Wei's falling out with Khun Sa could have happened in 1974 as the old warlord was arrested in Burma in 1969, released in 1974, and only in 1976 came down to the Thai border to rebuild his organization. Then, of course, Wei never joined the CPB and the party fell apart in 1989, not in 1996. Lemahieu concludes, not realizing the irony of what he had to say, by writing that the UNODC "encourages as many journalists as feasible to visit the Wa and our project zone. Indeed, nothing beats a personal visit to the project area in order to discover the discrepancy between the reality within the Wa and the virtual reality of what is being said and written outside the country." (*sic*)

The ignorance and incompetence of international anti-drug officials may be startling, but so is the overall hypocrisy of mostly Western nations when it comes to global narcotics suppression. In Asia, it is not forgotten that opium brought by Western traders enslaved millions of people in China and elsewhere during the colonial era. Just in time for Hong Kong's return to China on July 1, 1997, the Chinese movie industry released a mega production called *The Opium War*, which depicted Lin Zexu, the emperor's commissioner based in Guangdong and other southern provinces in the 1840s, as a national hero for trying to stop the importation of opium that the British were bringing in from India. The British, naturally, were brutal aggressors who defeated the Chinese, forced China to open its ports for opium, and turned Hong Kong into a British colony in 1842.

The origin of those wars can be traced back to the seventeenth century when Britain's East India Company began to fight its way into the highly lucrative and competitive markets of Asia. China, with its teeming millions, held the greatest attraction as it had goods, especially tea, that were becoming popular in Europe. But there was little the Chinese wanted from Britain In fact, they showed interest in only one item from Britain and British India: silver. By the early eighteenth century, India faced a shortage of silver and another commodity had to be found—and that was opium from the fields of India. Opium replaced silver as the currency of trade with the Chinese, and silver was not going back to India to pay for the opium.

The Chinese authorities tried, at least officially, to suppress the trade. Opium was devastating China's population as millions of people became addicted to the drug. Opium smoking had actually been banned by China in 1729, and cultivating and importing opium was specifically banned in 1799.[25] But these edicts were ignored by all Western merchants, and the ruling Qing Dynasty was too weak to enforce its policies. Moreover, the British were not the only traders marketing their opium. Americans sold Turkish opium to China and Persian opium was imported by any trader in a position to do so. The American merchant W. C. Hunter used one single phrase to describe the Chinese opium trade between 1835 and 1944: "We were all equally implicated."[26]

Then, in March 1839, Emperor Daoguang took decisive action and sent Lin Zexu to the south to stamp out the opium business. The British responded by bombarding the ports along China's southern coast to open them to British merchandise, which was primarily opium from India. The First Opium War ended with the Treaty of Nanjing in 1842. The Chinese, who were defeated by Britain's superior firepower, had to open five ports, including Shanghai, to foreign trade. And the island of Hong Kong became British.

Not everyone in London agreed with what the British military had done. William Gladstone, a young liberal politician who later became prime minister of Britain, said: "A war more unjust in origin, a war more calculated to cover this country with permanent disgrace, I do not know and have not read of."[27]

That did not prevent the British from fighting a Second Opium War from 1856 to 1860. Its final phase saw British and French forces charging into Beijing, where they looted and burned the emperor's famous summer palace. China had lost again, and the Kowloon peninsula on the mainland opposite Hong Kong island was ceded to the British. The enlarged colony of Hong Kong as well as Shanghai emerged as the most important transfer points for Indian opium entering the vast Chinese market. By then, India had also begun its own tea production, and the loser in the game was China. As the opium trade continued unabated, it soon produced more than one-fifth of government revenue in the British Indian empire, and new grandiose cities could be built.[28]

Panghsang and Mong La may have been built on income from the drug trade, but so were Hong Kong, Calcutta (Kolkata), Madras (Chennai), Bombay (Mumbai), and Saigon. It may be rather far-fetched to expect the world to accept the UWSA's non-drug related commercial enterprises as it has Jardine-Matheson, other Hong Kong conglomerates, and Britain's erstwhile East India Company, for we are living in different times with other values, but it is certainly not without precedent for companies that were once heavily engaged in the drug trade to turn to other more wholesome activities. Western policymakers must understand that many people in Asia see their narcotics policies as deeply hypocritical.

Britain was not the only Western power that used revenues from the opium trade to finance undertakings in India as well as colonies such as Singapore and Malaya. In French Indochina, there were 3,500 licensed opium dens and the government-administered Régie de l'Opium collected more than half of all revenues in the colony. Similar arrangements existed in the Dutch East Indies, now

Indonesia. Even there, opium was a government monopoly, and vast quantities of the drug were imported from the Middle East.[29] The consumers were mostly ethnic Chinese migrants, and so were the dealers who were referred to as 'tax farmers.' This did not indicate they were agriculturalists but that they had a government license which enabled them to sell opium in return for paying taxes to the colonial authorities.

But nothing could match China as a market. Towards the end of the nineteenth century, the country had tens of millions of opium addicts, and because supplies from India were insufficient to meet demand, large quantities of opium were soon produced in the Chinese interior as well. Opium was not entirely new to the area, but it had never before been grown on such an industrial scale as during the latter half of the nineteenth century.

The Panthay, or Hui, rebellion against the Chinese emperor in the mid- nineteenth century was crushed, but the fighting disrupted earlier trade flows, especially the export of minerals, and opium emerged as an alternative lucrative commodity that could be bought and sold. By the end of the nineteenth century, opium may even have become the main crop of the Chinese interior, and there was a huge demand for the drug to supplement insufficient imports from India. By the early twentieth century, China's annual opium production had risen to over 20,000 metric tons, with poppies grown mainly in Yunnan, Sichuan, Shaanxi, Gansu, Guizhou, and Shanxi provinces.[30]

It is unclear when large-scale poppy cultivation was introduced to the Wa Hills, but Hideyuki Takano, a Japanese writer and adventurer who lived there in the 1990s, believes that "the Wa people probably began producing opium in the latter half of the 19th century."[31] According to anthropologist Magnus Fiskesjö, as the imperial

Chinese authorities attempted to reinforce the prohibitions against opium in the mid- and late nineteenth century, "the production expanded even further in the mountains and in other inaccessible areas."[32] That would include areas such as the Wa Hills. Similarly, the cultivation of poppies spread to Kokang and the hills north of Kengtung in the eastern Shan States.

The first proposal for drastic action against the colonial opium trade came from American missionaries in China, who had seen how devastating opium smoking had been to large segments of society. They got support from President Theodore Roosevelt, and in 1909 representatives of thirteen countries met in Shanghai for the first international conference to discuss the opium problem. It led to the formation of the International Opium Commission tasked with the duty to oversee the trade. But it was toothless as no one was bound by any definite policy, and some key opium producing countries such as Turkey and Persia did not take an active part in it.[33]

Nevertheless, another opium conference was held in The Hague, the Netherlands, in 1911–12. The United Kingdom agreed to halt all importation of Indian opium by 1917, and the Shanghai Municipal Council closed down opium dens in the International Settlement, which was not formally a colony but an area of the city where foreigners resided and enjoyed extraterritorial rights. It was not a big loss, however. By then, opium revenues had turned Shanghai into China's most industrialized city and there were plenty of other sources of income. Moreover, the sale and consumption of opium continued in the 'native' parts of the city where a corrupt Chinese police force did little or nothing to stop it. On the contrary, the Shanghai police worked hand in hand with the criminal gangs which controlled the drug trade, gambling, and prostitution.

As Burma was conquered in stages by the British in the nineteenth century through the three Anglo-Burmese wars of 1824–26, 1852–53, and 1885, new rules for opium production were gradually introduced. An Opium Act was enacted in 1878, even before what is now northern Burma was taken over by the British.[34] Opium, imported from India, could be sold in government-licensed opium shops and the business was taxed by the colonial authorities, but it was not a major social problem in Burma proper or the adjacent Shan states, which came under British protection in the 1880s and 1890s. In fact, the main anthropological study of the Shan written during the colonial era, *Shans at Home* by Leslie Milne, has only one reference to opium: "No religious Shan takes opium, so it is not used openly as a medicine, but native doctors use it occasionally mixed with herbs."[35]

The 1878 Opium Act, which was amended in 1909, went into effect in 1910 and was supplemented by the 1938 Opium Rules, which outlined stiff penalties for illegal opium trading as "no person may transport opium unless such person can lawfully possess such opium"[36] and it could be sold only by "a licensed vendor."[37] But it was almost impossible to enforce those laws in Kokang and the Wa Hills, where local farmers grew poppies and Panthay (Hui) merchants bought the refined opium and sold it on to opium to buyers in China or Southeast Asia, including Siam (Thailand), Malaya, and Singapore.

A special Shan State Opium Order was promulgated in 1923, which at least in theory banned poppy cultivation in the Shan States. But, as researcher Robert Maule pointed out in his study of the issue, "the trans-Salween areas," that is, Kokang and the Wa Hills, "were excluded from the policy until more effective control has been established."[38] Burma was then a province of British India, and the "Secretary of State for India specifically warned the Burma

Government not to attempt any restrictive measures in Kokang if that would create unrest."[39] The local Kokang Chinese, who lived at an altitude where not even dry paddy farming was practicable, were dependent on various cash crops, notably tea and opium, to buy rice from the more developed valleys. In years when the opium crop failed because of frost or other natural disasters, "most of the people had to depend on roots and shoots."[40] The situation was similar in the Wa Hills, but there the British had even less influence than in partially controlled Kokang.

The rules that the British, with varying degrees of success, had introduced became totally irrelevant when the Japanese invaded the colony during World War II. The British and the Americans raised guerrilla forces to fight against the occupation, and most of the fighters were ethnic Kachin in the far north of the colony. Those forces needed goods and services, and the British paid for whatever they could obtain from local villagers in opium which they had brought with them from India. But then came the Americans, and the US Air Force began to fly in much larger quantities of Indian opium. As Ian Fellowes-Gordon, a British officer who served in the Kachin Hills during World War II, described in his excellent account of the fighting, the Americans "were doing it with typical efficiency, in ample, generous doses."[41] Whereas the British had paid for food and other goods in opium, the Americans now paid a number of the levies they had recruited in opium as well. As a result, Fellowes-Gordon wrote, "it was starting to circulate as a currency and it seemed as if, rather than being able to cut down the use of it, we would have to step up ours."[42]

The next Western involvement in the Southeast Asian drug trade came when Kuomintang forces retreated into northeastern Burma after their defeat in the Chinese civil war in 1949. American support for the Kuomintang was substantial because it coincided with the Korean War and, as such, became part of a larger geopolitical strategy: Claire Chennault's 'pincer movement' which, the Americans hoped, would lead to the fall of communism in China. But, like the British and the Americans during World War II, the Kuomintang also had to buy goods and services from the local people. The Kuomintang could not fly in opium from any neighboring country so they had to depend on local production in the areas of northeastern and eastern Shan states where they were ensconced. Income from the opium, sold to traders in Thailand, also paid for arms purchases from Burma's eastern neighbor. The Kuomintang's involvement in the opium trade was best described by one it its own generals, Duan Xiwen, in a 1967 interview with a British journalist: "Necessity knows no law. That is why we deal with opium. We have to continue to fight the evil of communism and to fight you must have an army, and an army must have guns, and to buy guns you must have money. In these mountains the only money is opium."[43]

The Kuomintang introduced a hefty opium tax, to be paid in kind, which forced the hilltribe farmers to grow even more to make ends meet. There were also other reasons for the opium boom of the 1950s—Burma's annual production was estimated at a mere 30 metric tons at independence in 1948 and by the mid-1950s had risen to several hundred metric tons—such as the influx of hilltribe refugees from Yunnan after the communist takeover in 1949. They were poor, arrived in a new country where they had to make a living, and there was a growing market for opium. When the Burmese army entered the Shan states to repel the Kuomintang invaders, the fighting made it difficult to transport 'normal' cash crops to the markets, and opium became a viable alternative as the merchants came to the villages to buy the produce.

In the 1960s, when the civil war spread to other areas of what had become Shan State and involved the Shan, the Kokang Chinese, and the Palaung, the traditional cash crop economy was in shambles, and the production of opium increased even further. The military takeover in Rangoon in 1962, and the introduction of the so-called 'Burmese Way to Socialism' led to the emergence of a black market where the most valuable medium of exchange was opium. Chao Tzang Yawnghwe, a prominent Shan analyst and former rebel leader, analyzed the phenomenon in a 1982 study:

> All businesses and banks … were nationalised [and] in such an economic vacuum there arose a black-market economy which for opium traffickers was a boon…. Opium was bought by them at very low prices from ragged cultivators, transported in armed caravans to the border and refined into heroin. And on the return trip to get more opium, Thai goods and commodities were taken back and sold in Shan State…. Rather than creating socialism, the Burmese Way to Socialism delivered the economy into the hands of the opium traffickers…. Thus, cultivation of opium, limited to the east of the Salween prior to 1963, not only spread all over Shan State, but to Kachin, Karenni and Chin states as well.[44]

Opium politics even became part of the military government's counterinsurgency program as the Ka Kwe Ye home guards were allowed to trade in opium to sustain their activities, privileges that also enabled traders like Luo Xinghan and Zhang Qifu, or Khun Sa, to make fortunes for themselves and become immensely rich.

In Thailand, where most of the opium was sold and many different dealers were involved in the trade, drugs became part of the local economy, especially in Chiang Mai and other northern cities, towns, and villages. An anonymous 'American living in Thailand' wrote in a letter to US congressman Lester Wolff in July 1977: "Profits from the sale of opium and heroin are generally reinvested in another illegal trade: basic dry goods and things like radios are brought from northern Thailand merchants for shipment across the border and illegal sale in Burma. If the narcotics trade is forcibly stopped, the economy in the area will be wrecked."[45] It could also be added that money derived from the drug trade paid for legitimate businesses in northern Thailand like the construction of hotels, supermarkets, and housing estates.

Throughout the 1950s and 1960s, US policymakers had blamed China for the region's opium boom. It was all part of a communist plot to undermine the moral standards of the West. The title of a major work that appeared at that time, says it all: *Psycho-Chemical Warfare: The Chinese Communist Drug Offensive Against the West.*[46] But those arguments were not convincing. The author produced, for instance, 'photographic evidence,' such as pictures of cardboard boxes with Chinese characters in which heroin had been concealed and confiscated, not forgetting that such characters are used by ethnic Chinese all over the region. The boxes in question also had writing in Thai, saying 'Boonrawd Brewery,' one of the main beer producers in Bangkok.

Whatever atrocities the communists had committed after their takeover of state power in China in 1949, there was no plot to flood the world with drugs. On the contrary, in the 1950s China had with brutal methods eradicated its own opium production. Poppy fields were cut down, dealers and even users were arrested and sent to reeducation camps, or simply executed. By the late 1950s, there were hardly any poppy fields left in China.

Then, in July 1971 US Assistant Secretary of State Marshall Green admitted that opium was not actually grown in China, as Washington had once claimed. Instead, Green said in an interview with the now defunct Hong Kong weekly *Far Eastern Economic Review*, opium was grown in a 'golden triangle' stretching from northeastern Burma to northern Thailand and northwestern Laos.[47] His somewhat surprising admission of the fact, which was known to most people in the region, came at a time when Washington was trying to win favor with Beijing. Indeed, in the same month as the article appeared, it was announced that then US president Richard Nixon would visit China the following February.

The new term, and it was the first time it was used, became an immediate hit. The name captured the imagination of the public as it evoked the lawless nature of the opium trade. Within a few years, the Golden Triangle—now with a capital 'G' and 'T'—came to epitomize all of Southeast Asia's opium-related problems. The name also caught on in Chinese (*jin sanjiao*) and Thai (*samliam thongkham*), and it is easy to understand why. In a place of constantly shifting borders and upheaval, only two currencies remained constant: opium and gold. Heavily armed mule convoys would take the raw opium from northern Burma down to Tachilek on the Thai border, where it was often sold in exchange for bars of pure gold.[48]

Thailand's dependence on drugs diminished over the years as other sectors of the economy, including tourism and manufacturing, took off, especially in the 1990s. Thailand's own opium production, which in the 1960s averaged 50–60 metric tons a year and was never as massive as in Burma or even Laos, also vanished completely as the Thai king initiated a number of development programs in the north.[49] But as the *ya ba* abuse spread like wildfire across Thailand in the 1990s and early 2000s, the country's drug problems were far from over, and it was not only Bang Ron and Wei Xuegang who benefited from UWSA protection.

In February 1997, a drug dealer named Li Yun-chung, who was wanted in the US in connection with a 486-kilogram heroin shipment seized in California in 1991, jumped bail in Bangkok and was spirited north by a relay of Mercedes cars. He spent a night in hiding in Mae Sai, and disguised as a local trader was driven across the border to Tachilek on the other side. From there he went on to Panghsang and was sheltered by the UWSA. Somehow, the Burmese military, under immense pressure from the Thais, managed to lure him back to Tachilek, where he was arrested, flown to Rangoon, and then handed over to the Thais.[50] The judge who had granted bail to Li was suspended and the fugitive himself was extradited to the US. The UWSA-controlled area, and even more so Mong La with all its casinos and other shady establishments like brothels, transvestite shows, and stores selling tiger skins and other parts of endangered species, were becoming criminal havens. That troubled not only the Thais but also the Chinese, who had close relations with the Wa but were, to say the least, wary of their involvement in the drug trade.

In 2018 and 2019, some unusual developments took place in Burma's section of the Golden Triangle. The production of opium was down, and so were the prices of raw opium and the more potent derivative heroin. Prices should go up when the supply of any commodity is down and demand remains the same, and drugs are no exception to that rule. The answer was found in China. For more than twenty years, China has been the main market for heroin produced in Burma, so the conclusion was that Chinese users were turning to other drugs: the powerful synthetic opiate fentanyl, which is produced in China, and cocaine imported from the Americas.

The Wa antiopium campaign had had its effects on Burma's overall output of opium, but that declining demand for heroin was another reason the area under poppy cultivation was shrinking. According to a 2019 survey done by the United Nations Office for Drugs and Crime (UNODC), it dropped to 37,300 hectares in 2018, down from 41,000 hectares in 2017, while the estimated total opium production dropped from 550 to 510 metric tons.[51] That meant a potential output of about 50 tons of heroin, significantly down from the 1990s and early 2000s when Burma's opium production was more than double.

Price trends were also a clear indication of falling demand for heroin. In 2019, an opium farmer in Kayah (Karenni) State would get 350,000 Burmese kyat, or US$240, for a *viss*, significantly more than in the 1990s, but almost the same in purchasing power parity. More tellingly, US$240 was only half of what the farmers could have fetched for a *viss* in 2013 or 2014. In the past, the merchants always came to the farmers to buy the crop; now farmers had to look up the merchants, and they often offered the farmers half the price in cash and the rest in methamphetamines.[52] The buyers of opium from Kayah State and southern Shan State were based in Namsang, a major town on the east–west highway through Shan State.

In Lashio, another town where opium was bought, the price dropped from a million kyat, or US$690, per *viss* in the early and mid-2010s to 600,000 (US$415) in 2019. In Mong Tun near the Thai border, where farmers were paid in Thai currency, the price per *viss* dropped from, 40,000–60,000 baht, or US$1,255–1,885, to 20,000 baht or US$630, and it was hard to find any buyers. It is clear that the demand for heroin had declined considerably.

The changing pattern of China's consumption of narcotics was clear in other basic statistics. In 2010, China had 1,545,000 registered drug users, with 1,065,000 of those addicted to heroin from Burma.[53] The actual figure, as most drug addicts are not registered with the authorities, could have been as many as 5–6 million, according to other independent researchers.[54] The number of registered drug addicts in China in 2016 was more at 2.5 million, of whom as many as 1.5 million were addicted to synthetic drugs, not heroin.[55]

In the 1990s and early 2000s, heroin accounted for 65–75 percent of all seized narcotics in China, and the Chinese marked the United Nations Anti-Drugs Day, June 26, with mass executions of drug offenders, including addicts. The consumption shift is in line with China's wider development into a more modern nation, where 'old' drugs like opium and heroin are no longer in vogue. As a result, Chinese addicts turned towards drugs such as ice, cocaine, and the locally made opiate fentanyl. Significant quantities of ice and fentanyl are produced in China and cocaine comes from South America. *The China Daily*, an official newspaper, reported in September 2018 that cocaine was being smuggled from South America to major ports on China's east coast before being moved to Guangdong, Hong Kong, and Macau.[56] That year, the Chinese police seized more than 1.3 metric tons of cocaine in a raid in Shenzhen, opposite Hong Kong.[57]

Despite those trends and falling prices, opium did not cease to be an important cash crop in parts of northern Burma. It is correct that apart from summoning Bao Youxiang and other Wa leaders to Kunming to be read the riot act by Chinese officials, China also supported the UWSA's crop substitution programs and this contributed to the decline in overall production, but it did not prevent opium farmers in other parts of Burma, such as western Shan, Kayah, Kachin, and Chin states, as well as the northern Sagaing Region from growing poppies, and the raw opium from there being refined into heroin. Even so, times had changed. In China, like in Thailand, other drugs had become more widely used.

There was one exception to the falling area under poppy cultivation and lower heroin prices. Prices remained high, and even increased, in Kachin State, where a *viss* of opium fetched 1.7 million kyat in 2017, or approximately US$1,300, and 2.5 million kyat, the equivalent of US$1,900, in 2018. Heroin addiction remains rampant in Kachin State and refineries are located in areas controlled by a remnant of Sakhon Ting Ying's New Democratic Army-Kachin, which became a government-recognized 'Border Guard Force' in 2009. As such, they could engage in any kind of business without interference from Burma's military authorities.

Although Burma's central authorities have always told the international community that they are committed to drug suppression, history indicates otherwise. From the days of the Ka Kwe Ye home guards to the situation today, drugs have been part of the government's counterinsurgency strategies, not law enforcement. Significantly, when then president Thein Sein initiated what he called a 'peace process,' which included talks with a number of Burma's ethnic armies, a main interlocutor who was introduced as 'U Sein Win' was identified by independent observers as none other than Wei Xuegang.[58] Wei also seemed to be the man not only the Burmese military trusted the most in its dealings with the Wa. As a local resident in Panghsang told US researcher Chin Ko-lin: "Wei Xuegang's relationship with the Burmese authorities is an ambiguous one; if Bao attacks Wei, Wei might turn to the Burmese authorities for help and team up with the Burmese and turn against Bao. Besides, the money from Wei is extremely important for Bao's financial well-being."[59]

As the UWSA grew stronger and better organized, the once Kuomintang-related druglord also emerged as China's favorite. In early 2020, he went to Kunming for private, and one would assume secret, talks with Chinese security officials. It was obvious that the Chinese had more faith in him than in the Wa, whose loyalty to China they could not always take for granted. After all, Wei, a fellow Chinese, could be expected to harbor some loyalty to his old homeland. The Wa, an ethnic minority also in China, have not always had a trouble-free relationship with the central authorities.

6

The Plan that Might Succeed

Whatever little most Chinese outside Yunnan know about the Wa comes mainly from a series of music videos where young girls, accompanied by young men beating drums, shake their long hair back and forth. The girls are dressed in red woven skirts with some kind of pattern which looks as if it could be of hilltribe origin and the young men are bare-chested. The problem is that those skirts are much shorter than the sarongs Wa girls would normally wear, and no female living in the hills where water is scarce would have hair that long because it would be impossible to keep it clean. Besides, young Wa men these days would not go around dressed in little more than a loincloth even when taking part in cultural events in their home villages.

Tellingly, these dances are not performed in a rural Wa setting but in purpose-built theaters in front of big audiences. The famous 'Wa hair dancers' are, in fact, the daughters of city cadres who are of Wa, Chinese, or mixed Wa-Chinese ancestry.[1] According to anthropologist Magnus Fiskesjö, the Chinese have created "an official socialist-era image of the Wa as a member of the happy family of nationalities within the Chinese nation: as exotic dancers full of primitive energy, now sanitised and harnessed under Communist Party guidance—the socialist-era version of Wa primitivity."[2]

In line with this thinking, ethnic theme parks have been established in several Chinese cities where one of the main attractions is to come and watch real Wa head-hunters performing exotic dances. Young Wa, because of their dark complexion, are hired to perform not only as wild Wa but also "as Africans, as Maori, and as American Indians."[3]

Those performers are Wa from Yunnan and Burma who have migrated to Chinese cities to find work in factories, and they take part in those spectacles to earn some extra money. But it is easy to imagine what the Wa dancers themselves think about their ethnicity and culture being exploited in this way. Moreover, according to Fiskesjö, "It is telling that Wa people use a Chinese loan word, *tiaowu* ('dance'), for all such Chinese-staged dances. They reserve their own indigenous word for 'dance' (*ngroh*) for their own revived social dancing, such as the traditional 'dancing in' of a new house.)"[4]

As China has abandoned its Marxist-Leninist ideology in favor of state and private capitalism, the concept of nationalism also has a new meaning. It is no longer a socialist brotherhood of nationalities which it used to be in theory, though not always in practice, but a pride in being Chinese and that China is really a nation-state. China's president Xi Jinping is the torchbearer of that idea, and he clearly sees himself as the third great leader in modern Chinese history. Mao Zedong liberated China from feudalism and oppression, created the People's Republic, and managed to unify the diverse country. Deng Xiaoping modernized China after Mao's death in 1976 and created a much more prosperous society based on 'socialism with Chinese characteristics' which, in effect, meant state-supervised cut-throat capitalism. Xi is going to turn China into the dominant world power and, as such, there is no room for internal divisions along ethnic or linguistic lines. In short, as the Hong Kong-based author and journalist Philip Bowring has pointed out, "Mao destroyed the old order, Deng laid the foundations for a modern economy, Xi is making China great again."[5]

James Millward, a China scholar and historian at Georgetown University in Washington, wrote an op-ed published in the *New York Times* on October 1, 2019, in which he argued that Xi, when he came to power in 2012, abandoned China's until recently relatively tolerant previous tradition of accepting ethnic diversity, in which no fewer than fifty-five nationalities were recognized in addition to the majority Han.[6] Instead, Xi's government began promoting a less tolerant pan-Chinese identity known as *zhonghua* while the Han language, previously known as *hanyu* became *guoyu*, or the 'national language.'[7] A major target for those new polices was the restive Turkic-Muslim Xinjiang region in the west with its traditional discontent with central authorities. In July 2019, China's ruling State Council issued a white paper entitled 'Historical Matters Concerning Xinjiang,' in which it claimed that Xinjiang has "long been an inseparable part of Chinese territory" and that the region's Uighur "formed through a long process of migration and integration."[8] They are "part of a Chinese civilization" and "Islam is neither the indigenous nor the sole belief system of the Uighurs," the paper stated.[9]

Non-Chinese historians acknowledge that the Uighurs are indeed a Turkic people related to similar ethnic groups in Central Asia. Control over the area where they live changed hands several times in history between foreign invaders and local warlords until China's Manchu-led Qing Dynasty conquered it and, in 1884, established a province called Xinjiang, or 'The New Frontier' in Chinese.

Today, bilingual education has been abolished not only in Xinjiang but also in other ethnic areas such as Tibet and parts of Yunnan. The Chinese are one people speaking one language. And China is one nation which includes Hong Kong, Macau, Taiwan, and all the islands and islets in the South China Sea. There is no room for diversity, or real autonomy for any part of the Great Chinese Nation.

The problem is that the unified nation state Xi wants to create never existed, and, as Millward wrote, "Concentration camps will not turn Uighurs and Kazakhs into faithful '*zhonghua*' Chinese who eat pork and disregard Ramadan. Violent policing will not make Hongkongers abandon calls for the autonomy promised in the territory's mini-Constitution. Religious repression and demonising the Dalai Lama will not endear Tibetans to the party. Military threats will not make Taiwanese feel closer to the mainland."[10]

Then there are 'the primitives' like the Wa with their drums and exotic dances. For a proud people like the Wa with a long history of de facto independence, this is nothing short of humiliation of the young performers and their families. Older Wa have not forgotten what happened in their hills in 1958, when newly arrived Chinese political commissars did their utmost to eradicate old traditions and beliefs, the very essence of their identity. The 'revival' of Wa culture, which is now taking place in a grotesque form solely for the purpose of entertainment, bears little resemblance to what it was in the past.

While the Wa in China are ruled by Beijing and those in the United Wa State Army (UWSA) in Burma are totally dependent on China for trade and the acquisition of weaponry, there is a deep, historically motivated distrust of the Chinese. That has deepened in more recent years with the promotion of ethnic theme parks, the hair-throwing dance, and similar absurdities. It is hardly surprising that the Wa in Burma in a small but not insignificant token of resistance use Vincent Young's romanized version of Wa, not the system the Chinese introduced in Yunnan in the 1950s.

Millward's article was appropriately titled 'What Xi Jinping Hasn't Learnt from China's Emperors,' and he argues that Xi's dream of a political and cultural homogeneity runs contrary to Chinese traditional approaches to diversity. However, the controversy surrounding the question of what kind of nation China should be is much older than Xi's coming to power in Beijing, as general secretary of the communist party in 2012 and as president in 2013.

It began when Dr. Sun Yat-sen and his republican revolutionaries rose in rebellion in 1911, overthrew the last Qing ruler in 1912, and inherited an empire which consisted of many nationalities and had no fixed borders. Imperial rule was concentrated in the court in Beijing, and the further away from that center the empire stretched, the weaker the central power became. Certain areas like Tibet may occasionally have paid tribute to the emperor, but that did not equate to recognition of sovereignty. Rather, it was a more like a 'bribe' that had to be paid in order to be left alone. The demand for clearly demarcated borders came with the arrival of Western colonial powers, which in the nineteenth century were busy carving up Asia between themselves: the Russians in the north and the west, the British in India in the south, and the French in the southeast. That, in turn, led to a number of border conflicts; that with India sparked a war in 1962 and remains unresolved even today.[11]

China's new republican rulers, as the renowned sinologist Maria Adele Carrai has pointed out, "shifted the locus of authority from a sacred and moral Heaven to the people, identified China as one nation among many, in equal relationship with the others, and began to use international law as the normal framework through which to conduct international relations."[12] However, what that 'nation' should consist of was not clear. Some republicans saw no reason to include non-Han areas while Sun Yat-sen sought to establish a 'union of nationalities,' which he identified as the Hans, Manchus, Mongols, Tibetans, and Uighurs.[13]

According to Sun, interim president of the new republic, that also meant that there was also a 'Chinese nation,' and that concept was used for the first time in a statement which he issued on January 5, 1912: "Now we have staged an uprising and the general situation has been settled. The Chinese nation is so brave to overthrow the autocratic government of the Qing dynasty and found the republic."[14] Never before had any official Chinese document talked about the existence of such a 'Chinese nation.' China was the Middle Kingdom, ruled by an emperor.

Mongolia, or 'Outer Mongolia' to distinguish it from 'Inner Mongolia' where Beijing had firmer control, had taken advantage of the upheaval and declared independence on December 1, 1911. Likewise, the 13th Dalai Lama issued a similar declaration of independence on February 13, 1913.[15] Chinese armies tried on several occasions to invade Tibet, but with limited success. Although foreign countries never recognized Tibet's independence, it continued to function as a de facto independent country throughout the republican period.

The Chinese did not intervene militarily in Mongolia, but its status as a separate nation was never recognized by the Republic of China. Maps produced in Taiwan, where the Republic lived on after the communist victory on the mainland in 1949, identified Mongolia as a Chinese province until the island began to act more as an independent entity in the early 2000s. It still officially is, but more recent maps of the Republic of China tend to be blurry when it comes to the mainland boundaries.

In the beginning, the Chinese communists had a more lenient view of the non-Han nationalities, which was affirmed in the Communist State Constitution of 1931:

> The right of self-determination of the national minorities in China, their right to complete separation from China, and to the formation of an independent state for each national minority. All Mongolians, Tibetans, Miao, Yao, Koreans and others living on the territory of China shall enjoy the full right to self-determination, i.e. they may either join the Union of Chinese Soviets or secede from it and form their own state as they may prefer.[16]

This policy was abandoned as soon as the communists seized power in Beijing and the People's Republic of China was proclaimed on October 1, 1949. The independence of Mongolia, now a people's republic allied with the Soviet Union, was recognized so as not create a rift in the communist camp. Diplomatic relations between Beijing and Ulan Bator were established as early as October 16, 1949. However, Tibet, bordering India, was a different matter. On October 7, 1950, the China's People's Liberation Army (PLA) entered Tibet, and on May 23, 1951, a 17-point 'Agreement for the Peaceful Liberation of Tibet' was signed between The Chinese and a representative of the 14th Dalai Lama. Tibet was, in effect, occupied, which led to an uprising in 1959 and the Dalai Lama's subsequent flight to India, where he remains in exile.

The PLA also marched into multiethnic Yunnan where some tribal people, among them the Wa, were largely unaware of what was happening in a country they did not even know they belonged to. The only Han Chinese the Wa had encountered before that were merchants who occasionally ventured into their hills. But border security, especially in view of Kuomintang forces encamped inside Burma on the other side, was of utmost importance and the Wa Hills were gradually brought under central control, first leniently, and after 1958 more brutally. 'The Menglian-Dai-Lahu-Va Autonomous County' was set up in 1954 in the area opposite what is now Panghsang and covering, as the name implies, tracts inhabited by Dai, or Shan, Lahu, and Wa. It was followed in 1955 by the creation of 'The Cangyuan Va Autonomous County' further to the north, and in 1964 by 'The Ximeng Va Autonomous County' between Menglian and Cangyuan.[17]

In the official version, this was done "in the course of practicing regional autonomy … many Va were trained, paving the way for implementing the Communist Party's united front policy, for further winning over and uniting with the patriots from the upper strata of the Vas, and for carrying out social reform in Va areas."[18] While some Wa were recruited, put in schools where they had to learn Chinese, and after that given some responsibilities in the local administration, those 'autonomous' counties were run by communist party cadres, and most of them were Han Chinese.

In Xi's China, with the introduction of *zhonghua* as the nationwide concept, and with the culture of a few 'primitive' peoples like the Wa being degraded to entertainment status in what amounts to human zoos, Han Chinese nationalism has been carried to the extreme. As Marxism-Leninism was discarded sometime in the late 1980s at least unofficially as the state ideology, nationalism replaced it. Under Xi, nationalism has been promoted more vigorously than it was under any of his predecessors in attempts to rally the people behind the top leadership and its policies. The same nationalism and visions of China's greatness are also the main driving forces behind Xi's multibillion US dollar Belt and Road Initiative (BRI).

Despite the radical transformation that China has undergone in the post-Mao era, however, the old chairman was never purged from official politics. His picture can be seen on Chinese banknotes and a huge Mao portrait hangs over Tiananmen, 'the Gate of Heavenly Peace,' in Beijing even today. As British historian and China expert Julia Lovell concludes, the Soviet Union could discard Stalin and still have Lenin as revolutionary founder; the Communist Party of China (CPC) has only Mao.[19]

That kind of respect, however, does not extend to those who were close to Mao when he was at the apex of his political power during the Cultural Revolution. The most notorious of them, Mao's dreaded intelligence chief Kang Sheng, is even considered a nonentity and his name is rarely mentioned in official circles. Only Chinese intelligence professionals recognize the crucial role he played in building the country's internal and external intelligence services.[20]

Kang Sheng was posthumously expelled from the CPC a few years after his death in 1976, and then slipped into official oblivion. His rule of terror was such that he was best forgotten. Massive Chinese support for overseas Maoist parties and insurrections may also have died with Kang, but some of the old comrades were not forgotten.

In her book about Maoist movements in various parts of the world, Julia Lovell suggested that after the leaders of the Communist Party of Burma (CPB) had been driven into exile in China in 1989, where they supposedly became marginal, impoverished figures "who could occasionally be glimpsed in the cities of south and west

China" and that their Mao jackets were tattered and their toes poked through their old cloth shoes.[21] She may have been right in saying that "the 'revolutionary diplomacy' of the Mao era has become an embarrassing memory, to be expunged in Orwellian style from the official record,"[22] but the rest is nonsense. China did look after the old CPB leaders as well as even some of the younger cadres who fled to China in 1989. As I witnessed when I visited them in Kunming, they had indeed been given government pensions and been provided with free accommodation in apartments in Kunming, while Thakin Ba Thein Tin and Ye Tun had private homes with staff looking after them in Changsha, where they lived in adequate comfort.[23]

However, the exiles were not allowed to engage in any kind of political work. Some of them did, though, and one exile in Tengchong in western Yunnan even maintains a bilingual Burmese and English website, which, however, does not appear to have been updated since 2016.[24] A few CPB members who were of Sino-Burmese descent were given Chinese citizenship. It should also be remembered that some of the veterans, and not only ethnic Wa who served as military officers in the CPB's army or former Red Guard volunteers from China, remained with the UWSA. One of them is Aung Myint, or Li Chu-le, a Sino-Burmese old-timer from central Burma who once served as Thakin Ba Thein Tin's top military adviser and later became a foreign liaison officer and spokesman for the UWSA.

Regardless of old loyalties, a new, more dynamic generation of leaders took over China in the 1980s and 1990s, and that was also reflected in new setups in the security services. The CPC had an effective intelligence apparatus even before it seized power in 1949, and the party's emphasis on security enabled it to identify and neutralize infiltrators among its own ranks, maintain control over its 'liberated areas' during the civil war, and eventually take over Beijing and proclaim its People's Republic. Shortly after the proclamation of the new regime, the now ruling CPC established the Ministry of Public Security, known as Gonganbu, which remained its main intelligence service until the Ministry of State Security (MSS) was established in 1983. The Cultural Revolution was not only over, it also led to a complete reversal of policies. Deng proclaimed that "reform is China's second revolution," and turned out to be exactly the 'capitalist roader' he had been condemned as when he was purged during the Cultural Revolution.[25] As China scholar David Ian Chambers writes, the post-Mao shakeup even reached the ranks of the intelligence services: "As rehabilitation began to gather momentum in the early 1980s, they culminated in the reappearance of once-purged intelligence cadres in their former units or alternative pre-retirement comfort posts. Countless solemn memorial meetings honoured the dead."[26]

The MSS consisted of a completely new breed of younger, better educated officers who were usually recruited before or during their university education. Many of them were graduates of the China Institute of Contemporary International Relations, the Beijing Institute of International Relations, the special training facility at the Jiangnan Social University in Suzhou, and the Zhejiang Police College, which drew students from across the country.[27]

The transformation could be noticed also in the workings of the powerful International Liaison Department of the Central Committee of the Communist Party of China (ILD/CPC). Originally established in 1951, it was once tasked with overseeing relations with foreign communist parties, those in power as well as fraternal movements all over the world, among them the CPB. Under Deng, it expanded its mission to include non-communist parties, which meant "any foreign political party that was willing to meet with it."[28]

Under Xi, those new policies have been refined. Official and semiofficial organs like the wire service *Xinhua*, the *China Daily*, and especially the *Guangming Daily*, have become important actors in China's drive to promote its views on the international stage. Gone are the surly, taciturn correspondents who hardly ever socialized with their foreign colleagues. The new ones tend to be younger, speak excellent English, and are active in international press clubs. One of their tasks is to promote Xi's BRI. Originally known as OBOR, short for the Silk Road Economic Belt and the 21st Century Maritime Silk Road, Xi called it "the greatest dream for the Chinese nation in modern history."[29] China's propaganda machinery began to promote it as a revival of ancient trade routes dating back to Marco Polo and the fabled Silk Road.

The problem, though, is that the existence of an ancient Silk Road along which desert caravans crossed from China through Central Asia and on to European markets is a popular myth of relatively recent origin. No historians dispute the fact that there was substantial trade between Europe and China dating back to medieval times. But whatever caravan trade there was through Central Asia, it did not to any large extent involve silk. According to British historian Susan Whitfield:

There was no 'Silk Road'. It is a modern label in widespread use only since the late 20th century and used since to refer to trade and interaction across Afro-Eurasia from roughly 200 BC to AD 1400. In reality, there were many trading networks over this period. Some of these dealt in silk, yarn and woven fabrics. Others did not.

Some started in China or Rome, but some in Central Asia, northern Europe, India or Africa—and many other places. Journeys were by sea, by rivers and by land, and some by all three.[30]

Bowring also argues that the trade "was mostly maritime, involved China but was mostly conducted by non-Chinese."[31] The early traders were Arabs and people from what is now the Indonesian archipelago, followed by the Portuguese in the fifteenth and early sixteenth centuries, and later the Dutch, French, British, and other Europeans. The Chinese explorer Zheng He, a eunuch from Yunnan whose fleets sailed across the Indian Ocean in the fifteenth century, was a rare exception. Historically, the Chinese were not great seafarers, nor did any Chinese merchants trudge through Central Asia with camels laden with silk or anything else. It was not until China turned into a major trading nation in the 1980s and 1990s that Chinese ships, after being absent for half a millennium, could be seen on the world's oceans.

So where did the notion of an ancient 'Silk Road' come from? It was first used in German and then in the plural, *Seidenstrassen* ('silk roads'), in an academic report published in Berlin in 1877 by German geographer Ferdinand von Richthofen, who had traveled extensively in Central Asia.[32] However, the term did not gain mainstream usage until one of von Richthofen's students, a Swede called Sven Hedin, literally followed his teacher's footsteps and in 1936 published a book called *The Silk Road*.[33] That was the first time the term appeared in English, and it caught on because it appealed to Western notions of the exotic East. It was Eurocentric, and as Hedin points out in his book, "The name 'Silk Road' is not Chinese and has never been used in China."[34] Indeed, it was likely first used officially in China in the

1980s when author Che Muqi published a book titled *The Silk Road: Past and Present*.[35] Lars Ellström, a prominent Swedish Sinologist who trekked the length of China from 2009 to 2011, sums it up: "Why is the term used in China today? It is good marketing for the nation and contributes to tourism."[36]

What was originally meant to be little more than a catchy book title has, since Hedin wrote it in 1936, assumed a life of its own and led to all kinds of theories—and myths—about cultural and economic exchanges between China and Europe, supposedly dating back to medieval times. A recent BBC documentary even called it "the world's first global superhighway where people with new ideas, new cultures and new religions made exchanges that shaped humanity."[37]

Pan Qi conjured up a 'southern Silk Road' in his 1985 article for the *Beijing Review* by inventing an old trade route down to Southeast Asia.[38] Again, there is no doubt that trade between China's southern regions and Southeast Asia existed in ancient times, but it involved tea, jade, and precious stones, not silk. In addition to that 'Silk Road,' there is also the supposed 'Maritime Silk Road' as well as a 'Pacific Silk Road,' and even an 'Ice Silk Road' connecting China with northern Russian ports in the Arctic Ocean all the way to Europe. Von Richthofen and Hedin could hardly have imagined what they would set in motion by using that term, which they probably did only in order to captivate the attention of their Western audiences.

Whatever the case, the BRI is a reality today, and Burma's key role in connecting China with the outside world actually predates Xi's plans by several decades. In 1993, a curious monument was erected in Jiegao, a two-square-kilometer enclave of Chinese territory south of the Ruili River, which otherwise forms parts of the border between China's Yunnan Province and Burma's Shan State. It shows four figures wheeling a circular object between them, their determined faces pointing south. The Chinese characters on the base say 'Unite! Blaze Paths! Forge Ahead!' Or, in more mundane terms, 'Southeast Asia here we come!'

The monument was placed there shortly after the Chinese had built a new wide bridge across the river, connecting the town of Ruili with Jiegao, which at that time consisted of little more than bamboo huts and rice fields. Only a few years later, the tiny enclave was packed with high-rise buildings, luxury hotels, stores selling all kinds of wares, and a huge jade market where buyers from all over China came to shop for the precious stone, which is found in its imperial green variety only in Hpakan in Burma's Kachin State. Every morning, caravans of trucks laden with Chinese consumer goods left Jiegao for points beyond: Muse right across the border, the towns of Lashio, Mandalay, and Rangoon, and even as far as Moreh on the Indian border. The research that China's economic intelligence operatives had done was paying off.

The next step for China was to construct pipelines through Burma, from the coast to the border near Ruili, through which oil and gas from fields in the Middle East were pumped into China. Then came plans to build a high-speed railway from Yunnan down to the deep-sea port of Kyaukphyu on the Bay of Bengal where the pipelines begin. That facility was also partly built by Chinese contractors, and Kyaukphyu, in turn, was only one of several ports on the Indian Ocean rim that China was involved in initiating and then taking part in constructing. Others were Gwadar in Pakistan and Hambantota in Sri Lanka. In August 2017, China opened its first overseas military base in Djibouti at the entrance to the Red Sea and shipping lanes through the Suez Canal.

In many ways, it all began with the establishment of new trade routes through Burma in the early 1990s. The Chinese must already have realized at the time that when it comes to trade none of their neighbors is as important as Burma. No other country can give China direct access to the Indian Ocean, bypassing the congested Malacca Strait and contested areas in the South China Sea. Border disputes and regional rivalry with India make access through that country impossible, and the Chinese-built highway connecting Xinjiang with Pakistan is clearly unsuitable for all-year traffic.

The times may have changed since the leaders in Beijing exported revolution, but what the CPB had failed to achieve for China on the battlefield—extend influence all the way to Southeast Asia—was accomplished by cross-border trade, diplomacy, and most importantly political and economic support for Burma's military government at a time when it was considered and treated as an international pariah. After the 1988 massacres of prodemocracy protesters, the United States, the European Union, Australia, and even Japan had imposed sanctions and boycotts on Burma, but China blocked any attempt to have the United Nations Security Council take action against the junta in Rangoon. When Western nations stopped trading with Burma, the border at Jiegao remained wide open. China also supplied Burma with badly needed military hardware. From the late 1980s to the mid-1990s, China exported an estimated US$1.2 billion worth of armaments to Burma, ranging from battle tanks, heavy artillery, and surface-to-air missiles to defense radars, jet fighters, transport aircraft, frigates, and patrol boats.[39]

Without all that assistance, combined with the China trade, the Burmese junta would probably not have survived. Western sanctions alone did not cause Burma to fall into the hands of the Chinese, as many foreign observers have argued. But Western policies certainly made it easier for China to implement its designs for Burma. This, in return, caused some in the West to criticize a policy of isolating Burma and "handing it over to China." These concerns were outlined as early as June 1997 in a *Los Angeles Times* article by Marvin Ott, an American security expert and former US Central Intelligence Agency analyst, who concluded: "Washington can and should remain outspokenly critical of abuses in [Burma]. But there are security and other national interests to be served ... it is time to think seriously about alternatives."[40]

However, the turn did not take place overnight. Between 2000 and 2008, the George W. Bush administration's bipartisan Burma policy not only maintained sanctions put in place by Congress during the previous Bill Clinton administration, but added new ones in an attempt to support Burma's democratic forces. In late 2007, the brutal suppression of a massive protest movement led by Buddhist monks led to more punitive measures being taken, and Burma's military leaders faced further international criticism over its disastrous response to Cyclone Nargis in 2008. While the Bush administration maintained a hard line against the regime's leadership, it also sought to take advantage of additional space to support civil society on the ground by expanding humanitarian assistance and other programs inside the country.

The revelation in the early 2000s that Burma and North Korea had established a strategic partnership helped to tip the balance in Washington. North Korea was reportedly providing Myanmar with tunneling expertise, heavy weapons, radar and air defense systems, and—it is alleged by Western and Asian intelligence agencies—even missile-related technology.[41]

Some leading foreign policy voices, such as then-Senator Jim Webb, began arguing that it was high time to shift tack and start to engage the Burmese leadership, which seemed bent on clinging on to power no matter the consequences. When the Barack Obama administration came into office in January 2009 on a platform of reversing Bush-era foreign policy, many saw an opening for a change in attitudes towards Burma as well. A general election had been held in November 2010, which ended formal junta rule by senior general Than Shwe and brought in a government led by Thein Sein.

That election, as well as a referendum held in 2008 to adopt a new constitution which had been drafted under military supervision, was blatantly rigged. The constitution was carefully written so it would preserve the military's 'leading role in national politics,' even if a truly civilian government were to assume office. A quarter of all parliamentary seats were reserved for the military, and no important clause in the constitution can be changed without more than three-quarters of the members of parliament voting in favor of such an amendment. In effect, the military has veto power over any attempt to change the 2008 constitution and thereby limit its power. What Burma went through in 2011–12 was not a 'transition to democracy,' as some Western analysts surmised, but the preservation of military rule behind a civilian façade.

That did not matter. It was seen as the opportunity that the West needed to mend fences with the Burmese leadership. Burma suddenly had a new face and was now a country ostensibly run by a constitution and a nominally civilian government, not a junta. With a new administration in Washington, it was the perfect time for Burma's still military-dominated leadership—Thein Sein had 'retired' from his position in the military to become president—to launch a charm offensive in the West, and for the United States and other Western countries to begin the process of détente. Both the US and Burmese leadership viewed pulling Burma from its uncomfortable Chinese embrace and close relationship with North Korea as a key element of this new era.

The Burmese-American historian Thant Myint-U has argued that "there is a myth in the West that Burma's reforms in 2011 were the result of a desire to tilt away from China. The truth was much more complex."[42] In fact, that is not a myth, and the reasons behind the generals' decision to improve relations with the West are not that difficult to understand.

In order to understand Burma's rather dramatic policy shift, it is instructive to look deeper into what was discussed in inner circles of the military in the early 2000s. Then condemned and isolated by the international community, the ruling military junta announced in August 2003 a seven-step 'Roadmap to Discipline-Flourishing Democracy.' That plan called for the drafting of a new constitution, which happened in 2008, and general elections, which were held in 2010. A new parliament would then be formed that that could "elect state leaders" charged with building "a modern, developed, and democratic nation."[43]

The 'roadmap' was made public and was followed almost to the letter. At the same time, a confidential 'master plan' outlined the need to change in order to lessen the heavy and increasingly uncomfortable dependence on China and improve relations with the West. A classified 346-page dossier titled 'A Study of Myanmar-U.S. Relations' was compiled as early as August 2004 and circulated internally among Burma's military leaders. It stated that the country's recent reliance on China as a diplomatic ally and economic patron had created a 'national emergency' that threatened the country's independence.[44]

The authors of the Burmese-language dossier are not known, but it is attributed to one 'Lt. Col. Aung Kyaw Hla,' who is identified as a researcher at the country's prestigious Defence Services Academy in Pyin Oo Lwin. However, it is unclear whether 'Aung Kyaw Hla' is a particular person or a codename used by a military think-tank. Anecdotal evidence suggests the latter. According to the dossier, Burma must normalize relations with the West after implementing the official roadmap and electing a government so that the regime can deal with the outside world on more acceptable terms.

Aung Kyaw Hla goes on to argue that although human rights are a concern in the West, the US would be willing to modify its policy to suit 'strategic interests.' Although the author does not specify those interests, it is clear from the thesis that he is thinking of common ground with the US vis-à-vis China. The author cites Indonesia under former dictator Suharto and communist-ruled Vietnam as examples of US foreign policy flexibility in weighing strategic interests against democratization and human rights.

If bilateral relations with the US were improved, the master plan suggests, Burma would also gain access to badly needed funds from the World Bank, the International Monetary Fund, and other global financial institutions. The country could then emerge from 'regionalism,' where it depended on the goodwill and trade of its immediate neighbors, including China, and enter a new era of 'globalization.'

The master plan clearly articulated the problems that must be addressed before Burma could lessen its reliance on China and become a trusted partner with the West. The main issue at the time of writing was the detention of prodemocracy icon Aung San Suu Kyi, who Aung Kyaw Hla wrote was a key 'focal point': "Whenever she is under detention pressure increases, but when she is not, there is less pressure." While the report implies Suu Kyi's release would improve ties with the West, the plan's ultimate aim, which it spells out clearly, is to 'crush' the opposition.

The dossier concluded that the regime could not compete with the media and nongovernmental organizations run by Burmese exiles, but if US politicians and lawmakers were invited to visit the country, they could help to sway international opinion in the regime's favor. In the years leading up to the policy shifts in 2011 and 2012, many Americans, including some congressmen, did indeed visit Burma and often proved less critical of the regime than they previously had been. In the end, it seems that Burma's military leaders successfully managed to engage the US rather than vice versa.

A breakthrough came in September 2011 when Thein Sein announced that his government had decided to suspend a controversial US$3.6 billion hydroelectric power project in Kachin State. Located at Myitsone where the Mali Hka and Nmai Hka converge to form the Irrawaddy, it was a joint venture between the China Power Investment Corporation, Burma's Ministry of Electric Power, and the Asia World Company, a conglomerate founded by former opium warlord Luo Xinghan and his family. Some 600 square kilometers of forest land would have been flooded if the dam were built, and the 6,000 megawatts of electricity it was planned to generate would have been primarily exported to China.

The US had quietly supported opposition to the dam, and as a result of that and other moves by Thein Sein, including the release of political prisoners, the lifting of press censorship, thus allowing the

National League for Democracy (NLD) and other parties to operate openly, and initiating a peace process, relations with the United States improved rapidly, exactly along the lines suggested by Aung Kyaw Hla in 2004. In early December 2011, US Secretary of State Hillary Clinton paid a high-profile visit to Burma, the first such trip by a top-ranking Washington official in more than fifty years.

Both China and North Korea were high on the agenda during Clinton's visit. Subsequently, strategic and economic concerns have risen up the bilateral agenda even as human rights and democratization have been steadily deemphasized. As a result, the two old adversaries, Burma and the United States, increasingly ended up on the same side of the fence in the struggle for power and influence in Southeast Asia. Burma was no longer seen by the United States and elsewhere in the West as a pariah state that has to be condemned and isolated.

Clinton's visit to Myanmar was followed by a visit by President Obama in November 2012, who returned to Rangoon two years later as the country finally took its turn as chair of the Association of Southeast Asian Nations (ASEAN). In May 2013, Thein Sein became the first Myanmar head of state to visit the United States since the old dictator Ne Win was there in 1966.

Aung San Suu Kyi was released shortly after the 2010 elections, and she became a member of parliament after a by-election in April 2012. Then, in November 2015, her NLD scored a landslide victory in the national elections and Aung San Suu Kyi became State Counselor, which made her de facto head of state. By the time she arrived in Washington for a state visit in September 2016, US-Burma relations had been almost completely normalized. On the occasion of her visit, she and President Obama announced the lifting of all remaining economic sanctions.

The developing friendship between Burma and the United States prompted China to start searching for new ways to shore up its relationship with Burma. In 2012, academic-style journals in China ran several articles analyzing what went wrong with Beijing's Burma policy and what could and should be done to rectify it. One proposed measure was to launch a public relations campaign in Burma aimed at overhauling China's current negative image in the country.

Beijing also began furiously reaching out to other elements of Burmese society, including the NLD and other democrats, utilizing the CPC's 'government-to-government', 'party-to-party', and 'people-to-people' policies to widen the CPC's contacts which until then had been limited to the circle of regime leaders and their business cronies.

In addition to these 'soft power' tools, Beijing had through its contacts with the UWSA and other ethnic armies the ability to either facilitate or frustrate any efforts by Burma's leaders to assert control over the country and establish durable peace. In 2011, China began carefully implementing this mix of hard and soft power tools to maintain a position of influence with both the Thein Sein and Aung San Suu Kyi governments.

Burma was also prepared in its efforts to maintain its independence. To strengthen its position vis-à-vis China, Burma turned not only to the US but also to its partners in ASEAN, which it chaired in 2014. Even more significantly, when General Min Aung Hlaing, who was appointed commander-in-chief of Burma's military in March 2011, went on his first foreign trip in mid-November, he did not go to China but instead to China's traditional enemy, Vietnam. Myanmar and Vietnam share the same fear of their common, powerful northern neighbor, so it is reasonable to assume that Min Aung Hlaing had a lot to discuss with his Vietnamese hosts.

While the Burmese government seeks to build deeper relations with other nations in the region, stark domestic challenges continue to hinder meaningful economic or political developments at home. As history has shown, China's dual-track policy—'government-to-government' and 'party-to-party'—has maintained distinct leverage and influence over Burma's rebel groups as well as the government, further complicating the peace process that Thein Sein initiated in 2011. The distinction between 'government-to-government' and 'party-to-party' may seem artificial in a country like China where there is only one party, and that party controls the government. But it has enabled the Chinese to maintain relations with the Burmese government, the NLD, and groups like the UWSA.

The Chinese government consistently denies reports of interfering in Burma's ethnic conflicts, but Beijing's tacit support for the UWSA tells a different story.[45] China's interest in the talks between Burma's government, its military, and the country's many ethnic armed groups is also not motivated by a desire to find a final solution to decades of civil war. China does not seek peace, it wants stability which it can use to its geostrategic advantage. In the case of Burma, that means maintaining and strengthening the economic corridor from Yunnan down to the Bay of Bengal and the port at Kyaukphyu, which gives China access to the Indian Ocean.

Maintaining the status quo by keeping the UWSA strong enough to deter the Burmese military from attacking it, gives China the advantage it needs to maintain influence, and it would be foolish to give it up. In other words, minister in the president's office Aung Min's warning to the demonstrators in Monywa in November 2012 was well founded. Even at that time, Burma had every reason to be wary of China, and was aware of the cards it could play to regain the influence in Burma that was partly lost under the Thein Sein government.

Thein Sein's peace process was far from the first attempt to negotiate an end to Burma's civil wars. There had been the 1963 peace parley, meetings with the CPB and the Kachin Independence Army (KIA) in 1980, and numerous talks with various ethnic armies that led to a series of ceasefire agreements in the late 1980s and early 1990s. This time, however, the talks became an international affair as dozens of foreign, mainly Western, peacemakers flocked to the country. They brought with them millions of dollars in aid packages, organized seminars, and arranged study tours for ethnic leaders to Northern Ireland, Colombia, Guatemala, and South Africa as well as their own home countries—Switzerland, Norway, Sweden, Finland, and the Netherlands.

However, given their lack of actual insight into the issues that had kept the civil wars alive for decades, the Western peacemakers were before long outmaneuvered by the Chinese, who from the very beginning had also taken an active part in the so-called 'peace process.' None of the Westerners could exercise the same degree of influence over the ethnic armies, or for that matter the central government. China also had direct, geostrategic interests in Burma—access to the Indian Ocean—while for the foreigners participation in the talks was little more than an exercise in promoting their own perceptions of peacemaking, human rights, and democracy.

Besides, it was not clear what the talks were all about because any concession to ethnic minority claims, such as the reintroduction of a federal system, would be impossible as the 2008 constitution cannot be changed unless the military wants it. They have time on their side, and again made it clear that it is their duty to uphold the constitution, not to change it. Even former president Thein Sein, once hailed by some Western writers as 'Burma's Gorbachev' because of the changes he introduced, told the people to vote in the November 2020 election for candidates who would "take care of race and religion as well as the military, which tirelessly fulfils its national duties."[46] It is also known, the ex-president said, that efforts are being made "to weaken the military that protects our country … [and] our country is likely to be devoured by outsiders, under excuses of democracy and human rights."[47] Thein Sein was not a reformer but a military man, and the Chinese knew much better than any Western diplomat, democracy advocate, or peacemaker how to deal with him and other military leaders as well as its civilian politicians, and how to play their cards in the so-called 'peace process.'

China's official delegate to the peace talks is Sun Guoxiang, Beijing's special envoy for Asian affairs, and he has repeatedly expressed support for the process. As a Foreign Ministry official, he is playing only one role in China's multilayered foreign policy. Sun's positive message, with constant references to 'amicable talks' and 'friendly neighbourly relations' are only the surface layer of that policy.[48]

The second layer consists of the ILD/CPC, which maintains close contacts with groups such as the UWSA, the Myanmar National Democratic Alliance Army in Kokang, the Mong La-based National Democratic Alliance Army (Eastern Shan State), and the KIA.

The third layer is the PLA, which maintains links with other militaries across the world. Apart from selling weapons to foreign governmental and nongovernmental clients, directly or through front companies, it provides beneficiaries such as the UWSA with a wide variety of armaments. As we have seen, those armaments are then shared with other ethnic armed groups in Burma.

China may have transformed its economic system from rigid socialism to free-wheeling capitalism, but politically it remains an authoritarian one-party state where the CPC is above the government and the military. The old policy of a fictitious distinction between 'party-to-party' and 'government-to-government' relations, which dates back to Maoist times, has remained unchanged.

Consequently, China's main man in dealing with Burma's many political actors is not Sun but rather Song Tao, head of the ILD/CPC. Song was educated at Monash University in Melbourne, Australia, from September 1988 to August 1991, at a time when the Tiananmen Square massacres took place.[49] The fact that he did not defect shows that he was immensely loyal to the CPC. He served as assistant to the Chinese ambassador to India in the early 2000s before becoming ambassador himself to Guyana and the Philippines. In October 2015, Song took part in a high-profile visit to North Korea and the following month took over the post of ILD/CPC chief from Wang Jiarui, a CPC veteran who was in charge of maintaining relations with communist parties in North Korea, Cuba, and Vietnam.

In recent years, Burma and North Korea have been Song's most important assignments. It is worth noting that he visited Pyongyang with an 'art troupe' in mid-April, shortly after the North Korean leader Kim Jong-un had been to Beijing as part of China's attempts to force him to the negotiating table with the United States and South Korea, with China playing its own games from behind the scenes.

While Song is not a high-profile figure like Sun, he is known to work actively in the background and prefers to meet Burmese politicians and army officers in Beijing rather than Burma's new capital, Naypyitaw. However, he did go to Naypyitaw in 2016 and 2017, where he met Aung San Suu Kyi and General Min Aung Hlaing. Moreover, 'party-to-party' relations have been maintained with the NLD as well as the military-backed Union Solidarity and Development Party (USDP). The CPC's position above the government in Beijing as well as the PLA in the Chinese hierarchy explains why China can publicly praise Burma's peace process while quietly providing the UWSA with heavy weaponry. Support for the UWSA and its allies serves as a 'stick' in Beijing's relationship with Burma, while diplomacy and promises of aid and investment are the 'carrot.'

In order to show that they, and only they, would be able to help the Burmese government solve its internal ethnic problems, the Chinese have also been instrumental in helping the UWSA set up the oddly named seven-member Federal Political Negotiation and Consultative Committee (FPNCC), which was formed on April 19, 2017.[50] It effectively replaced an earlier, mainly Thailand-based alliance called the United Nationalities Federal Council, which fell apart after several of its members had made peace with the government.

Launched on October 15, 2015, the government has called for what it termed a 'Nationwide Ceasefire Agreement' (NCA). However, it was not nationwide and only three of the ten groups have signed it—the three with any armed forces: the Karen National Union (KNU) and its Karen National Liberation Army (KNLA), the Democratic Karen Buddhist Army, and the Restoration Council of Shan State. The other seven are more like NGOs or tiny militias than real rebel armies. By contrast, the seven members of the FPNCC represent more than eighty percent of all armed rebels in the country. They have refused to sign the NCA, arguing that political talks must come before any agreement is formalized with the government.[51]

That conclusion is based partly on the experiences of the Kachin Independence Army (KIA), which did sign a ceasefire agreement in 1994, but instead of the promised talks, the Burmese army began attacking them in June 2011. Since then, the war in the far north has become even more intense, with more than 100,000 Internally Displaced Persons, and the Burmese military for the first time in the history of the civil war using helicopter gunships and jet fighters to attack rebel positions.

Significantly, the FPNCC has called upon China to supervise the peace process, including overseeing all talks with the government. "China's positive involvement in Myanmar's (Burma's) peace process has become more important and cannot be averted," the FPNCC said in a statement released on March 28, 2018.[52] This follows an August 24, 2017 FPNCC press release, which stated that "to be successful, we request China to [be] more involved in [the] Myanmar (Burma) peace process."[53] The FPNCC has also declared support for China's BRI to seize influence over Burma's future direction.

After a brief hesitation during the 2011–15 transition from direct military to quasidemocratic rule, China is once again reasserting its influence in Burma, and it is doing so through its time-tested multilayered policies. China's role in the peace process was clearly demonstrated when, on May 18, 2018, leaders of all seven members of the FPNCC were summoned to Kunming for talks with Sun Guoxiang. Sun made it clear that China would not accept any fighting near the border, which had occurred when the Palaung Ta'ang National Liberation Army (TNLA) attacked a casino near Muse on May 12, this being the reason why the Chinese summoned the FPNCC to Kunming. Among those killed were two Chinese nationals.

Sun also urged the FPNCC to take part in further talks with the government and the military. Even if they would not be accepted as participants and therefore not allowed to speak, he suggested that they could distribute their demands in writing. Perhaps more significantly, he told them to stay clear of any Western peacemaking outfits. "Whenever the West gets involved, it only leads to more conflict," he said.[54] Only China would be able to act as an arbiter in the ongoing peace talks.

While China exerts influence over the FPNCC as a group as well as its individual members, it would be wrong to view them as Chinese puppets. Their reluctance to sign the NCA is one example of this, as are attempts by some of the groups, notably the KIA, to reach out to Western governments and NGOs. In April 2014, General Gun Maw, the deputy commander-in-chief of the KIA, traveled to the United States, where he met State Department officials and urged the US to play a role in Burma's peace process.[55] But that, and the lack of expected US involvement, could also be why he was sidelined in January 2016.[56] In January 2018, the Kachin elected N Ban La as their new leader and he is seen as more aligned to China and less keen to win sympathy from the West.

Nevertheless, interviews with lower- and middle-ranking Kachin officers suggest that not everyone in the movement shares his policy of steering it closer to China and the UWSA. Even N Ban La admitted in an interview that many Kachin are apprehensive of the fact that several UWSA leaders have been indicted by US courts for their involvement in the Golden Triangle drug trade.[57] The KIA and the UWSA are partners in the FPNCC.

Sentiment among the other FPNCC members is more difficult to ascertain. They are dependent on the UWSA for arms and ammunition and there is no difference of opinion when it comes to rejecting the NCA in its present form. But no other group is as close to China's security services as the UWSA. In private conversations, they express a desire to diversify international contacts, and acknowledge their inability to do so because of Chinese pressure and the dominant role China has come to play in the peace process.[58]

On the other hand, Singapore researcher Andrew Ong points out in a recent article that the Wa are not as dependent on the Chinese as many outside observers have suggested. The UWSA is also connected with business interests elsewhere in Burma:

> With telecommunications systems and somewhat a stable kyat only a [*sic*] relatively recent phenomena in Myanmar [Burma], the UWSA has for decades relied on Chinese currency and Chinese markets for its rubber and mining industries, construction technology, and communication networks. Yet since the 1990s, the UWSA has demonstrated a creativity and ability to navigate different routes, markets, and investments to buttress its self-reliance. Collaborations between Wa-owned companies and other Myanmar [Burmese] conglomerates point to strong business ties with elites in Yangon [Rangoon] and Mandalay.[59]

The UWSA has used proxies such as Ho Chin Ting alias Ai Haw alias Hsiao Haw to invest in enterprises such as Yangon Airways and a chain of hotels in Burma, among them the luxurious Thanlwin Hotel in Rangoon. Ai Haw is the principal owner and managing director of Yangon Airways.[60] Any armed conflict with the Burmese army would put such investments in jeopardy, and keeping those has become even more important as the UWSA is switching from producing narcotics to more legitimate business pursuits, such as tin mining and prospecting for rare earth metals. Therefore, the UWSA is more interested in maintaining the status quo than joining forces with the KIA, the TNLA, and other allies in their fights against the Burmese army. The KIA leader N Ban La is known to have asked the UWSA to launch attacks on the Burmese army to relieve the pressure on his forces when they came under attack, but the UWSA turned down the request.[61]

The FPNCC has also acted independently in the peace process. On April 19, 2017, it issued a 47-page counterproposal in Burmese and English, the essence of which is that "all ethnic revolutionary armed forces may participate in the political dialog and political negotiations and finally enter into Federal Political Agreement" (*sic*). 'Finally' indicates that political talks would have to be held first and an agreement signed later. The statement also calls for the withdrawal of the Burmese military from "conflict areas of national minorities."[62]

The statement reflects deep suspicions of the authorities' intentions with the talks, and already in September 2015, before the NCA was announced, the Kachin Baptist Convention (KBC) issued a statement urging the KIA not to sign the NCA without political guarantees and stating that unless political goals were materialized, "KBC opposes disarming."[63]

As the most influential civil society organization among the predominantly Christian Kachin, the KBC apparently did not want the KIA to repeat the same mistake as was made when it signed a ceasefire agreement with central authorities in 1994 and then came under attack, ironically only a few months after the then Thein Sein government had announced its 'peace process.' Since then, fighting has spread to Kokang, to Palaung areas in northern Shan State, and to Rakhine State, where a new force, the Arakan Army, fought battles with the Burmese army. Overall, Burma has not seen such heavy fighting since the 1980s.

The Wa position in the talks is that they want an official Wa State to be carved out of Shan State, amendments to the NCA and Burma's 2008 constitution, and recognition of the Wa-controlled areas on the Thai border.[64] It may be impossible for any Burmese government to concede to the last demand as it would mean recognition of the forcible eviction of thousands of Shan from that area. As for the other demands, the Burmese military has shown no interest in even discussing those issues. China may be the only viable interlocutor, but there are, after all, possible channels for other mediators through which they could balance the UWSA's reliance on China as the sole middleman.[65]

Ong, the Singapore researcher, identifies the World Food Program (WFP), which has worked in the Wa Hills since 2004, as one of the avenues for securing ties with the Wa. He points out, though, that the WFP's programs have been scaled down owing to "lack of funding and shifting priorities."[66] He also argues that premature rumors of the willingness of the UWSA to sign the NCA have created confusion among its allies, and "is part of the motivation to create a unified stance under the FPNCC."[67] Ong asks for a more nuanced approach to the Wa, which would include increased development assistance to lessen their dependence on China.

Any direct international involvement in this would mean a fundamental change in attitudes towards the UWSA, which may not be possible for the US in light of the 2005 indictments. It is, however, possible to work indirectly through local NGOs, civil society groups, and the Wa church, even if Christians have recently come under pressure from the UWSA leadership. On September 9, 2018, the UWSA, apparently acting on orders from China, issued a statement instructing all of its military officers and administrators to "find out what the [Christian] missionaries are doing and what are their intentions."[68]

Church workers were detained and churches demolished during a campaign that is believed to have been prompted by Chinese suspicion against possible influence from foreign missionaries, or that those missionaries would use the Wa Hills as a base for spreading their gospel to China.[69] Hardly coincidentally, the announcement came after John Cao, an ethnic Chinese pastor and a permanent US resident, was arrested in March that year for illegally crossing the Sino-Burmese border. In June, he was sentenced to seven years in prison on immigration-related charges. Cao, a prominent figure in China's 'house church movement,' where believers gather at home rather than in officially approved and tightly controlled churches, first became active in the Wa Hills in 2013. There is no reason to believe that Cao was more than a philanthropic church worker, but the Chinese as well as some of the UWSA leaders saw the emergence of faith-based organizations and movements as a challenge to their authority. The territory controlled by the UWSA is not run along any democratic lines. There is only one party, the United Wa State Party, and Bao Youxiang, in his capacity as chairman of the administration, general secretary of the party, and commander of the armed forces, is the paramount leader, not unlike Xi Jinping in China.

Even so, UWSA's leaders have indicated that they would welcome ties with non-Chinese actors. As for now, they have no choice but to work closely with the Chinese. China and the Wa leaders also share a common interest in avoiding any armed confrontation between the UWSA and the Burmese army. But the UWSA position, to maintain the status quo, is untenable in the long run. No country would want to accept an entirely self-governing state within its boundaries. The Chinese realize this, and are putting pressure on the UWSA to enter into some kind of deal—not the NCA, which is unworkable—with the central government. Consequently, there is also an obvious conflict of interest between the Chinese and the UWSA, and with no 'third party' involved with the Wa, China would remain their only choice.

At the same time, it would be unrealistic to expect the Chinese to compromise on its geostrategic interests and lessen the ties they have with the UWSA and its allies. Some dramatic events in August 2017 also played to the advantage of the Chinese. Hundreds of thousands of Muslim Rohingya from northern Rakhine State fled to Bangladesh following a Burmese army crackdown on a small insurgent group called the Arakan Rohingya Salvation Army (ARSA), which had attacked a number of police stations in Rakhine State. The refugees brought with them tales of systematic murder, burning of villages, and mass rape of Rohingya women and girls. Rather than tracking down the ARSA, the Burmese military unleashed its fury on the civilian Rohingya population.

The West condemned the carnage, and as the refugees were hoarded into squalid, makeshift camps in Bangladesh, Gambia, a small, Muslim-majority state in West Africa, brought the case before the International Court of Justice in The Hague. Burma stood accused of genocide, and to the astonishment of many of her former admirers, Aung San Suu Kyi went to The Hague to claim otherwise. The Rohingya crisis turned Burma from having been the darling of the West after the 2011–12 reforms into an international pariah. Aung San Suu Kyi was also stripped of a number of international awards she had received when she was seen as a model fighter for democracy and human rights. However, the NLD's landslide victory in the November 2020 elections was largely the result of Suu Kyi's immense popularity among the country's Burman Buddhist majority as well as in many ethnic areas, where she is seen as the only person outside the military who is capable of leading the country. The International Crisis Group concluded in a report after the election: "While the Rohingya crisis has demolished her image abroad, her personal defence of Myanmar [Burma] against accusations of genocide at the International Court of Justice in The Hague in 2019 has, on the contrary, enhanced her aura at home, as has her prominent leadership of the response to the COVID-19 pandemic."[70]

Spurned by the West, Aung San Suu Kyi turned to China for sympathy and assistance. She traveled to Beijing to meet Xi, and was promised political support as well as loans and credits. The situation was back to square one with the West condemning the Burmese regime and reimposing sanctions, while China, once again, lent support and made it clear that it would block any attempts by the UN Security Council to take action against Burma.

But mistrust of China runs deep in Burma among the population at large, and especially among the country's armed forces. Years of fighting the CPB have left deep scars in the minds of many senior army officers, and no one in the top military leadership would want to see a return to the days when 'Lt. Col. Aung Kyaw Hla,' whoever he was, felt compelled to write his rather alarmist thesis. The Chinese are well aware of that and, for their long-term game plan—an economic and strategic corridor from Yunnan down to the Indian Ocean—to succeed, they need the UWSA.

But can China really count on the Wa? The Burmese Wa and their UWSA may be Chinese puppets, but as history as well as more recent developments have shown, they are no Chinese stooges. They have their own political and social goals, and only time will tell whether they will get their state and be able to live in harmony with all other nationalities in the Union of Burma—and lessen their present, heavy dependence on a much stronger eastern neighbor that has never treated them fairly.

Notes

Chapter 1: The Wa. Wild Men of the Mountains

1. Minutes from the hearings were published as *Frontier Areas Committee of Enquiry 1947: Part II* (1947). Rangoon: Government Printing. See also Tualchin Neihsial (ed.) (1998), *Burma: Frontier Areas Committee of Enquiry Report*. New Delhi: Inter-India Publications (first printed in the United Kingdom in 1947 by His Majesty's Stationery Office.) I have here used 'Burma' as the name for the country. It was only in 1989 that the then ruling military junta decided to call it 'Myanmar' even in English texts (it has always been *myanma* or *bama* in the Burmese language, the former being a more formal name and the latter used in colloquial speech). At the same time, the names of many local places were changed as well, among them Maymyo, which became Pyin Oo Lwin.
2. *Frontier Areas Committee of Enquiry 1947*, p. 175.
3. *Ibid.* p. 35.
4. *Ibid.* p. 36.
5. *Ibid.* pp. 37, 39.
6. *Ibid.* p. 190.
7. *Ibid.*
8. For an account of the relationship between the Lawa (or Lua) and the Shan and the northern Thai, see Sarassawadee Ongsakul, *History of Lanna* (2005). Chiang Mai: Silkworm Books, pp. 30–32.
9. G. F. Hudson, *The Wa People of the Burma-China Border* (1957), St. Anthony's Papers, 11, Far Eastern Affairs. London: Chatto & Windus, p. 128.
10. Sarassawadee (2005), p. 32.
11. Sir J. George Scott (1932), *Burma and Beyond*. London: Grayson & Grayson, p. 292.
12. *Ibid.* p. 292.
13. Quoted in Taryo Obayashi (1966), 'Authropogonic Myths of the Wa in Northern Indo-China.' *Hitotsubasji Journal of Social Studies*, vol. 3, no. 1, p. 45. Available at https://hermes-ir.lib.hit-u.ac.jp/rs/bitstream/10086/8490/24/HJsoc0030100430.pdf (accessed February 5, 2019).

14. *Ibid.* p. 46.

15. Quoted in *ibid.* p. 59.

16. Scott (1932), p. 292.

17. Alan Winnington (1959), *The Slaves of the Cool Mountains: The Ancient Social Conditions and Changes Now in Progress on the Remote South-Western Borders of China.* London: Lawrence & Wishart, p. 131. Zhuge Liang is spelled Chu Ko-liang in Winnington's book.

18. Ma Jianxiong (1913), 'Clustered Communities and Transportation Routes: The Wa Lands Neighboring the Lahu and the Dai on the Frontier.' *Journal of Burma Studies*, vol. 17, no. 1, p. 107. Available at http://www.ha.cuhk.edu.hk/Papers%202013/Ma%20 Jianxiong_Clustered%20Communities%20and.pdf (accessed March 5, 2019).

19. Sao Saimong Mangrai (1965), *The Shan States and the British Annexation.* Ithaca: Cornell University Southeast Asia Program, p. 271.

20. Magnus Fiskesjö (2014), 'Wa Grotesque: Headhunting Theme Parks and the Chinese Nostalgia for Primitive Contemporaries,' *Ethnos: Journal of Anthropology*, vol. 80 (August), p. 3. Available at https://www.tandfonline.com/doi/abs/10.1080/00141844. 2014.939100 (accessed April 16, 2020).

21. Winnington (1959), p. 131.

22. *Ibid.* p. 133.

23. Scott (1932), pp. 296–97.

24. *Ibid.* p. 299.

25. Hudson (1957), p. 129.

26. Magnus Fiskesjö (2010a), 'Mining, History, and the Anti-state Wa: The Politics of Autonomy between Burma and China,' *Journal of Global History*, vol. 5, no. 2, p. 248. Available at https://www.cambridge.org/core/journals/journal-of-global-history/ article/mining-history-and-the-antistate-wa-the-politics-of-autonomy-between-burma-and-china/9044696A0E0155EA8CE7A824054B8371 (accessed March 5, 2019).

27. Saimong (1965), pp. 263–64, and Sao Sanda Simms (2017), 'Great Lords of the Sky: Burma's Shan Aristocracy.' Self-published under *Asian Highlands Perspectives*, no. 48, pp. 415–16.

28. Magnus Fiskesjö (2000), *The Fate of Sacrifice and the Making of Wa History.* Unpublished Ph.D. thesis, University of Chicago, p. 49.

29. *Ibid.*

30. *Ibid.* p. 50.

31. Ma Yin (ed.) (1989), *China's Minority Nationalities.* Beijing: Foreign Languages Press, p. 278.

32. *Ibid.* pp. 278–79.

33. Magnus Fiskesjö (2012), 'Kinesiska perspektiv på Wa-folkets historia' (in Swedish), *Kina Rapport* (March 13), p. 80.

34. Sir Charles Crosthwaite (1912). *The Pacification of Burma.* London: Edward Arnold, p. 128. Available online at https://archive.org/stream/pacificationofbuoocrosrich/ pacificationofbuoocrosrich_djvu.txt (accessed March 12, 2019).

35. For a succinct history of Shan-Burmese relations during the British era, see Chao Tzang Yawnghwe [1987] (2010), *The Shan of Burma: Memoirs of a Shan Exile*. Second, revised edition, Singapore: Institute of Southeast Asian Studies, pp. 47–90.

36. Hudson (1957), pp. 129–30.

37. *Ibid.* p. 130.

38. G. E. Harvey (1933), *1932 Wa Précis: A Précis Made in the Burma Secretariat of all Traceable Records Relating to the Wa States*. Rangoon: Office of Superintendent, Government Printing and Stationery, Burma, p. 40.

39. Hudson (1957), p. 129.

40. Dorothy J. Solinger (1977), 'Minority Nationalities in China's Yunnan Province: Assimilation, Power, and Policy in a Socialist State,' *World Politics*, vol. 30, no. 1 (October), p. 12. Available at https://www.researchgate.net/publication/259380631_Minority_Nationalities_in_China's_Yunnan_Province_Assimilation_Power_and_Policy_in_a_Socialist_State (accessed March 5, 2019).

41. Wil O. Dijk (2006), *Seventeenth-century Burma and the Dutch East India Company, 1634–1680*. Singapore: Singapore University Press, p. 191.

42. *Ibid.* p. 175.

43. *Ibid.*

44. See Tian Jinchen, 'One Belt and One Road: Connecting China and the World' (2017), paper prepared for McKinsey and Company (April 19). Available at https://www.mckinsey.com/industries/capital-projects-and-infrastructure/our-insights/one-belt-and-one-road-connecting-china-and-the-world (accessed March 20, 2018). Tian mentions how Zhang Qian 'helped establish the Silk Road,' but there is nothing about his attempts to reach India.

45. For the plans to build a railway to China, see John L. Christian (1940), 'Trans-Burma Trade Routes to China,' *Pacific Affairs*, vol. 13, no. 2, pp. 185–87. Available at https://www.jstor.org/stable/2751052?seq=1#page_scan_tab_contents (accessed March 15, 2019).

46. *Ibid.* p. 186.

47. *Ibid.* p. 187.

48. *Ibid.* p. 188. See also H. G. Deignan (1934), *Burma: Gateway to China*. Washington: The Smithsonian Institution, p. 15.

49. Frank Owen (1984), *The Campaign in Burma*. Dehra Dun: Natraj Publishers, p. 76.

50. John LeRoy Christian (1945), *Burma and the Japanese Invader*. Bombay: Thacker & Company, p. 360.

51. See San C. Po (1928), *Burma and the Karens*. London: Elliot Stock, p. 23. See also Bertil Lintner [1994] (2011), *Burma in Revolt: Opium and Insurgency Since 1948*. Fourth edition, Chiang Mai: Silkworm Books, pp. 49–51.

52. Alfred W. McCoy (1972). *The Politics of Heroin in Southeast Asia*. New York: Harper Torchbooks, p. 304.

53. 'The Young Family's Work with the Wa People.' Available at http://www.humancomp.org/wadict/young_family.html (accessed January 10, 2019).

54. *Ibid.*

55. Hudson (1957), p. 133.

56. Samara Yawnghwe (2013), *Maintaining the Union of Burma 1946–1962: The Role of the Ethnic Nationalities in a Shan Perspective.* Bangkok: Institute of Southeast Asian Studies, Chulalongkorn University, p. 120.

57. Sai Aung Tun (2009), *History of the Shan State: From Its Origins to 1962.* Chiang Mai: Silkworm Books, p. 203.

58. *Ibid.* p. 195.

59. Chatichai Choonhavan later became a Thai politician and served as the country's prime minister from 1988 to 1991.

60. Sai Aung Tun (2009), pp. 201–2.

61. *Ibid.* p. 200.

62. *Ibid.*

63. Communication with Andrew Ong, a Singapore scholar and Wa expert, March 26, 2019.

64. Yang Li, *The House of Yang: Guardians of an Unknown Frontier.* Sydney: Bookpress, 1997, p. 51.

65. For the full text of the Panglong Agreement, see http://www.ibiblio.org/obl/docs/panglong_agreement.htm and for download, http://www.myanmar-law-library.org/law-library/laws-and-regulations/constitutions/the-panglong-agreement-1947.html (both accessed March 20, 2019).

66. The full text of the 1947 Constitution is available at http://www.myanmar-law-library.org/law-library/laws-and-regulations/constitutions/1947-constitution.html (accessed March 20, 2019). Chapter IX:178 states that "The Provisions of Chapter X of this Constitution shall not apply to the Kachin State." Chapter IX:181 (10) says that "The Provisions of Chapter X of this Constitution shall not apply to the Karen State."

67. David Lawitts (2015), 'The Grand Old Man of Chiang Mai: The Life of Harold Young.' *Chiang Mai City Life* (April 1). Available at https://www.chiangmaicitylife.com/citylife-articles/the-grand-old-man-of-chiang-mai-the-life-of-harold-young/ (accessed March 15, 2019).

68. *Ibid.*

69. Lintner [1994] (2011), p. 127.

70. US Congress, House. Committee on Un-American Activities (1958), *International Communism (Communist Encroachment in the Far East):* 'Consultations with Maj.-Gen. Claire Lee Chennault, United States Army.' 85th Congress, 2nd Session, April 23, pp. 9–10.

71. *Kuomintang Aggression Against Burma* (1953). Rangoon: Ministry of Information, p. 95.

72. Robert Taylor (1973), *Foreign and Domestic Consequences of the Kuomintang Intervention in Burma.* Ithaca: Cornell University Southeast Asia Program, Data Paper no. 93, p. 49.

73. McCoy (1972), p. 133.

74. Elaine T. Lewis (1957), 'The Hill Peoples of Kengtung State', *Practical Anthropology,* vol. 4, no. 5, p. 224.

75. *Ibid.* pp. 224, 226.
76. Winnington (1959), p. 129.
77. Justin Watkins and Richard Kunst (2006), 'Writing of the Wa Language,' *The Wa Dictionary Project.* London: School of Oriental and African Studies (July 30). Available at http://www.humancomp.org/wadict/wa_orthography.html (accessed January 10, 2020).
78. Fiskesjö (2000), p. 35.
79. *Ibid.*
80. Fiskesjö (2014), p. 8.
81. *Ibid.*
82. For this period in Shan rebel history, see Lintner [1994] (2011), pp. 195–97, and Chao Tzang Yawnghwe [1987] (2010), pp. 109–11.
83. For a map of the border and the areas that were ceded to China, see Josef Silverstein (1977), *Burma: Military Rule and the Politics of Stagnation.* Ithaca: Cornell University Press, p. 174. For an account of the early years of the Kachin rebellion, see Lintner, [1994] (2011), pp. 199–101.

Chapter 2: The Plan that Failed

1. Interview with then CPB chairman, Thakin Ba Thein Tin, Panghsang, December 23, 1986.
2. H. N. Ghoshal assumed the Burmese name Ba Tin when he was elected to the CPB's Central Committee in 1946, but was then referred to as *yebaw* ('comrade') Ba Tin, never, as Martin Smith writes in his book *Burma: Insurgency and the Politics of Ethnicity* (1991). London: Zed Press, p. 46. 'Thakin Ba Tin'. I made the same mistake in the first edition of my book *The Rise and Fall of the Communist Party of Burma* (1990). Ithaca: Cornell University Southeast Asia Program), but corrected it on the online version (https://www.amazon.com/dp/B00ME6AZWQ) when a CPB veteran pointed out my mistake. Dr. Naag also had a Burmese name, *yebaw* Tun Maung.
3. Sao Sanda Simms (2017), *Great Lords of the Sky: Burma's Shan Aristocracy,* p. 30. Self-published under *Asian Highlands Perspectives,* no. 48, p. 9. Available at http://www.lulu.com/shop/sao-sanda-simms/ahp-48-great-lords-of-the-sky-burmas-shan-aristocracy/hardcover/product-23272477.html (accessed January 10, 2020).
4. Hans-Bernd Zöllner (2006), *Myanmar Literature Project,* Working Paper no. 10: 2, Universität Passau, pp. 38–39. Available at https://www.burmalibrary.org/docs11/mlp10.02-op.pdf (accessed January 10, 2020).
5. 'Express Letter from the Chief Secretary to the Govt. of Burma, Police Department, No. 173-C-34,' dated March 17, 1934 and reproduced in *Communism in India: Unublished Documents 1925–1934* (1980). Calcutta: National Book Agency, pp. 177–78. The document does not give the Chinese name for the newspaper, which ceased publication in November 1929.

6. This version of the fate of Aung San and Hla Myaing alias Bo Yan Aung was told to me by several communist veterans during my stay at the CPB's Panghsang headquarters from December 18, 1986 to March 22, 1987.

7. Interview with Kyaw Zaw, Panghsang, January 1, 1987.

8. Bertil Lintner (1990), pp. 9–10, and Bertil Lintner [1994] (2011), *Burma in Revolt: Opium and Insurgency Since 1948*. Fourth edition, Chiang Mai: Silkworm Books, pp. 75–76.

9. Some writers erroneously refer to the two parties as the CPB (White Flag) and the CPB (Red Flag). No communist party would call itself 'white flag' because it was a derogatory term used by Thakin Soe who accused the party of being 'revisionist.' The main party was always called the CPB. It is also incorrect to refer to Thakin Soe's party as the CPB (Red Flag). He was an internationalist and, therefore, did not include 'Burma' in the name of his party but called it the Communist Party (Red Flag). Moreover, the name Burmese Communist Party (BCP), which appeared in government publications and in writings by some academics, was never used by the CPB. It was always the Communist Party of Burma in English.

10. Interview with Thakin Ba Thein Tin, Panghsang, December 23, 1986. *Yebaw* is Burmese for 'comrade' and was often used to denote certain leading party members.

11. For the most comprehensive account of the murders in Rangoon's Secretariat, see Kin Oung (1993), *Who Killed Aung San?* Bangkok: White Lotus. A second, expanded edition was published in 1996.

12. Fleischman, Klaus (ed.) (1989b), *Documents on Communism in Burma 1945–1977*. Hamburg: Mitteilungen des Instituts für Asienkunde, p. 124.

13. Smith (1991), p. 103.

14. *Ibid.* p. 446.

15. *Ibid.*

16. Interview with Thakin Ba Thein Tin, Panghsang, December 23, 1986. Interview with Khin Maung Gyi, Panghsang, December 28, 1986.

17. Smith (1991), p. 446.

18. Mao Zedong (1967), *Selected Works, Volume IV*. Beijing: Foreign Languages Press, pp. 157–76.

19. Interview with Thakin Ba Thein Tin, Panghsang, December 24, 1986.

20. Interview with Aye Ngwe, Panghsang, January 4, 1987.

21. For a chronology of Sino-Burmese relations, see *China's Foreign Relations: A Chronology of Events 1949–1988* (1989). Beijing: Foreign Languages Press, pp. 207–15.

22. Interview with Khin Maung Gyi, Panghsang, December 28, 1987. A copy of that thesis is in my possession.

23. Interview with Thakin Ba Thein Tin, Panghsang, December 24, 1986, and with Pegu Yoma survivors Aung Sein and Than Maung, Panghsang, December 25, 1986.

24. *A Short Outline of the History of the Communist Party of Burma*, official party document dated June 1964 and printed in Beijing. A copy is in my possession.

25. Interview with San Thu, Panghsang, January 5, 1987.

26. Interview with one of those ethnic Chinese party members, who requested anonymity, Panghsang, December 5, 1987.

27. *A Short Outline*, p. 5.

28. Interview with Thakin Ba Thein Tin, Panghsang, December 24, 1986.

29. Interview with Aung Sein, Panghsang, December 25, 1986.

30. 'Key Developments in China's 1966–1976 Cultural Revolution' (2016), *Associated Press* (June 2), available at https://apnews.com/dbf0fd79a3d14b1c91c4d98b17704240/key-developments-chinas-1966-1976-cultural-revolution (accessed January 11, 2020).

31. Those sixteen points are available at https://www.marxists.org/subject/china/peking-review/1966/PR1966-33g.html (accessed January 11, 2020).

32. Interview with Pegu Yoma survivors Aung Sein and Than Maung, Panghsang, December 25, 1986.

33. Interview with Thakin Ba Thein Tin, Panghsang, December 24, 1986.

34. Interview with Pegu Yoma survivors Aung Sein and Than Maung, Panghsang, December 25, 1986

35. Several authors have assumed that Thakin Than Myaing was executed during the Cultural Revolution (for instance, Klaus Fleischmann (1989a), *Die Kommunistische Partei Birmas: Von den Anfängen bis zur Gegenwaht*, Hamburg: Mitteilungen des Instituts für Asienkundse, p. 421.) That is incorrect. Several party members I met in Panghsang in 1986–87 told me that he was alive and living in Chengdu. He died in China in the 1990s.

36. Interview with Thakin Ba Thein Tin, Panghsang, December 24, 1986.

37. See, for instance, Josef Silverstein (1997), *Burma: Military Rule and the Politics of Stagnation*. Ithaca: Cornell University Press, pp. 178–79. See also Martin Smith (1991) pp. 224–27, and Martin Smith (1994), *Ethnic Groups in Burma: Development, Democracy and Human Rights*. London: Anti-Slavery International, p. 59. The situation "became even more desperate in 1968, following anti-Chinese riots in Rangoon, Mao Zedong ordered full-scale backing to the CPB."

38. David Steinberg, 'Burma Under the Military: Towards a Chronology' (1981), *Contemporary Southeast Asia*, vol. 3, no. 3 (December), p. 262.

39. This account of CPB conquests during 1968 to 1970 is based on interviews with party veterans Kyaw Sein, Hla Pe, Lukm Zau, and Mong Ko, November 19–20, 1986.

40. Interview with Lao Er Ji Pyao, Man Hpai, April 4, 1987.

41. Interview with Mya Thaung, Mong Mau, December 4, 1986.

42. *Miandian Lianbang Wa Bang Zhi* (A Record of the Wa State of the Union of Burma). (2018), The United Wa State Party, Panghsang, pp. 652–53. Also interview with Zhao Yilai, Mong Mau, December 11, 1986. Zhao Yilai's name can also be spelled Chao Ngi Lai or, with Burmese phonetics, Kyauk Nyi Laing. His Wa name was Ta Lai. Bao Youxiang can also be spelled Bao Yuchang and his Wa name is Ta Pang.

43. *Ibid.* p. 675.

44. Interview with Mya Thaung, Mong Mau, December 4, 1986.

45. Interview with ex-officer Aung Myint (not his real name), Bangkok, October 10, 1992.

46. *Ibid.*

47. See Adrian Cowell's and Chris Menges' excellent 1973 film, *The Opium Warlords*, which contains an interview with Khun Hseng, Khun Sa's uncle. While listening to intercepted radio massages, he gets the following information: "At present the Burmese troops are also moving in to help the Kokang Ka Kwe Ye (Luo's Kokang militia) to carry down the opium." That the Burmese army in the early 1970s directly participated in defending the opium convoys from the north to the Thai border has also been confirmed by several former Burmese army officers I have interviewed in Bangkok.

48. Magnus Fiskesjö, in his otherwise excellent research, makes the mistake of assuming that CPB cadres who had been driven out of central Burma established the northeastern base area. See Magnus Fiskesjö (2012), 'Kinesiska perspektiv på Wa-folkets historia,' *Kinarapport* (in Swedish), (March), p. 82. Available at http://tidskrift.nu/artikel.php?Id=7986 (accessed January 10, 2010).

49. Interview with Kyaw Mya, Panghsang, December 29, 1986.

Chapter 3: The Wa and the Communist Party of Burma

1. This Panglong should not be confused with the market town of Panglong in central Shan State, where Aung San and representatives of the Shan, Kachin, and Chin signed an agreement on February 12, 1947 to set up a federal union after independence. This Panglong is a predominantly Panthay, or Chinese Muslim, town and for many years it was where many prominent opium traders resided.

2. Interview with Zhao Yilai, Mong Mau, December 4, 1986.

3. Interview with Mya Thaung, political commissar of the northern Wa Hills, Mong Mau, December 4, 1986.

4. According to Falise Thierry, a Belgian photojournalist who visited the Wa Hills in 1993. See https://www.bangkokpost.com/thailand/special-reports/312577/as-seen-through-the-lens-of-an-insider and https://www.gettyimages.com/detail/news-photo/members-of-the-united-wa-state-army-display-a-human-skull-news-photo/165249418.

5. Tom Kramer (2007), *The United Wa State Party: Narco-Army or Ethnic Nationalist Party?* Washington: East-West Center, p. 16.

6. Bertil Lintner (2011), *Burma in Revolt: Opium and Insurgency Since 1948.* Fourth edition, Chiang Mai: Silkworm Books, p. 272.

7. The news about Naw Seng's death, based on a CPB radio broadcast, was prominently displayed in the Burmese government's newspaper, *The Working People's Daily*, April 27, 1972.

8. Klaus Fleischmann (ed,) (1989), *Documents on Communism in Burma 1945–1977.* Hamburg: Mitteilungen Des Instituts für Asienkunde, pp. 185–86.

9. John Byron and Robert Pack (1992), *The Claws of the Dragon: Kang Sheng, the Evil Genius Behind Mao and His Legacy of Terror in People's China*. New York: Simon & Schuster, p. 324.

10. According to the CPB's own statistics collected in 1986, there were 263,029 people in the CPB-controlled areas, of whom 122,399 were male and 140,630 female. Although the large disparity in the numbers between the sexes (18,231) could not be attributed to war casualties alone, it nevertheless is a clear indication of the heavy toll the fighting had taken.

11. Interview with Mya Thaung, Mong Mau, December 4, 1986.

12. *Beijing Review*, July 30, 1976.

13. *Ibid.*

14. *Beijing Review*, September 30, 1976.

15. *Beijing Review*, November 26, 1976.

16. To further please the Chinese, on September 7, 1979 Burma announced at a meeting in Havana, Cuba that it was leaving the Non-Aligned Movement. The Burmese delegate, President San Yu, criticized the Vietnamese invasion of Cambodia, which led to the ouster of the Khmer Rouge.

17. See Thakin Ba Thein Tin (1978), *The Entire Party! Unite and March to Achieve Victory!* (translation from the Burmese). Panghsang, CPB's printing press, p. 4.

18. A Wa woman I met in the area in February 1986 told me she had named her young son 'Township Officer.' When I asked her why, she replied that "he's very lazy, doesn't want to do anything, and he never comes when I call him."

19. *The Spirit of 1948–1949 was one of self-reliance and enduring hardships* (translation from the Burmese) (1979), Panghsang: CPB's printing press, August.

20. Interview with Khin Maung Gyi, Panghsang, December 28, 1986.

21. *The Working People's Daily*, May 10, 1989.

22. Interview with Brang Seng, Pa Jau (Kachin headquarters), August 12, 1986. *The Working People's Daily* of May 10, 1989, however, claims that "the KIA held firm their right to secede," but that statement is not supported by meeting documents and independent sources.

23. Interview with Ye Tun, Panghsang, December 31, 1986.

24. That discussion was still ongoing when I was in Panghsang from December 1986 to March 1987.

25. See *China's Foreign Relations: A Chronology of Events 1949–1988* (1989). Beijing: Foreign Languages Press, p. 21, and Wikipedia https://en.wikipedia.org/wiki/Five_Principles_of_Peaceful_Coexistence (accessed January 10, 2020).

26. News release, *The People's Voice of Burma, the Organ of the Communist Party of Burma*, Panghsang, April 20, 1986.

27. *Ibid.*

28. *Ibid.*

29. This discussion was still ongoing when I stayed at Panghsang from December 1986 to March 1987.

30. For a breakdown of representation in the politburo and the central committee, see Bertil Lintner (1990), *The Rise and Fall of the Communist Party of Burma*. Ithaca: Cornell University Southeast Asia Program, pp. 71–73.

31. Interview with Brang Seng, Pa Jau, August 12, 1986.

32. I was present at the battle of Hsi-Hsinwan when it began in November 1986.

33. This was obvious when I trekked through the CPB's base areas in 1986 and 1987. The soldiers who escorted me were often quite blunt in their comments about leaders who they called 'the Red Burmese' as opposed to 'the White Burmese,' or the government's army.

34. Luo is a major character in Adrian Cowell's and Chris Menges' documentary, *The Opium Warlords*, which was shot in Shan State in 1972–73.

35. See A Special Correspondent (1981), 'The Return of Lo Hsing-han,' *Focus* Bangkok (August). I was that 'Special Correspondent' and the article was based on several interviews with Shan and Kokang rebel leaders, including Sao Sai Tu, who was arrested along with Luo Xinghan (Lo Hsing-han).

36. Interview with Mya Thaung, Mong Mau, December 4, 1986.

37. Interview with CPB central committee member Soe Thein, January 5, 1987.

38. *Ibid.*

39. SWB [Summary of World Broadcasts], FE/0164B/1, May 30, 1988. The same account was also published as a booklet (in Burmese) by the CPB's printing press in Panghsang. A copy of that booklet is in my possession.

40. For surprisingly accurate biographies of those two party members, see the military government's otherwise error-ridden publication, *Burma Communist Party's Conspiracy to take over State Power* (1989). Rangoon, pp. 77–79.

41. *The Working People's Daily*, November 20, 1989. A transcript of the entire discussion was published in *The Working People's Daily* of November 18, 19, 20, and 21, 1989. Surprisingly, the government published this in order to prove that the CPB was behind Burma's prodemocracy movement.

42. According to correspondence I received from Panghsang in April 1989.

43. *Miandian Lianbang Wa Bang Zhi* (A Record of the Wa State of the Union of Burma) (2018), The United Wa State Party, Panghsang, pp. 652–53.

44. This was first reported by me as 'Rebels with a cause' (1989a), *Far Eastern Economic Review*, March 30.

45. SWB, FE/0439B/1, April 20, 1989.

46. FBIS [Foreign Broadcast Information Service]-EAS-89-081, April 28, 1989.

47. Hand-written minutes from this meeting were passed on to the me during my visit to Jinghong, southern Yunnan, in May 1989.

48. According to numerous conversations between CPB soldiers which I overheard during my stay in the CPB's base area from November 1986 to April 1987.

49. Julia Lovell (2019), *Maoism: A Global History*. London: The Bodley Head, p. 426.

Chapter 4, The Growth of the United Wa State Army

1. Interviews with former CPB cadres in Yunnan, April 1989.

2. Interview with Aung Gyi, Rangoon, April 21, 1989.

3. For an account of Olive Yang and her exploits, see Bertil Lintner [1994] (2011), *Burma in Revolt: Opium and Insurgency Since 1948*. Boulder, Colorado: Westview Press (1994), pp. 100, 155, 186–87, 297, 376, 414, and fourth edition (2011), Chiang Mai: Silkworm Books, pp. 120, 190, 230–31.

4. For instance, see *The Working People's Daily*, Rangoon, April 23, 1989.

5. Interview with Ai Pao, Wa leader in exile in Thailand, Chiang Mai, April 19, 1989.

6. Soe Tun Ni, 'All that glitters is not gold-2,' *The Working People's Daily*, May 10, 1989.

7. *The Working People's Daily*, December 5, 1989.

8. See, for instance, https://en.wikipedia.org/wiki/United_Wa_State_Army (accessed January 25, 2020); and Paul Keenan (2008), *By Force of Arms: Armed Ethnic Groups in Burma*. New Delhi: Vij Books India, p. 72.

9. For those agreements, see https://www.bbc.com/news/world-asia-23300441, and https://www.mmpeacemonitor.org/1499

10. Washington: US State Department's International Narcotics Control Strategy Report (April 1993), pp. 262–64. Available at https://books.google.co.th/books/about/International_Narcotics_Control_Strategy.html?id=kVnkAAAAMAAJ&redir_esc=y (accessed January 15, 2020).

11. Drug Enforcement Administration, Intelligence Division: "Drug Intelligence Brief: The Price Dynamics of Southeast Asian Heroin," (February 2001), p. 3.)

12. For details about the locations of those laboratories, see Bertil Lintner (1993), 'The Politics of the Drug Trade in Burma,' *Occasional Paper no. 33*, Indian Ocean Centre for Peace Studies, University of Western Australia, pp. 50–57, and Bertil Lintner (1991), 'Cross-Border Drug Trade in the Golden Triangle (S.E. Asia),' *Territory Briefing no. 1*, International Boundaries Research Unit, University of Durham, UK, p. 12 (map.)

13. Sarassawadee Ongsakul (2005), *History of Lanna*. Chiang Mai: Silkworm Books, pp. 30–32.

14. Alfred McCoy (2003), *The Politics of Heroin: CIA Complicity in the Global Drug Trade*. New York: Lawrence Hill Books, p. 440. See also Tom Kramer (2007), *The United Wa State Party: Narco-Army or Ethnic Nationalist Party?* Washington: East-West Center, p. 22.

15. See Bertil Lintner and Michael Black (2009), *Merchants of Madness: The Methamphetamine Explosion in the Golden Triangle*. Chiang Mai: Silkworm Books, pp. 153–54. Those details were obtained from internal Thai police records.

16. Those figures were given to me by Xiao Minlaing, Panghsang, August 28, 2019.

17. I was able to see this for myself when I visited the Wa Hills in August 2019.

18. Hans Steinmüller (2020), 'The Moral Economy of Militarism: Peasant Economy, Military State and Chinese Capitalism in the Wa State of Myanmar,' *Social Anthropology* (February 4), p. 11. Available at https://onlinelibrary.wiley.com/doi/full/10.1111/1469-8676.12755 (accessed February 7, 2020).

19. *Ibid.*

20. Interview with Xiao Minlaing, Panghsang, August 28, 2019.

21. Chin Ko-lin (2009), *The Golden Triangle: Inside Southeast Asia's Drug Trade*. Ithaca: Cornell University Press, p. 35, and interview with Xiao Minliang, Panghsang, August 28, 2019.

22. Chin (2009), pp. 35–36.

23. Bertil Lintner (1994b), 'Turf War in the Triangle,' *Far Eastern Economic Review* (January 20).

24. See Lintner (1993), pp. 31–32, 56, 60, and Bertil Lintner (1995b), 'New Menace in the Golden Triangle,' *Reader's Digest* (December), pp. 23–26. The information in those two publications is based on numerous interviews with local people in the area and international drug enforcement officials.

25. Jake Brunner, Kirk Talbott and Chantal Elkin (1988), *Logging Burma's Frontier Forests*. Washington: World Resources Institute, p. 21.

26. *A Choice for China* (2005). Global Witness report, October. Available at https://cdn.globalwitness.org/archive/files/library/a_choice_for_china_low_res.pdf (accessed January 15, 2020).

27. Quoted in *A Disharmonious Trade: China and the Continued Destruction of Burma's Northern Frontier Forests* (2009), Global Witness report, October, p. 12. Available at https://www.globalwitness.org/en/archive/disharmonious-trade-china-and-continued-destruction-burmas-northern-frontier-forests/ (accessed January 15, 2020).

28. Song Qingrun (2015), 'Myanmar Must Restore Peace on China Border,' *China Daily* (March 29).

29. See, for instance, Yun Sun (2019), 'Why China is Sceptical About the Peace Process,' *Frontier Myanmar* (October 3). Available at https://frontiermyanmar.net/en/why-china-is-sceptical-about-the-peace-process (accessed January 15, 2020); and her 2018 paper, *China's Role in Myanmar's Internal Conflicts*. Washington: The United States Institute of Peace, p. 7. Available at https://www.usip.org/sites/default/files/2018-09/ssg-report-chinas-role-in-myanmars-internal-conflicts.pdf (accessed January 15, 2020).

30. See Bertil Lintner (1995a), 'The Drug Trade in Southeast Asia,' *Jane's Intelligence Review, Special Report no. 5* (April), p. 14

31. Zhou Yongming (1999), *Anti-Drug Crusades in Twentieth-Century China: Nationalism, History, and State Building*. Lanham: Rowman & Littlefield, p. 163. See also Bertil Lintner (2011), *Burma in Revolt: Opium and Insurgency Since 1948*. Chiang Mai: Silkworm Books, pp. 400–1.

32. *Ibid.* p. 401, quoting *The People's Armed Police News*, December 13, 1992.

33. Zhou (1999), p. 164.

34. *Ibid.* p. 165.

35. See, for instance, Andrew Forbes and David Henley (1997), *The Haw: Traders of the Golden Triangle*. Chiang Mai: Teak House Publications; Chang Wen-Chin (2014), *Beyond Borders: Stories of Yunnanese Chinese Migrants in Burma*. Ithaca: Cornell University Press; Ann Maxwell Hill (1998), *Merchants and Migrants: Ethnicity and Trade among Yunnanese Chinese in Southeast Asia*. New Haven: Yale University Southeast Asia Studies; and Chiranan Prasertkul (1989), *Yunnan: Trade in the Nineteenth Century: Southwest China's Cross-boundaries Functional System*. Bangkok: Institute of Asian Studies, Chulalongkorn University, 1989.

36. See Chapter One.

37. See Lintner (1991), p. 25, and Bertil Lintner (1994a), 'Burma: China's New Gateway: Route for Trade, Arms and Immigrants', *Far Eastern Economic Review* (cover story), December 22.

38. Bertil Lintner (2019), *The United Wa State Army and Burma's Peace Process*. Washington: The United States Institute of Peace, p. 17. Available at https://www.usip.org/publications/2019/04/united-wa-state-army-and-burmas-peace-process (accessed January 20, 2020); and Anthony Davis (2019). 'It's party time for Myanmar's largest armed ethnic faction,' *Asia Times*, April 9. Available at https://www.asiatimes.com/2019/04/article/anthony-davis-wa-story/ (accessed January 20, 2020).

39. Lintner (2019), p. 15.

40. Hans Steinmüller (2018), 'Conscription by Capture in the Wa State of Myanmar: Acquaintances, Anonymity, Patronage, and the Rejection of Mutuality,' *Comparative Studies in Society and History*, vol. 61, no. 3, pp. 508–34. Available at http://eprints.lse.ac.uk/90635/ (accessed January 20, 2020).

41. Interview with Xiao Minliang, Panghsang, August 28, 2019. He was unwilling to disclose the number of troops, so the figure 20,000–25,000 is based on observations by political analysts in Rangoon and Bangkok.

42. Min Zin (2013), 'When the Chinese Press down,' *The Irrawaddy* (August 14). Available at https://www.irrawaddy.com/opinion/guest-column/when-the-chinese-press-down.html (accessed January 20, 2020).

43. Interviews with former CPB members and EAO leaders, Ruili, March 2018.

44. Andrew Ong (2020), 'Engaging the UWSA: Countering Myths, Building Ties.' Available at https://teacircleoxford.com/2018/08/20/engaging-the-uwsa-countering-myths-building-ties/ (accessed January 20, 2020).

Chapter 5, The United Wa State Army and Drugs: A Chinese Dilemma

1. US Drug Enforcement Administration, News release, January 24, 2005. Available at https://www.dea.gov/sites/default/files/pubs/states/newsrel/nyco12405.html (accessed January 25, 2020).

2. *Ibid.*

3. *Ibid.*

4. *Ibid.*

5. *Ibid.*

6. For a complete list of the names on the unsealed as well as the sealed list, see Bertil Lintner (2019), *The United Wa State Army and Burma's Peace Process*. Washington: The United States Institute of Peace, p. 11, Available at https://www.usip.org/sites/default/files/2019-07/pw_147-the_united_wa_state_army_and_burmas_peace_process.pdf (accessed January 10, 2020).

7. Interview with Xiao Minliang, deputy leader of the United Wa State Party, Panghsang, August 28, 2019.

8. For this breakdown of prices here and below, see Bertil Lintner (1998), 'Drugs and the Asian Crisis,' *The Asia-Pacific Magazine*, no. 13 (December).

9. Chin Ko-lin (2009), *The Golden Triangle: Inside Southeast Asia's Drug Trade*. Ithaca: Cornell University Press, p. 232.

10. Chin Ko-lin and Sheldon X. Zhang (2015), *The Chinese Heroin Trade: Cross-Border Drug Trafficking in Southeast Asia and Beyond*. New York: New York University Press, p. 112.

11. A Special Correspondent (1981), 'The Return of Lo Hsing-han,' *Focus*, Bangkok (August).

12. Tom Allard (2019), 'The Hunt for Asia's El Chapo,' *Reuters* (October 14). Available at https://www.reuters.com/investigates/special-report/meth-syndicate/ (accessed April 5, 2020).

13. *Ibid.*

14. Quoted in Tom Kramer (2007), *The United Wa State Party: Narco-Army or Nationalist Party?* Washington: East-West Center, p. 34.

15. Tom Kramer (2005), 'A Downward Spiral: Proposed opium bans could spark humanitarian crisis,' *Irrawaddy*, vol. 13, no. 10 (October). Available at https://www.tni.org/my/node/12410 (accessed March 25, 2020).

16. Interview with Saw Lu, Chiang Mai, May 25, 1993.

17. *Ibid.*

18. The document is available at https://www.burmalibrary.org/sites/burmalibrary.org/files/obl/docs/BONDAGE.htm (accessed April 10, 2020).

19. For all those quotes, see the above weblink.

20. Dennis Bernstein and Leslie Kean (1996), 'People of the Opiate,' *Baltimore Sun* (December 22). Available at https://www.baltimoresun.com/news/bs-xpm-1996-12-22-1996357002-story.html (accessed April 10, 2020).

21. See Alfred McCoy (1972), *The Politics of Heroin in Southeast Asia*. New York: Harper Torchbooks, p. 4.

22. Kate Hodal (2013), 'Meth drug makers lure children in Thailand with sweet-coated yaba pills,' *The Guardian* (August 27). Available at https://www.theguardian.com/world/2013/aug/27/meth-drugs-yaba-lure-children-thailand (accessed April 10, 2020).

23. Andrew Marshall and Anthony Davis, 'Speed Tribe: Inside the world of Wa—Asia's deadliest drug cartel,' *Time* (December 16). Available at http://content.time.com/time/world/article/0,8599,2056076,00.html (accessed April 10, 2020).

24. A copy of the letter, which no longer is available on the Internet, is in my possession.

25. McCoy, Alfred (1991), *The Politics of Heroin: CIA Complicity in the Global Drug Trade*. New York, Lawrence Hill Books, p. 82.

26. J. M. Scott (1969), *The White Poppy: A History of Opium*. New York: Funk & Wagnalls, pp. 84–85.

27. Richard Hughes (1968), *Borrowed Place, Borrowed Time: Hong Kong and Its Many Faces*. London: Andre Deutsch, p. 41.

28. Maurice Collis (1946), *Foreign Mud*. London. Faber & Faber, p. 303.

29. For a history of the Dutch opium trade in the East Indies, see James R. Rush (1990), *Opium to Java: Revenue Farming and Chinese Enterprise in Colonial Indonesia, 1860–1910*. Ithaca: Cornell University Press.

30. Samuel Merwin (1908), *Drugging a Nation*. New York: Fleming H. Revell Company, p. 9.

31. Hideyuki Takano (2002), *The Shore Beyond Good and Evil: A Report from Inside Burma's Opium Kingdom*. Tokyo: Kotan Publishing, p. 79.

32. Magnus Fiskesjö (2000), 'The Fate of Sacrifice and the Making of Wa History.' Unpublished Ph.D. thesis, University of Chicago, p. 193.

33. Martin Booth (1996), *Opium: A History*. London: Simon & Schuster, p. 181.

34. For a complete collection of Burma's opium acts and rules, see *The Opium Manual: Containing the Opium Act and the Rules and Directions thereunder in force in Burma*, (1964). Rangoon: Superintendent, Central Press.

35. Leslie Milne [1910] (1970), *Shans at Home*. London: John Murray. Reprint, New York: Paragon Book Reprint Corp., p. 180.

36. *The Opium Manual*, p. 25.

37. *Ibid.* p. 27.

38. Robert Maule (2002), 'British Policy Discussions on the Opium Question in the Federated Shan States,' *Journal of Southeast Asian Studies* (June), p. 204. Available at https://www.jstor.org/stable/20072412?seq=1 (accessed April 10, 2020).

39. *Ibid.*

40. British intelligence document quoted in Sai Kham Mong (2005), *Kokang and Kachin in the Shan State (1945–1960)*. Bangkok: Institute of Asian Studies, Chulalongkorn University, p. 67.

41. Ian Fellowes-Gordon (1957), *The Amiable Assassins: The Story of the Kachin Guerrillas of North Burma*. London: Robert Hale Limited, p. 87.

42. *Ibid.*

43. *Weekend Telegraph*, London, March 10, 1967. Quoted in McCoy (1972), p. 319.

44. Chao Tzang Yawnghwe (1982), 'Politics of Burma and Shan State: Effects on Thailand and North Thailand,' *Political Science Review*, Chiang Mai University, Thailand (September).

45. *Hearings Before the Select Committee of Narcotics Abuse and Control, House of Representatives, 95th Congress* (1978), Washington: Government Printing Office, pp. 215–16.

46. Stanton Candlin (1973), *Psycho-Chemical Warfare: The Chinese Communist Drug Offensive Against the West.* New Rochelle, New York: Arlington House.

47. T. D. Allman (1971), 'A Wonderland of Opium,' *Far Eastern Economic Review* (July 24).

48. Bertil Lintner (2003), 'Dark Journey,' *Far Eastern Economic Review* (May 8).

49. For a breakdown of Thailand's opium production from 1961 to 1999, see Ronald Renard (2001), *Opium Reduction in Thailand 1970–2000: A Thirty-Year Journey.* Chiang Mai: Silkworm Books, p. 36.

50. Bertil Lintner and Rodney Tasker (1997), 'Caged but dangerous,' *Far Eastern Economic Review* (June 5).

51. United Nations Office for Drugs and Crime (UNODC) (2019), 'Myanmar opium cultivation continues to drop as regional drug markets change' (January 11). Available at https://www.unodc.org/southeastasiaandpacific/en/myanmar/2019/01/myanmar-opium-survey-report-launch/story.html (accessed April 12, 2020).

52. Interviews with people close to the opium trade, Chiang Mai, March 12, 2019.

53. Chin Ko-lin and Sheldon X. Zhang (2015), p. 199.

54. Elizabeth J. Cohen and Joseph J. Amon (2008), 'Health and Human Rights Concerns in Detention in Guangxi Province, China,' *Plos Medicine*, vol. 5, no. 12 (December 9). Available at https://journals.plos.org/plosmedicine/article/file?id=10.1371/journal.pmed.0050234&type=printable (accessed April 10, 2020).

55. Jamie Ducharme (2019), 'Trump Said China Doesn't Have a Drug Problem. The Data Tells a Different Story,' *Time* (February 15). Available at https://time.com/5530597/trump-china-drug-problem/ (accessed April 12, 2020); and Chin Ko-lin and Sheldon X. Zhang (2016), 'A People's War: China's Struggle to Contain its Illicit Drug Problem.' *Foreign Policy at Brookings* (July). Available at https://www.brookings.edu/wp-content/uploads/2016/07/A-Peoples-War-final.pdf (accessed April 12, 2020).

56. Zheng Caixiong (2018), '1.3 tons of cocaine seized in crackdown in drug gang in Shenzhen,' *China Daily* (September 14). Available at http://www.chinadaily.com.cn/a/201809/14/WS5b9b43d3a31033b4f4656124.html (accessed April 12, 2020).

57. *Ibid.*

58. Aung Zaw (2020), 'Shadowy Drug Lord Wei Hsueh-kang's [Wei Xuegang] Influence Still Felt in Myanmar's Wa Region and Beyond,' *The Irrawaddy* (March 9). Available at https://www.irrawaddy.com/opinion/commentary/shadowy-drug-lord-wei-hsueh-kangs-influence-still-felt-myanmars-wa-region-beyond.html (accessed April 10, 2020).

59. Chin Ko-lin (2009), *The Golden Triangle: Inside Southeast Asia's Drug Trade.* Ithaca: Cornell University Press, p. 141.

Chapter 6, The Plan that Might Succeed

1. Magnus Fiskesjö (2014), 'Wa Grotesque: Headhunting Theme Parks and the Chinese Nostalgia for Primitive Contemporaries,' *Ethnos: Journal of Anthropology*, vol. 80 (August), p. 10. Available at https://www.tandfonline.com/doi/abs/10.1080/0014184 4.2014.939100 (accessed April 16, 2020).

2. *Ibid.* p. 10.

3. *Ibid.* p. 17.

4. *Ibid.* pp. 10–11.

5. Philip Bowring (2017), 'China's Silk Road Illusions,' *The New York Review of Books* (October 25). Available at https://www.nybooks.com/daily/2017/10/25/chinas-silk-road-illusions/ (accessed April 16, 2020).

6. James Millward, James (2019), 'What Xi Jinping Hasn't Learnt from China's Emperors,' *The New York Times* (October 1). Available at https://www.nytimes.com/2019/10/01/opinion/xi-jinping-china.html (accessed April 15, 2020).

7. *Ibid.*

8. 'Historical Matters Concerning Xinjiang.' Available at http://www.xinhuanet.com/english/2019-07/21/c_138244704.htm (accessed April 16, 2020).

9. *Ibid.*

10. Millward (2019).

11. For an account of that border conflict and war, see Bertil Lintner (2018), *China's India War: Collision Course on the Roof of the World*. New Delhi: Oxford University Press.

12. Maria Adele Carrai (2019), *Sovereignty in China: A Genealogy of a Concept Since 1840*. Cambridge: Cambridge University Press, p. 107.

13. Ting Tsz Kao. 1980. *The Chinese Frontiers*. Aurora, Illinois: Chinese Scholarly Publishing Company, p. 148.

14. Zheng Dahua (2019), 'Modern Chinese nationalism and the awakening of self-consciousness of the Chinese Nation,' *International Journal of Anthropology and Ethnology*, vol. 3, no. 11. Available at https://link.springer.com/article/10.1186/s41257-019-0026-6#Sec7 (accessed April 20, 2020).

15. See https://www.sftindia.org/campaign/13th-february/ (accessed April 18, 2020). For the full text of the announcement, which was made public on February 14, see https://en.wikisource.org/wiki/Proclamation_of_Independence_of_Tibet (accessed April 18, 2020).

16. Carrai (2019), p. 127.

17. Ma Yin (ed.) (1989), *China's Minority Nationalities*. Beijing: Foreign Languages Press, p. 279.

18. *Ibid.* pp. 279–80.

19. Julia Lovell (2019), *Maoism: A Global History*. London: The Bodley Head, p. 427.

20. I. C. Smith, and Nigel West (2012), *Historical Dictionary of Chinese Intelligence*. Lanham: The Scarecrow Press, p. 133.

21. Lovell (2019), p. 426.

22. *Ibid.* p. 427.

23. I have visited several CPB exiles in Kunming and other towns in Yunnan on numerous occasions, and found all of them well-clothed and well-fed.

24. See https://www.cp-burma.org/

25. 'Reform is China's Second Revolution' (1985), *China Daily* (March 28). Available at https://www.chinadaily.com.cn/china/19thcpcnationalcongress/2010-10/21/content_29714471.htm (accessed April 16, 2020).

26. Dr. David Ian Chambers (2012), 'The Past and Present State of Chinese Intelligence Historiography', *Studies in Intelligence*, vol. 56, no. 3 (September).

27. Smith and West (2012), p. 181.

28. Anne-Marie Brady (2003), *Making the Foreign Serve China: Managing Foreigners in the People's Republic*. Lanham: Rowman and Littlefield, p. 200.

29. Elizabeth C. Economy (2018), *The Third Revolution: Xi Jinping and the New Chinese State*. New York: Oxford University Press, p. 3.

30. See Whitfield's blog with an introduction to the book she edited: *Silk Roads: Peoples Cultures and Landscapes*, Oakland: University of California Press, 2019. The blog is available at https://silkroaddigressions.com/ (accessed April 10, 2020.)

31. Email to me from Philip Bowring, January 18, 2020. See also his book *Empire of the Winds: The Global Role of the Winds*. London: I.B. Tauris, 2018.

32. Tamara Chin (2013), 'The Invention of the Silk Road', *The University of Chicago Press Journals*, vol. 40, no. 1 (Autumn), p. 196. Available at https://www.jstor.org/stable/10.1086/673232?seq=1#metadata_info_tab_contents (accessed April 10, 2020).

33. Sven Hedin (1936), *The Silk Road*. London: George Routledge & Sons.

34. *Ibid.* p. 226.

35. Che Muqi states on the cover to his *The Silk Road: Past and Present*, Beijing: Foreign Languages Press, 1989, that "In ancient China, the Silk Road ran across Eurasia for thousands of kilometres. For more than a thousand years after the second century B.C. a great flow of silk and silk fabrics was transported from China to the West over the road, hence the Silk Road. The economy, culture and arts of Western countries were also introduced to China by this road. The Silk Road once played a great role in promoting friendly relations and economic and cultural exchanges between China and European, Asian and African countries.' This is pure propaganda, not backed up by any independent historical research.

36. E-mail from Lars Ellström, January 10, 2020.

37. See "The Silk Road", BBC, February-April, 2020, https://www.bbc.co.uk/programmes/p03qb13o (accessed on August 25, 2020.)

38. See Chapter One.

39. For a complete list of Chinese supplies of military materiel, see Andrew Selth (1995), *Burma's Arms Procurement Programme*, Working Paper no. 289 (September). Canberra: Strategic and Defence Studies Centre, Australian National University.

40. Marvin Ott (1997), 'Don't Push Myanmar Into China's Orbit,' *The Los Angeles Times* (June 9). Available at http://articles.latimes.com/1997-06-09/local/me-1645_1_southeast-asia (accessed April 10, 2020).

41. First reported by Bertil Lintner and Shawn Crispin (2003), in 'Dangerous Bedfellows,' *Far Eastern Economic Review* (November 20).

42. Thant Myint-U (2019), *The Hidden History of Burma: Race, Capitalism and the Crisis of Democracy in the 21st Century.* London: Atlantic Books, p. 157.

43. For an overview of the 'roadmap', see David Arnott, *Burma/Myanmar: How to Read the Generals' "Roadmap": A Brief Guide With Links to the Literature.* Available at http://www.ibiblio.org/obl/docs/how10.htm (accessed April 10, 2020); and Khin Maung Win, address at a Myanmar Institute of Strategic and International Studies seminar in Rangoon, January 27–28, 2004. Available at http://burmatoday.net/burmatoday2003/2004/02/040218_khinmgwin.htm (accessed April 10, 2020).

44. A copy of the dossier is in my possession. All quotes from it here are my translations from the original in Burmese.

45. Sui-lee Wee (2015), 'Myanmar official accuses China of meddling in rebel peace talk,' *Reuters* (October 8). Available at http://www.reuters.com/article/us-myanmar-china-idUSKCN0S22VT20151008 (accessed April 15, 2020).

46. San Yamin Aung (2020), 'Myanmar's Ex-President Tells Voters to Protect Race, Religion, Military in 2020 Election,' *The Irrawaddy* (January 7). Available at https://www.irrawaddy.com/news/burma/myanmars-ex-president-tells-voters-protect-race-religion-military-2020-election.html (accessed April 10, 2020).

47. *Ibid.*

48. This account of China's policy toward the Wa, Burma, and China's involvement in the peace process is based on discussions with several former CPB members who worked with Chinese officials for years and now are close to the UWSA leadership. For security reasons, the time and place of my meetings with them cannot be disclosed.

49. For a biography of Song Tao, see https://en.wikipedia.org/wiki/Song_Tao_(diplomat)

50. Its members are the United Wa State Army, Myanmar National Democratic Alliance Army, National Democratic Alliance Army-Eastern Shan State, Kachin Independence Army, Ta'ang National Liberation Army, Arakan Army, and Shan State Army (not to be confused with the army of the Restoration Council of Shan State, which uses the same name).

51. Interviews with leaders of the Ta'ang National Liberation Army (TNLA), Ruili, China, March 10, 2018. Leaders and member of the KIA have expressed the same views in several discussions with me ever since their ceasefire with the government broke down in June 2011.

52. Nyein Nyein (2018), "Northern Alliance Seeks Continued Support from China in Peace Process Negotiations," *The Irrawaddy* (March 29). Available at https://www.irrawaddy.com/news/burma/northern-alliance-seeks-continued-support-china-peace-process-negotiations.html

53. Bertil Lintner (2017), 'China looms large over Myanmar war and peace,' *Asia Times* (November 28). Available at http://www.atimes.com/article/china-looms-large-myanmar-war-peace/

54. Minutes from the meeting are in my possession.

55. 'Gun Maw (2014) urges US to play role in Burma's peace process. *The Democratic Voice of Burma* (April 22). Available at http://www.dvb.no/news/gun-maw-urges-us-to-play-role-in-burmas-peace-process-burma-myanmar-kachin/39806

56. Joe Kumbun (2017), "The Tripartite Power Struggle in the KIO," *The Irrawaddy* (June 30). Available at https://www.irrawaddy.com/opinion/guest-column/tripartite-power-struggle-kio.html

57. Bertil Lintner (2018a), 'Spurned by West, Myanmar's Kachins look to China,' *Asia Times* (January 24) Available at http://www.atimes.com/article/spurned-west-myanmars-kachin-look-china/

58. Interview with TNLA leaders, Ruili, March 10, 2018.

59. Andrew Ong (2018a), 'Engaging the UWSA: Countering Myths, Building Ties,' *The Tea Circle* (August 20). Available at https://teacircleoxford.com/tag/uwsa/

60. Interview with a former (now retired) high-ranking Burmese military intelligence officer, Rangoon, August 30, 2018. See also http://www.mmpeacemonitor.org/stakeholders/myanmar-peace-center/169-uwsa

61. Interview with a source close to the UWSA, Ruili, March 9, 2018.

62. A copy of the proposal is in my possession.

63. Lintner (2018a). The article contains an interview with N Ban La during which these issues were discussed.

64. Ong (2018a).

65. *Ibid.*

66. *Ibid.*

67. *Ibid.*

68. A copy of the Chinese-language statement is in my possession.

69. See Bertil Lintner (2018b), 'Why China fears Myanmar's Christians,' *Asia Times* (September 17). Available at http://www.atimes.com/article/why-china-fears-myanmars-christians/ and http://www.mizzima.com/news-domestic/uwsa-detains-several-christian-clergy-members. That China is worried about the influence Western missionaries may have on the Wa was confirmed in an email to the author from a source in Yunnan, September 18, 2018.

70 https://www.crisisgroup.org/asia/south-east-asia/myanmar/another-landslide-victory-aung-san-suu-kyis-party-myanmar-what-cost (accessed on November 15, 2020.)

Abbreviations and Glossary

AA — Arakan Army. Rebel group active in Rakhine and Shan States.

AFPFL — Anti-Fascist People's Freedom League. Burma's main political party in the 1940s and 1950s.

BIA — Burma Independence Army. Army allied with Japan which fought for independence for the colony from British rule. Set up in Bangkok in 1941.

BNUP — Burma National United Party. Set up by the Wa after the April 1989 mutiny.

BRI — Belt and Road Initiative. A global, multibillion-dollar Chinese program aimed at infrastructure development.

BSPP — Burma Socialist Programme Party. Burma's only legally permitted political party from the 1962 coup to the 1988 prodemocracy uprising. Became the National Unity Party after 1988 (not to be confused with the BNUP).

CPB — Communist Party of Burma. Founded in 1939. Defunct after a mutiny within the rank-and-file of its army in 1989.

CPC — Communist Party of China. China's ruling party since 1949.

CPI — Communist Party of India.

CP(RF)   Communist Party (Red Flag). Radical breakaway communist party in Burma led by Thakin Soe.

DEA   Drug Enforcement Administration. A US federal law enforcement agency under the Department of Justice.

FPNCC   Federal Political Negotiation and Consultative Committee. Seven-member committee set up on April 19, 2017. An alliance of seven ethnic armed organizations in Myanmar.

ILD   International Liaison Department. Section of the Communist Party of China set up to maintain relations with foreign political parties and organizations. Sometimes referred to as the International Liaison Department of the Central Committee of the Communist Party of China (ILD/CPC).

KBC   Kachin Baptist Convention. Baptist denomination among Myanmar's Kachin people, affiliated with the Baptist World Alliance and the World Council of Churches.

KDA   Kachin Democratic Army. Breakaway faction from the KIA in northern Shan State.

KIA   Kachin Independence Army. Kachin rebel army set up in 1961.

KIO   Kachin Independence Organisation. Political wing of the KIA.

KKY   Ka Kwe Ye (Burmese for 'defense'). Home guard units set up by the Burmese army in the 1960s. Allowed to trade in opium in exchange for fighting the insurgents.

KNLA   Karen National Liberation Army. Armed wing of the KNU.

KNU   Karen National Union. Karen rebel group. Founded in 1947 as a legal political organization, went underground in 1949.

MNDAA   Myanmar National Democratic Alliance Army. Former CPB units in Kokang.

MSS   Ministry of State Security. Established in 1983. China's main intelligence, security, and secret police agency.

MTA   Mong Tai Army. One of Khun Sa's armies. Disbanded when he surrendered in 1996. The remnants formed the RCSS.

NDAA (ESS)   National Democratic Alliance Army (Eastern Shan State). Former CPB units in eastern Shan State.

NDA-K   New Democratic Army-Kachin. Name used by the former CPB units in Kachin State, now defunct.

NDF   National Democratic Front. Alliance of ethnic rebel armies in Myanmar, founded in 1976, now defunct.

NLD   National League for Democracy. Burmese prodemocracy party set up in 1988. Formed a government in 2015.

PKI   Partai Komunis Indonesia. Communist Party of Indonesia. Had representatives in the CPB's area in the 1970s.

PLA   People's Liberation Army (of China). Armed forces of the People's Republic of China.

RCSS   Restoration Council of Shan State. Successor to Khun Sa's MTA. Its army uses the name SSA but should not be confused with the original SSA which was set up in 1964.

SSA   Shan State Army. Shan rebel army founded in 1964.

SSPP   Shan State Progress Party. Political wing of the SSA, set up in 1971.

SUA   Shanland United Army. Khun Sa's first army, set up in 1972.

SURA   Shan United Revolutionary Army. Shan rebel army which merged with Khun Sa's forces in 1985.

TNLA   Ta'ang National Liberation Army. Palaung rebel army.

UNODC   United Nations Office on Drugs and Crime.

USDP   Union Solidarity and Development Party. Pro-military political party in Burma.

UWSA   United Wa State Army. Armed wing of the UWSP.

UWSP   United Wa State Party. Founded when the BNUP and WNC merged in 1989.

WCA   Wa Central Authority.

WNA   Wa National Army. Armed wing of the WNO.

WNC   Wa National Council. Officially the administrative wing of the WNO, in reality a separate organization. Merged with the BNUP in 1989 and became part of the UWSP/UWSA.

WNO   Wa National Organisation. Non-communist Wa army based on the Thai border, set up in 1974.

Dramatis Personae

AUNG SAN (1915–1947). Born as Htein Lin in Natmauk, central Burma. Burma's independence hero. First general secretary of the Communist Party of Burma (CPB) in 1939. Sent to China to contact Mao Zedong's communists but ended up with the Japanese. Leader of the legendary 'Thirty Comrades' who underwent Japanese military training in the 1940s. Four of those thirty later joined the CPB's insurgent army. Assassinated by a group of plotters led by U Saw, a right-wing politician, on July 19, 1947.

BA THEIN TIN, THAKIN (1914–1995). Joined the CPB in 1939. Went underground in 1948. Left for China in 1953. De facto leader of the CPB in the 1960s and became its official chairman in 1975. Driven into exile in China in 1989. Died in Changsha, Hunan Province, in 1995.

BANG RON alias **SURACHAI NGERNTHONGFOO**. Sino-Thai druglord. Set up one of Thailand's largest methamphetamine production and distribution networks until the Thai police raided his home in 1998. Escaped to Burma where he linked up with the Wei brothers (see below).

BAO YOUXIANG (BAO YUCHANG) alias **TA PANG** (1949–). Wa leader who joined forces with the CPB in 1969. Alternate member of the CPB's central committee in 1985. One of the leaders of the 1989 mutiny and became the first commander of the UWSA. General secretary of the UWSP and chairman of the Wa government since 2004. Younger brother of Bao Youri and elder brother of Bao Youliang. A fourth brother (younger), Bao Youhua, died in 2007.

BRANG SENG, MARAN (1930–1995). Former headmaster of the Baptist High School in Myitkyina. Went underground in 1963 and served as chairman of the Kachin Independence Organisation from 1975 until his death in Yunnan, China, in 1995.

DUAN XIWEN (TUAN SHI-WEN) (1912–1980). Nationalist Chinese general. Took part in the efforts to build up a 'secret' Kuomintang army in Burma in the 1950s. Retreated to the Thai border where he and his men established Mae Salong northwest of Chiang Rai as their main base. Died in a Bangkok hospital.

KANG SHENG (1898–1975). Oversaw the work of the intelligence and security apparatus of the Communist Party of China (CPC) in the 1940s and again during the Cultural Revolution in the 1960s and 1970s. Also responsible for the CPC's contacts with overseas communist parties, including the CPB.

KHIN NYUNT (1939–). Hard-line Burmese general, head of the country's intelligence services. Led the crackdown on the prodemocracy movement in the late 1980s and 1990s. Burma's prime minister from

2003 until he was purged in 2004. Now lives in retirement in Rangoon (Yangon).

KHUN SA alias **ZHANG QIFU** (1934–2007). Sino-Shan druglord. Began his career as a government-recognized militia commander. Arrested by the Burmese in 1969, released in 1974. Head of the Shanland United Army and merged his forces with the forces of Shan warlord Moh Heng in 1985. The joint forces became known as the Mong Tai Army. Surrendered in 1996 and moved to Rangoon (Yangon), where he died.

LI MI (1902–1973). Nationalist Chinese general. Fled to Hong Kong after the communist takeover in China in 1949, then transferred to Thailand and the Shan states of Burma where he built up a resistance army that was supposed to enter China and fight the communists. Left for Taiwan in the 1950s.

LI WENHUAN (LEE WEN-HUAN) (1917–2000). Nationalist Chinese general. Fled to Burma after the communist takeover in China in 1949. Became a prominent Golden Triangle druglord, whose forces were based at Tam Ngob, northwest of Chiang Mai, northern Thailand. Died in Chiang Mai.

LI ZIRU (1948–2005). Chinese from Baoshan, Yunnan. One of the Chinese Red Guard volunteers who came across the border to fight alongside the CPB in the late 1960s. Headed (together with Bao Youxiang) the CPB's 683 Brigade in central Shan State in the 1980s. Joined the 1989 mutiny and became one of the leaders of the United Wa State Party. Died of a heart attack in Panghsang.

LIN MINGXIAN alias **SAI LEÜN** alias **U SAI LIN**. Sino-Shan, born around 1950 in Panghsai on the Shan State border with China. Grew up partly in China. Joined the CPB with other Red Guard volunteers in the late 1960s. One of the leaders of the 1989 mutiny. Became the leader of the National Democratic Alliance Army (eastern Shan State) with its headquarters at Mong La on the Chinese border. Married to Peng Jiasheng's daughter.

LUO XINGHAN (LO HSING-HAN) (1935–2013). Kokang Chinese warlord and heroin trafficker. Head of a government-recognized militia unit. Went underground in 1973 and was arrested on the Thai side of the border shortly afterwards. Extradited to Burma and sentenced to death. Released during a general amnesty in 1980 and set up a new militia force. Became a prominent businessman in Burma and acted as go-between for the government in negotiations with the CPB mutineers in 1989. Died in Rangoon (Yangon).

MAHASANG (1946–2007). The second son of Sao Maha, the *saohpa* of the Wa state of Vingngun. Head of a government-recognized militia unit allied with Luo Xinghan, and went underground with him in 1973. Stayed on the Thai border where he set up the Wa National Organisation/Army in 1974. Allied with Mo Heng's Shan United Revolutionary Army and remnants of the Kuomintang. Went to Panghsang after the 1989 mutiny but was arrested by the mutineers. Managed to escape and went back to Thailand. Died in Chiang Mai.

NAW KHAM (1969–2013). Ethnic Shan leader of a predominantly Lahu militia. Was first allied with Khun Sa, then an independent operator in the Mekong River region. Major drug trafficker. Arrested by Lao officials in 2012 and extradited to China where he was sentenced to death and executed.

NAW SENG (1922–1972). Kachin. Led resistance against the Japanese occupation in the 1940s and joined the Burmese army after World War II. Went underground in 1949 and retreated into China in 1950 where he stayed in a people's commune in Guizhou Province. He and his around 200–300 Kachin warriors became known as the *Guizhou laobing* and returned to Burma in 1968 as the main force of the CPB's army. Died under mysterious circumstances in the Wa Hills.

NE WIN alias **THAKIN SHU MAUNG** (1911–2002). Sino-Burmese. Belonged to the rightist faction of the Dohbama Asiayone and the Thirty Comrades. Received intelligence training by the Japanese and became chief of staff of the Burmese army in 1949. Headed a caretaker government from 1958 to 1960. Staged a coup in 1962 and ruled the country as dictator until he resigned in 1988. Died in Rangoon (Yangon).

PENG JIASHENG (PHEUNG KYA-SHIN) (1931–). Kokang Chinese. Officer in Jimmy Yang's Kokang Revolutionary Force, which merged with some Shan groups to become the Shan State Army in 1964. Contacted by the CPB in 1967 and joined its army but never the party. Initiated the 1989 mutiny by breaking away from the CPB in March 1989. His younger brother Peng Jiafu (1936–2017), was also a prominent former CPB military commander who joined the 1989 mutiny.

SAW LU alias **SAUL** alias **TA PLUIK** (1942–). Wa. Studied at Gordon Seagrave's missionary school in Namkham, northern Shan State, and at a Baptist school in Myaungmya in the Irrawaddy delta. Headed a government-recognized militia unit in Saohpa in the Wa Hills in the mid-1960s and fought against the CPB in 1969. Was forced out by Wa forces allied with the CPB and moved to Lashio. Arrested by Burmese authorities in 1992 and charged with cooperating with the US Central Intelligence Agency and the Drug Enforcement Administration. Later released. Made it to the Wa Hills and served as international liaison officer for the UWSP until he was ousted in 1995.

SONG TAO (1955–). Chinese diplomat born in Jiangsu Province, currently serving as the head of the International Liaison Department of the Communist Party of China. Attended Monash University in Melbourne, Australia from 1988 to 1991 after which he served as Chinese ambassador to Guyana and the Philippines. A major mover and shaker behind the scenes in China's relations with North Korea and Burma.

SUN GUOXIANG (1953–). Chinese diplomat, born in Shanghai. Beijing's special envoy for Asian affairs, which included liaising with the Burmese government and Burma's ethnic armies. The public face of China's Burma policy and as such not nearly as powerful as Song Tao.

TIN YEE alias **NE WIN** (1922–?). CPB member. Went to China in 1951 and returned to Burma in 1968. Chief of general staff of the CPB's army from 1986 until the 1989 mutiny when he fled to China. Hated by the Wa because of his use of human-wave tactics in battles with government forces.

TING YING, SAKHON. Kachin of the Ngoshan tribe. Joined the Kachin Independence Army in 1960s, but broke away in 1968 and joined the Communist Party of Burma. Set up the New Democratic Army-Kachin after the 1989 mutiny and entered into a ceasefire agreement with the government. Later head of a government-recognized militia force.

WEI XUEGANG (WEI HSUEH-KANG) alias **PRASIT [CHARNCHAI] CHIWINITIPANYA** alias **SEIN WIN** (1946–). Chinese from Yunnan whose family fled to the Wa Hills after the communist takeover in China in 1949. He and his brothers Wei Xuelong and Wei Xueyin were based in Vingngun and connected with the Kuomintang-CIA spy network. Fled to the Thai border when the CPB drove them out of the Wa Hills in the early 1970s. First allied with Khun Sa's drug trafficking organization, then with the Wa National Organisation/Army/Council and eventually with the United Wa State Party/Army. Was indicted (along with his brothers and the Bao brothers) on drug trafficking charges by a US federal court in 2005.

XIAO MINLIANG (1949–). Wa from Cangyuan in China and educated there. Joined the CPB's military in 1969 and the party in 1970 and served as a commander in the forces in central Shan State until the 1989 mutiny. Vice chairman of the Wa government when it was established in 1995.

YANG, JIMMY alias **YANG ZHENSHENG** alias **YANG KYIN-SEIN** (1920–1985). Kokang Chinese. Belonged to the ruling family in Kokang and elected a member of the Burmese parliament in 1950. Founded the Kokang Revolutionary Force in 1963, which merged with some Shan groups to form the Shan State Army in 1964. Later joined forces with the remnants of the Kuomintang. Settled in Thailand and moved to France in 1973. Returned to Burma during a general amnesty in 1980 and died in Rangoon (Yangon).

YANG MAOLIAN (1951–). Kokang Chinese. Military officer in the CPB's army. Joined the 1989 mutiny but fought against Peng Jiasheng for control over Kokang. His younger brother Yang Maoxian was executed in Kunming in 1994 for trafficking in heroin to China.

YANG, OLIVE alias **YANG JINXIU** alias **YANG KYIN-HSUI** (1927–2017). Younger sister of Jimmy Yang. Arrested in 1952 for supporting the Kuomintang. Released in 1957 and then returned to Kokang where she built up her own private army. The first militia commander who organized lorry convoys that carried opium to the Thai border. Arrested again in 1963 and released in 1968. Played a role (together with Luo Xinghan and Aung Gyi, a retired Burmese army brigadier-general) in negotiating the 1989 peace treaty between the central government and the CPB mutineers.

YAWT SERK (1959–). Born in Mong Nawng near Loilem, Shan State. Former junior commander in Khun Sa's army and now leader of the Restoration Council of Shan State (RCSS), an ethnic Shan group which signed a ceasefire agreement with the government on October 15, 2015.

ZHANG SUQUAN alias **SAO HPALANG** (1927–2011). Chinese from Manchuria. Joined the Kuomintang and fought with its forces in Burma and Laos. Khun Sa's chief of staff and the main military strategist of the Shanland United Army as well as the Mong Tai Army. Surrendered with Khun Sa in 1996 and became a prominent businessman in Rangoon (Yangon).

ZHANG ZHIMING alias **KYI MYINT** (1950–). Chinese from Wanding, Yunnan. Joined the CPB as a Red Guard volunteer in 1968 (along with Li Ziru and Lin Mingxian) and rose to become a prominent military commander. Joined the 1989 mutiny and now a high-ranking officer in the National Democratic Alliance Army-Eastern Shan State, based at Mong La.

ZHAO GUOAN (1949–). Chinese from Nansan, Yunnan. Joined the CPB as a volunteer in the late 1960s and later served as supply officer under Li Ziru and Bao Youxiang in the CPB's 683 Brigade. Now in charge of foreign affairs for the Wa authorities.

ZHAO YILAI alias **CHAO NGI LAI** alias **KYAUK NYI LAING** alias **TA LAI** (1940–2009). Wa from a small village near the Chinese border. Had his own guerrilla force in the 1960s until he joined forces with the CPB in 1969. Became the most prominent Wa in the CPB and was elected an alternate member of its central committee in 1985. Led the 1989 mutiny together with Bao Youxiang. First leader of the UWSP and today considered the 'father of the Wa nation.' Died in a hospital in Lancang, Yunnan, and buried in Saohpa in the northeastern Wa Hills.

Bibliography

Books

Aung Tun, Sai. 2009. *History of the Shan State: From Its Origins to 1962*. Chiang Mai: Silkworm Books.

Ba Thein Tin, Thakin. 1978. *The Entire Party! Unite and March to Achieve Victory!* (translation from the Burmese). Panghsang: CPB's printing press.

Backus, Charles. 1981. *The Nan-chao Kingdom and T'ang China's Southwest Frontier*. Cambridge: Cambridge University Press.

Barton, G. E. 1933. *Barton's 1929 Wa Diary*. Rangoon: G.B.P.C.O.

Bo Yang. 1987. *Golden Triangle: Frontier and Wilderness*. Hong Kong: Joint Publishing Co.

——————. 1996. *The Alien Realm*. London: Janus Publishing.

Booth, Martin. 1996. *Opium: A History*, London: Simon & Schuster.

Bowring, Philip. 2018. *Empire of the Winds: The Global Role of Asia's Great Archipelago*. London: I.B. Tauris.

Brady, Anne-Marie. 2003. *Making the Foreign Serve China: Managing Foreigners in the People's Republic*. Lanham: Rowman and Littlefield, 2003.

Brunner, Jake, Kirk Talbott and Chantal Elkin. 1998. *Logging Burma's Frontier Forests*. Washington: World Resources Institute.

Byron, John, and Robert Pack. 1992. *The Claws of the Dragon: Kang Sheng, the Evil Genius Behind Mao and His Legacy of Terror in People's China*. New York: Simon & Schuster.

Candlin, Stanton. 1973. *Psycho-Chemical Warfare: The Chinese Communist Drug Offensive Against the West*. New Rochelle, New York: Arlington House.

Carrai, Maria Adele. 2019. *Sovereignty in China: A Genealogy of a Concept Since 1840*. Cambridge: Cambridge University Press.

Chang Wen-Chin. 2014. *Beyond Borders: Stories of Yunnanese Chinese Migrants of Burma*. Ithaca: Cornell University Press.

Chin Ko-lin. 2009. *The Golden Triangle: Inside Southeast Asia's Drug Trade*. Ithaca: Cornell University Press.

Chin Ko-lin and Sheldon X. Zhang. 2015. *The Chinese Heroin Trade: Cross-Border Drug Trafficking in Southeast Asia and Beyond*. New York: New York University Press.

China's Foreign Relations: A Chronology of Events 1949–1988. 1989. Beijing: Foreign Languages Press.

Chiranan Prasertkul. 1989. *Yunnan Trade in the Nineteenth Century: Southwest China's Cross-boundaries Functional System*. Bangkok: Institute of Asian Studies, Chulalongkorn University.

Chouvy, Pierre-Arnaud. 2009. *Opium: Uncovering the Politics of the Poppy*. London: I.B. Tauris.

————, (ed.) 2013. *An Atlas of Trafficking in Southeast Asia: The Illegal Trade in Arms, Drugs, People, Counterfeit Goods and Natural Resources in Mainland Southeast Asia*. London: I.B. Tauris.

Christian, John LeRoy. 1945. *Burma and the Japanese Invader*. Bombay: Thacker & Company.

Cochrane, Wilbur Willis. [1915] 1981. *The Shans*. 2 vols. Rangoon: Superintendent, Government Printing, Burma. Reprint, New York: AMS Press.

Collis, Maurice. 1946. *Foreign Mud*. London: Faber & Faber.

Colquhoun, Archibald Ross. [1885] 1970. *Amongst the Shans*. London: Field and Tuer. Reprint, New York: Paragon Book Reprint Corp.

Communist Party of Burma. 1964. *A Short Outline of the History of the Communist Party of Burma*. Beijing.

Crosthwaite, Sir Charles. 1912. *The Pacification of Burma*. London: Edward Arnold.

Deignan, H. G. 1934. *Burma: Gateway to China*. Washington: The Smithsonian Institution.

Dijk, Wil O. 2006. *Seventeenth-century Burma and the Dutch East India Company, 1634–1680*. Singapore: Singapore University Press.

Economy, Elizabeth C. 2018. *The Third Revolution: Xi Jinping and the New Chinese State*. New York: Oxford University Press.

Faligot, Roger. 2019. *Chinese Spies: From Chairman Mao to Xi Jinping*. London: Hurst and Company.

Fellowes-Gordon, Ian. 1957. *The Amiable Assassins: The Story of the Kachin Guerrillas of North Burma*. London: Robert Hale Limited.

FitzGerald, C. P. 1972. *The Southern Expansion of the Chinese People*. New York: Praeger Publishers.

Fleischmann, Klaus. 1989a. *Die Kommunistische Partei Birmas: Von den Anfängen bis zur Gegenwart*. Hamburg: Instituts für Asienkunde.

————, (ed.). 1989b. *Documents on Communism in Burma 1945–1977*. Hamburg: Instituts für Asienkunde.

Forbes, Andrew, and David Henley. 1997. *The Haw: Traders of the Golden Triangle*. Chiang Mai: Teak House Publications.

Gibson, Richard M., with Wenhua Chen. 2011. *The Secret Army: Chiang Kai-shek and the Drug Warlords of the Golden Triangle*. Singapore: John Wiley and Sons.

Hanks, Jane Richardson, and Lucien Mason Hanks. 2001. *Tribes of the North Thailand Frontier*. New Haven: Yale University Southeast Asia Studies.

Harvey, G. E. 1933. *1932 Wa Précis: A Précis Made in the Burma Secretariat of all Traceable Records Relating to the Wa States*. Rangoon: Office of Superintendent, Government Printing and Stationery, Burma.

Hill, Ann Maxwell. 1998. *Merchants and Migrants: Ethnicity and Trade among Yunnanese Chinese in Southeast Asia*. New Haven: Yale University Southeast Asia Studies.

Hoskins, Janet (ed.). 1996. *Headhunting and the Social Imagination in Southeast Asia*. Stanford: Stanford University Press.

Hudson, G. F. 1957. *The Wa People of the Burma-China Border*. St. Anthony's Papers, 11, Far Eastern Affairs. London: Chatto & Windus.

Hughes, Richard. 1968. *Borrowed Place, Borrowed Time: Hong Kong and Its Many Faces*. London: Andre Deutsch.

Israeli, Raphael. 2017. *The Muslim Midwest in Modern China: The Tale of Hui Communities in Gansu (Lazhou, Linxia, and Lintan) and in Yunnan (Kunming and Dali)*. San Jose: Resource Publications.

Jelsma, Martin, Tom Kramer, and Pietje Vervest (eds.). 2005. *Trouble in the Triangle: Opium and Conflict in Burma*. Chiang Mai: Silkworm Books.

Keenan, Paul. 2013. *By Force of Arms: Armed Ethnic Groups in Burma*. New Delhi: Vij Books India.

Kham Mong, Sai. 2005. *Kokang and Kachin in the Shan State (1945–1960)*. Bangkok: Institute of Asian Studies, Chulalongkorn University.

Kin Oung. 1993. *Who Killed Aung San?* Bangkok: White Lotus. Second, expanded edition, 1996.

Kramer, Tom. 2007. *The United Wa State Party: Narco-Army or Ethnic Nationalist Party?* Washington: East-West Center.

Kuhn, Delia, and Ferdinand Kuhn. 1962. *Borderlands*. New York: Alfred A. Knopf.

Lintner, Bertil. 1990. *The Rise and Fall of the Communist Party of Burma*. Ithaca: Cornell University Southeast Asia Program.

——————. [1990] 1996. *Land of Jade: A Journey from India through Northern Burma to China*. Kiscadale Publications. Third edition, Bangkok: Orchid Press.

——————. [1994] 2011. *Burma in Revolt: Opium and Insurgency Since 1948*. Boulder, Colorado: Westview Press. Fourth edition, Chiang Mai: Silkworm Books.

——————. 2015. *Great Game East: India, China and the Struggle for Asia's Most Volatile Frontier*. New Haven: Yale University Press.

——————. 2018. *China's India War: Collision Course on the Roof of the World*. New Delhi: Oxford University Press.

——————. 2019. *The United Wa State Army and Burma's Peace Process*. Washington: The United States Institute of Peace. https://www.usip.org/sites/default/files/2019-07/pw_147-the_united_wa_state_army_and_burmas_peace_process.pdf_

Lintner, Bertil, and Michael Black. 2009. *Merchants of Madness: The Methamphetamine Explosion in the Golden Triangle*. Chiang Mai: Silkworm Books.

Lovell, Julia. 2019. *Maoism: A Global History*. London: The Bodley Head.

Ma Yin (ed.). 1989. *China's Minority Nationalities*. Beijing: Foreign Languages Press.

Mao Zedong. 1967. *Selected Works, Volume IV*. Beijing: Foreign Languages Press.

Marshall, Andrew. 2002. *The Trouser People: A Story of Burma in the Shadow of the Empire*. London: Viking Penguin.

Mattis, Peter, and Matthew Brazil. 2019. *Chinese Communist Espionage: An Intelligence Primer*. Annapolis, Maryland: Naval Institute Press.

McCoy, Alfred W. 1972. *The Politics of Heroin in Southeast Asia*. New York: Harper Torchbooks. Republished as *The Politics of Heroin: CIA Complicity in the Global Drug Trade*. New York: Lawrence Hill Books, 1991, 2003.

McGregor, Richard. 2012. *The Party: The Secret World of China's Communist Leaders*. London: Penguin Books.

Merwin, Samuel. 1908. *Drugging a Nation*. New York: Fleming H. Revell Company.

Milne, Leslie. [1910] 1970. *Shans at Home*. London: John Murray. Reprint, New York: Paragon Book Reprint Corp.

Min Zin (ed.). 2018. *China's Multi-Layered Engagement Strategy and Myanmar's Reality: The Best Fit for Beijing's Preferences*. Yangon: Institute for Strategy and Policy.

Neihsial, Tualchin (ed.). [1947] 1998. *Burma: Frontier Areas Committee of Enquiry Report*. United Kingdom: His Majesty's Stationery Office. Reprint, New Delhi: Inter-India Publications.

Owen, Frank. 1984. *The Campaign in Burma*. Dehra Dun: Natraj Publishers.

Pasuk Phongpaichit, Sungdish Piriyarangsan, and Nualnoi Treerat. 1998. *Guns, Girls, Gambling, Ganja: Thailand's Illegal Economy and Public Policy*. Chiang Mai: Silkworm Books.

Po, San C. 1928. *Burma and the Karens*. London: Elliot Stock.

Renard, Ronald. 1996. *The Burmese Connection: Illegal Drugs and the Making of the Golden Triangle*. Boulder: Lynne Rienner Publishers.

—————. 2001. *Opium Reduction in Thailand 1970–2000: A Thirty-Year Journey*. Chiang Mai: Silkworm Books.

Rush, James R. 1990. *Opium to Java: Revenue Farming and Chinese Enterprise in Colonial Indonesia, 1860–1910*. Ithaca: Cornell University Press.

Scott, J. M. 1969. *The White Poppy: A History of Opium*. New York: Funk & Wagnalls.

Scott, James C. 2009. *The Art of Not Being Governed: An Anarchist History of Upland Southeast Asia*. New Haven: Yale University Press.

Scott, Sir J. George. 1900. *Gazetteer of Upper Burma and the Shan States in Five Volumes*. Rangoon: Superintendent, Government Printing, Burma.

—————. 1932. *Burma and Beyond*. London: Grayson & Grayson.

Scott, James George. 1935. *Burma and Beyond*. London: Grayson & Grayson.

Silverstein, Josef. 1977. *Burma: Military Rule and the Politics of Stagnation*. Ithaca: Cornell University Press.

—————. 1980. *Burmese Politics: The Dilemma of National Unity*. New Brunswick: Rutgers University Press.

Simms, Sao Sanda. 2017. *Great Lords of the Sky: Burma's Shan Aristocracy.* Self-published under *Asian Highlands Perspectives,* no. 48.

Smith, Charles. 1984. *The Burmese Communist Party in the 1980s.* Singapore: Institute of Southeast Asian Studies.

Smith, I. C., and Nigel West. 2012. *Historical Dictionary of Chinese Intelligence.* Lanham: The Scarecrow Press.

Smith, Martin. 1991. *Burma: Insurgency and the Politics of Ethnicity.* London: Zed Press.

—————. 1994. *Ethnic Groups in Burma: Development, Democracy and Human Rights.* London: Anti-Slavery International.

Takano, Hideyuki. 2002. *The Shore Beyond Good and Evil: A Report from Inside Burma's Opium Kingdom.* Tokyo: Kotan Publishing.

Taylor, Robert. 1973. *Foreign and Domestic Consequences of the Kuomintang Intervention.* Ithaca: Cornell University Southeast Asia Program, Data Paper no. 93.

Telford, James Haxton. 1937. *Animism in Kengtung State.* Rangoon: Burma Research Society.

Thant Myint-U. 2006. *The River of Lost Footsteps: Histories of Burma.* New York: Farrar, Straus and Giroux.

—————. 2011. *Where China Meets India: Burma and the New Crossroads of Asia.* New York: Farrar, Straus and Giroux.

—————. 2019. *The Hidden History of Burma: Race, Capitalism and the Crisis of Democracy in the 21st Century.* London: Atlantic Books.

Ting Tsz Kao. 1980. *The Chinese Frontiers.* Aurora, Illinois: Chinese Scholarly Publishing Company.

Tinker, Hugh. 1966. *The Union of Burma.* London: Oxford University Press.

Trager, Frank. 1966. *Burma: From Kingdom to Republic.* London: Pall Mall Press.

Tullis, LaMond. 1995. *Unintended Consequences: Illegal Drugs and Drug Policies in Nine Countries.* Boulder, Colorado: Lynne Rienner Publishers.

United Wa State Party. 2018. *Miandian Lianbang Wa Bang Zhi* (in Chinese: A Record of the Wa State of the Union of Burma). Panghsang.

Watson, Francis. 1966. *The Frontiers of China.* London: Chatto & Windus.

Whitfield, Susan (ed.). 2019. *Silk Roads: Peoples Cultures and Landscapes.* Oakland: University of California Press.

Winnington, Alan. 1959. *The Slaves of the Cool Mountains: The Ancient Social Conditions and Changes Now in Progress on the Remote South-Western Borders of China.* London: Lawrence & Wishart.

Yang Li. 1997. *The House of Yang: Guardians of an Unknown Frontier.* Sydney: Bookpress.

Yawnghwe, Chao Tzang. [1987] 2010. *The Shan of Burma: Memoirs of a Shan Exile.* Second, revised edition, Singapore: Institute of Southeast Asian Studies.

Yawnghwe, Samara. 2013. *Maintaining the Union of Burma 1946–1962: The Role of the Ethnic Nationalities in a Shan Perspective.* Bangkok: Institute of Asian Studies, Chulalongkorn University.

Yun Sun. 2018. *China's Role in Myanmar's Internal Conflicts.* Washington: The United States Institute of Peace.

Zheng Lan. 1981. *Travels Through Xishuangbanna: China's Subtropical Home of Many Nationalities.* Beijing: Foreign Languages Press.

Zhou Yongming. 1999. *Anti-Drug Crusades in Twentieth-Century China: Nationalism, History, and State Building.* Lanham: Rowman & Littlefield.

Burmese Government Publications

Bulletin of Narcotics. 1992. Rangoon: The Central Committee for Drug Abuse Control, Ministry of Home Affairs.

Burma and the Insurrections. 1949. Rangoon: Government of the Union of Burma Publications.

Drug Suppression in Myanmar. 1992. The Central Committee for Drug Abuse Control, Ministry of Home Affairs.

Frontier Areas Committee of Enquiry 1947: Part II. 1947. Rangoon: Government Printing.

The Kachin Hills Manual. 1924. Rangoon: Superintendent, Government Printing, Burma.

The Kachin Hills Manual. 1959. Rangoon: Superintendent, Government Printing and Stationery, Union of Burma.

Kuomintang Aggression Against Burma. 1953. Rangoon: Ministry of Information.

The Opium Manual: Containing the Opium Act and the Rules and Directions thereunder in force in Burma. 1964. Rangoon: Superintendent, Central Press.

Shan States and Karenni: List of Chiefs and Leading Families. Simla: Government of India Press, 1943.

Superintendent, Government Printing and Stationery. 1960. 'Agreement between the Government of the Union of Burma and the Government of the People's Republic of China on the Question of the Boundary Between the Two Countries.' Rangoon: Ministry of Information.

Papers and Articles

Allard, Tom. 2019. 'The Hunt for Asia's El Chapo.' *Reuters* (October 14). https://www.reuters.com/investigates/special-report/meth-syndicate/

Allman, T. D. 1971. 'A Wonderland of Opium.' *Far Eastern Economic Review* (July 24).

Associated Press, 2016. 'Key Developments in China's 1966–1976 Cultural Revolution.' https://apnews.com/dbf0fd79a3d14b1c91c4d98b17704240/key-developments-chinas-1966-1976-cultural-revolution

Aung Zaw. 2020. 'Shadowy Drug Lord Wei Hsueh-kang's [Wei Xuegang] Influence Still Felt in Myanmar's Wa Region and Beyond.' *The Irrawaddy* (March). https://www.irrawaddy.com/opinion/commentary/shadowy-drug-lord-wei-hsueh-kangs-influence-still-felt-myanmars-wa-region-beyond.html

Black, Michael. 'The UWSA: From Drugs to Guns.' Unpublished paper by Thailand-based researcher, in author's possession.

Bernstein, Dennis, and Leslie Kean. 1996. 'People of the Opiate.' *Baltimore Sun*, (December 22).

Bowring, Philip. 2017. 'China's Silk Road Illusions.' *The New York Review of Books* (October 25). https://www.nybooks.com/daily/2017/10/25/chinas-silk-road-illusions/

British Intelligence, 1960. 'The Sino-Burmese Border Question: Research Backgrounder.' Hong Kong. Mimeograph, in author's possession.

Buchanan, John. 2016. 'Militias in Myanmar.' The Asia Foundation (July). https://asiafoundation.org/wp-content/uploads/2016/07/Militias-in-Myanmar.pdf

Central Intelligence Agency. 1971. 'Intelligence Report: Peking and the Burmese Communists, the Perils and Profits of Insurgency.' Langley: Directorate of Intelligence (July). https://www.cia.gov/library/readingroom/docs/esau-52.pdf

Chambers, Dr. David Ian. 2012. 'The Past and Present State of Chinese Intelligence Historiography.' *Studies in Intelligence*, vol. 56, no. 3 (September).

Chao Tzang Yawnghwe. 1982. 'Politics of Burma and Shan State: Effects on Thailand and North Thailand.' *Political Science Review*, Chiang Mai University, Thailand (September).

Chin Ko-lin and Sheldon X. Zhang. 2016. 'A People's War: China's Struggle to Contain its Illicit Drug Problem.' *Foreign Policy at Brookings* (July). https://www.brookings.edu/wp-content/uploads/2016/07/A-Peoples-War-final.pdf

Chin, Tamara. 2013. 'The Invention of the Silk Road.' *The University of Chicago Press Journals*, vol. 40, no. 1 (Autumn). https://www.jstor.org/stable/10.1086/673232?seq=1#metadata_info_tab_contents

Christian, John L. 1940. 'Trans-Burma Trade Routes to China.' *Pacific Affairs*, vol. 13, no. 2.

Cohen, Elizabeth J., and Joseph J. Amon. 2008. 'Health and Human Rights Concerns in Detention in Guangxi Province, China. *Plos Medicine*, vol. 5, no. 12 (December 9). https://journals.plos.org/plosmedicine/article/file?id=10.1371/journal.pmed.0050234&type=printable

Davis, Anthony. 2013. 'Orient Excess: Drug production in Myanmar.' *IHS Jane's* (July 8), and *Jane's Intelligence Review*, no. 8. https://biblio.parlament.ch/libero/WebOpac.cls?VERSION=2&ACTION=DISPLAY&RSN=371533&DATA=PDB&TOKEN=bJS5H7kJpS1063&Z=1&SET=3

————. 2019. 'It's party time for Myanmar's largest armed ethnic faction.' *Asia Times* (April 9).

Ducharme, Jamie. 2019. 'Trump Said China Doesn't Have a Drug Problem. The Data Tells a Different Story.' *Time* (February 15). https://time.com/5530597/trump-china-drug-problem/

Fiskesjö, Magnus. 2000. 'The Fate of Sacrifice and the Making of Wa History.' Unpublished Ph.D. thesis, University of Chicago.

————. 2010a. 'Mining, History, and the Anti-state Wa: The Politics and Autonomy between Burma and China.' *Journal of Global History*, vol. 5, no. 2, pp. 241–64. https://doi.org/10.1017/S1740022810000070

Fiskesjö, Magnus. 2010b. 'Participant Intoxication and Self-Other Dynamics in the Wa Context.' *The Asia Pacific Journal of Anthropology*, vol. 11, no. 2, pp. 111–27. https://www.tandfonline.com/doi/abs/10.1080/14442211003720588

————. 2011. 'Slavery as the Commodification of People: Wa "Slaves" and Their Chinese "Sisters".' *Focaal: Journal of Global and Historical Anthropology*, vol. 59, pp. 3–18. https://www.berghahnjournals.com/view/journals/focaal/2011/59/focaal590101.xml

————. 2013a. 'Gifts and Debts: The Morality of Fieldwork in the Wa Lands on the China-Burma Frontier.' In Sarah Turner (ed.), *Red Stamps and Gold Stars: Fieldwork Dilemmas in Upland Socialist Asia*. Vancouver: University of British Columbia Press, pp. 60–79.

————. 2013b. 'Introduction to Wa Studies.' *The Journal of Burma Studies*, vol. 17, no. 1, pp. 1–27. https://muse.jhu.edu/article/509834/pdf

————. 2014. 'Wa Grotesque: Headhunting Theme Parks and the Chinese Nostalgia for Primitive Contemporaries.' *Ethnos: Journal of Anthropology*, vol. 80 (August), pp. 1–27. https://www.tandfonline.com/doi/abs/10.1080/00141844.2014.939100

Global Witness. 2005. 'A Choice for China.' https://cdn.globalwitness.org/archive/files/library/a_choice_for_china_low_res.pdf

Hearings Before the Select Committee of Narcotics Abuse and Control, House of Representatives, 95th Congress. 1978. Washington: Government Printing Office, pp. 215–16.

Hodal, Kate. 2013. 'Meth drug makers lure children in Thailand with sweet-coated yaba pills.' *The Guardian* (August 27). https://www.theguardian.com/world/2013/aug/27/meth-drugs-yaba-lure-children-thailand

Kramer, Tom. 2005. 'A Downward Spiral: Proposed opium bans could spark humanitarian crisis.' *Irrawaddy*, vol. 13, no. 10 (October). https://www.tni.org/my/node/12410

Kumbun, Joe. 2017. 'The Tripartite Power Struggle in the KIO.' *The Irrawaddy* (June 30. https://www.irrawaddy.com/opinion/guest-column/tripartite-power-struggle-kio.html

Lawitts, David. 2015. 'The Grand Old Man of Chiang Mai: The Life of Harold Young.' *Chiang Mai City Life* (April 1).

Lewis, Elaine T. 1957. 'The Hill Peoples of Kengtung State.' *Practical Anthropology*, vol. 4, no. 5.

Lintner, Bertil. 1987a. 'War in the North, an insurgent who's who, the KIO's grip, Rangoon fights war of attrition in the north.' *Far Eastern Economic Review*, cover story (May 28).

————. 1987b. 'The rise and fall of the communists, A product of moneylending, Political line-up of the CPB, Tax revenue from opium helps finance the party, Peking's support continues but at a much reduced rate.' *Far Eastern Economic Review* (June 4).

————. 1989a. 'Rebels with a cause.' *Far Eastern Economic Review* (March 30).

Lintner, Bertil. 1989b. 'Left in disarray, An inside job'. *Far Eastern Economic Review* (June 1).

——————. 1991. 'Cross-Border Drug Trade in the Golden Triangle (S.E. Asia)'. *Territory Briefing no. 1*, International Boundaries Research Unit, University of Durham, UK.

——————. 1993. 'The Politics of the Drug Trade in Burma'. *Occasional Paper no. 33*, Indian Ocean Centre for Peace Studies, University of Western Australia.

——————. 1994a. 'Burma: China's New Gateway. Route for Trade, Arms and Immigrants'. *Far Eastern Economic Review*, cover story (December 22).

——————. 1994b. 'Turf War in the Triangle'. *Far Eastern Economic Review* (January 20).

——————. 1995a. 'The Drug Trade in Southeast Asia'. *Jane's Intelligence Review, Special Report no. 5* (April).

——————. 1995b. 'New Menace in the Golden Triangle'. *Reader's Digest* (December), pp. 23–26.

——————. 1998. 'Drugs and the Asian Crisis'. *The Asia-Pacific Magazine*, no. 13 (December).

——————. 2003. 'Dark Journey'. *Far Eastern Economic Review* (May 8).

——————. 2017. 'China looms large over Myanmar war and peace'. *Asia Times* (November 2). http://www.atimes.com/article/china-looms-large-myanmar-war-peace/

——————. 2018a. 'Spurned by West, Myanmar's Kachins look to China'. *Asia Times* (January 24). http://www.atimes.com/article/spurned-west-myanmars-kachin-look-china/

——————. 2018b. 'Why China fears Myanmar's Christians'. *Asia Times* (September 17). http://www.atimes.com/article/why-china-fears-myanmars-christians/

——————. 2019a. 'Myanmar's Wa seek peace through strength'. *Asia Times* (April 17). https://www.asiatimes.com/2019/04/article/myanmars-wa-seek-peace-through-strength/

——————. 2019b. 'Myanmar's Wa hold the key to peace'. *Asia Times* (September 6). https://www.asiatimes.com/2019/04/article/myanmars-wa-seek-peace-through-strength/

——————. 2019c. 'Why Myanmar's Wa always get what they want'. *Asia Times* (September 18). https://www.asiatimes.com/2019/09/article/why-myanmars-wa-always-get-what-they-want/

Lintner, Bertil, and Shawn Crispin. 2003. 'Dangerous Bedfellows'. *Far Eastern Economic Review* (November 20).

Lintner, Bertil, and Rodney Tasker. 1997. 'Caged but dangerous'. *Far Eastern Economic Review* (June 5).

Ma Jianxiong. 2013. 'Clustered Communities and Transportation Routes: The Wa Lands Neighboring the Lahu and Dai on the Frontier'. *Journal of Burma Studies*, vol. 17, no. 1, pp. 81–119. https://muse.jhu.edu/article/509837

Marshall, Andrew and Anthony Davis. 2002. 'Speed Tribe: Inside the world of Wa—Asia's deadliest drug cartel'. *Time* (December 16). http://content.time.com/time/world/article/0,8599,2056076,00.html

Maule, Robert. 2002. 'British Policy Discussions on the Opium Question in the Federated Shan States,' *Journal of Southeast Asian Studies* (June), p. 204. https://www.jstor.org/stable/20072412?seq=1

Millward, James. 2019. 'What Xi Jinping Hasn't Learnt from China's Emperors.' *The New York Times* (October 1). https://www.nytimes.com/2019/10/01/opinion/xi-jinping-china.html

Milsom, Jeremy D. 2010. 'Conflicting Agendas: Illicit Drugs, Development and Security in the Wa Special Region of Myanmar.' Melbourne: Department of Resource Management and Geography, School of Land and Environment, University of Melbourne.

Min Latt. 'Burma in Battle.' Unpublished manuscript about the Communist Party of Burma, mimeograph, early 1950s, in author's possession.

Min Zin. 2013. 'When the Chinese Press Down.' *The Irrawaddy* (August 14).

Obayashi, Taryo. 1966. 'Authopogonic Myths of the Wa in Northern Indo-China.' *Hitosubashi Journal of Social Studies*, vol. 3, no. 1, pp. 43–66.

Ong, Andrew. 2018a. 'Engaging the UWSA: Countering Myths, Building Ties.' *The Tea Circle* (August 20). https://teacircleoxford.com/tag/uwsa/

————. 2018b. 'Producing Intransigence: (Mis)understanding the United Wa State Army in Myanmar.' *Contemporary Southeast Asia*, vol. 40, no. 3, pp. 449–74.

Ott, Marvin. 1997. 'Don't Push Myanmar Into China's Orbit.' *The Los Angeles Times* (June 9). http://articles.latimes.com/1997-06-09/local/me-1645_1_southeast-asia

Pan Qi. 1985. 'Opening to the Southwest: An Expert Opinion.' *Beijing Review*, vol. 35 (September 2).

San Yamin Aung. 2020. 'Myanmar's Ex-President Tells Voters to Protect Race, Religion, Military in 2020 Election.' *The Irrawaddy* (January 7). https://www.irrawaddy.com/news/burma/myanmars-ex-president-tells-voters-protect-race-religion-military-2020-election.html

Selth, Andrew. 1995. *Burma's Arms Procurement Programme*. Working Paper no. 289 (September). Canberra: Strategic and Defence Studies Centre, Australian National University.

Solinger, Dorothy J. 1977. 'Minority Nationalities in China's Yunnan Province: Assimilation, Power, and Policy in a Socialist State.' *World Politics*, vol. 30, no. 1 (October).

Song Qingrun. 2015. 'Myanmar Must Restore Peace on China Border. *China Daily* (March 29).

A Special Correspondent. 1981. 'The Return of Lo Hsing-han.' *Focus*, Bangkok (August).

Steinberg, David. 1981. 'Burma Under the Military: Towards a Chronology.' *Contemporary Southeast Asia*, vol. 3, no. 3 (December), p. 262.

Steinmüller, Hans. 2019. 'Conscription by Capture in the Wa State of Myanmar: Acquaintances, Anonymity, Patronage, and the Rejection of Mutuality.' *Comparative Studies in Society and History*, vol. 61, no. 3, pp. 508–34. http://eprints.lse.ac.uk/90635/1/Steinm%C3%BCller_Conscription-by-capture.pdf

Steinmüller, Hans. 2020. 'The Moral Economy of Militarism: Peasant Economy, Military State and Chinese Capitalism in the Wa State of Myanmar.' *Social Anthropology* (February 4). http://eprints.lse.ac.uk/103170/

Tian Jinchen. 2017. 'One Belt and One Road: Connecting China and the World.' Paper prepared for McKinsey and Company (April 19).

United Nations Office for Drugs and Crime (UNODC). 2019. 'Myanmar opium cultivation continues to drop as regional drug market change' (January 11).

Watkins, Justin, and Richard Kunst. 2006. 'Writing of the Wa Language,' *The Wa Dictionary Project*, London: School of Oriental and African Studies (July 30).

Worobec, Stephen Francis. 1984. 'International Narcotics Control in the Golden Triangle of Southeast Asia.' Ph.D. thesis, Claremont, California: Claremont Graduate School.

Yun Sun. 2019. 'Why China is Sceptical About the Peace Process.' *Frontier Myanmar* (October 3).

Zheng Caixiong. 2018. '1.3 tons of cocaine seized in crackdown in drug gang in Shenzhen.' *China Daily* (September 14). http://www.chinadaily.com.cn/a/201809/14/WS5b9b 43d3a31033b4f4656124.html

Zheng Dahua. 2019. 'Modern Chinese nationalism and the awakening of self-consciousness of the Chinese Nation.' *International Journal of Anthropology and Ethnology*, vol. 3, no. 11. https://link.springer.com/article/10.1186/s41257-019-0026-6#Sec7

Index

CPSIA information can be obtained
at www.ICGtesting.com
Printed in the USA
BVHW060946120222
628820BV00002B/6